THE CITY AS SUBURB

Center Books on American Places

George F. Thompson, series founder and director

THE CITY AS SUBURB

A *History of* NORTHEAST BALTIMORE SINCE 1660

Eric L. Holcomb

Center for American Places
Santa Fe, New Mexico,
and Staunton, Virginia

PUBLISHER'S NOTES: *The City as Suburb: A History of Northeast Baltimore since 1660* is the second volume in the series *Center Books on American Places*, created and developed by the Center for American Places. The book was brought to publication in an edition of 1,200 hardcover copies with the generous support of William F. Holcomb and the Friends of the Center for American Places, for which the publisher is most grateful. The publisher extends special thanks to Philip J. Merill of Nanny Jack and Co. for bringing this project to its attention. For more information about the Center for American Places and the publication of *The City as Suburb: A History of Northeast Baltimore since 1660*, please see page 266.

©2005 Center for American Places
All rights reserved.
Published 2005. First edition.
Printed in China on acid-free paper.

Center for American Places, Inc.
P.O. Box 23225
Santa Fe, New Mexico 87502, U.S.A.
www.americanplaces.org

Distributed by the University of Virginia Press
www.upress.virginia.edu

9 8 7 6 5 4 3 2 1

Library of Congress Cataloging-in-Publication Data is available from the publisher upon request.

ISBN 1-930066-29-5

CONTENTS

Acknowledgments	vii
Foreword by Kathleen G. Kotarba	ix
Introduction	xiii
Before There Was a City, *1659–1781*	3
Creation of Borderland Communities, *1781–1852*	15
A Thriving Borderland Region, *1852–1898*	59
The Tentacles of the City	85
Democratizing the Suburban Dream, *1898–1941*	119
Mainstreets	169
Diversity in City Suburbia: Subdivisions Mature into Neighborhoods	185
Walking through Today, *1945–2005*	229
Notes	247
Index	259
About the Author	265

Looking south into the neighborhood of Lauraville from Mary Garrett Elementary School. Baltimore City skyline is in the background. (Photo by Robert Wallace)

ACKNOWLEDGMENTS

DEDICATED to my family—my wife Tracy, my brother Craig, and especially my Father, in sweet and loving memory of my Mother.

Robert Wallace, the original book designer and shanghaied photographer, traipsed through each section of Northeast Baltimore and captured several of the current images of this book. Most of all, he was a provider of common sense, which at times I lacked.

However, if it weren't for the hundreds of friends, colleagues, strangers, and neighbors of Northeast Baltimore, I would not have discovered its history. The staff at the Baltimore City Commission for historical and Architectural Preservation and the librarians in the Maryland Room at the Pratt Library aided and abetted me. Thank you Kathleen Kotarba, Brigitte Fessenden, Walter Leon and David McPherson, Jeff Korman, Eva Slezak, Layne Bosserman, Lee Lears, Mendy Gunter, and Sondra Guttman. Mary Markey at the Maryland Historical Society helped me. Also, Rebecca Gundy and Tony Roberts of the Baltimore City Archives as well as Marge Shipley, Elmer Haile, and Jim Long of the Baltimore County Historical Society greatly helped us. Also Philip J. Merrill of Nanny Jack and Co. was of tremendous help.

As important, the citizens of Northeast Baltimore came to my aid. The Harbel Senior Committee, under the direction of Jack Ray, created a group of dynamic citizens that provided a wealth of information. Thank you, Mrs. Stotler, Cynthia Tommey, Gayle Johnson Adams, Henry Szymanski, Ms. Cleo Stewart, Andrew Richwein, Edgar Muller, Ruth Gilka, Mary clare simon, Ed Balles, Mrs. Mary Barstow, Paul Baer, Elsie P. Bill, Bill Underwood, Forrest Gesswein, and Pastor Kretzschman. Julie Johnson of the Hamilton Branch Library also helped immensely.

Other neighbors supplied essential information: Bob and Betty Mayes, Tom Chaulkley, Francis Werneth, Will Colhouer, and the wonderful folks at the St. Johns United Methodist Church. Thanks go to Joyce Cook who graciously lent us her family photographs.

Jack Hennessy graciously loaned his grandfather's photographs for the book. James H. Lewis, Jack's grandfather, was born and raised in East Baltimore. When he married he moved to Gardenville and raised his family on Southern Avenue. He was an amateur photographer and captured, for us, rare glimpses of early twentieth-century Baltimore.

Folks at Baltimore Heritage and fellow colleagues always contributed tidbits, insights, and suggestions: Karen Lewand, John McGrain, Jim Wollon, Charles B. Duff, Jack Breihan, Steve Allen, Dr. Jessica Elfenbein, Peter Pearre, Councilman John Cain, Dr. Ron Mattson, and Dr. Randall Beirne.

FOREWORD

THE GROWTH of Northeast Baltimore illustrates the American transition from settlement to suburb. Here we witness a model that has played out again and again on this continent. By revealing the unseen layers of a rich history, Eric Holcomb presents the features of this model that are unique to this corner of the world. It is a specific and loving portrait.

A history of Northeast Baltimore, by necessity, explores the beauty in the relationship between buildings and the land. In this region, the Piedmont Plateau descends into the Tidewater, shaping the characteristics of all future development. In the nineteenth century, the region is considered by many to be the embodiment of the "Picturesque." By the twentieth century, the area offers prototypical suburban design that incorporates both planned and natural landscapes.

Country estates of Baltimore merchants and the utilitarian plots of the truck farmer existed side by side. From the era of the earliest known farm, that of the Gatch Family (1737), into the twentieth century, there were distinct alliances of landowners. While the estates of the wealthy merchants were havens of retreat, their owners' interests remained with the mercantile fortunes of the City. The affiliations of truck farmers remained with county interests and, in many cases, with those of rural villages. In studying this dichotomy, it becomes clear that there is an agricultural underpinning that lends structure to the face of Northeast Baltimore. We are presented with a borderland whose characteristics changed dramatically with the development of an early and large American city.

As one reflects upon the history of Lauraville and Gardenville, it is startling to realize that these suburban neighborhoods located within modern Baltimore City were prototypical farm villages of the nineteenth century. At one time they were the nucleus for thriving and self-sufficient farm communities. While these two communities retain an identifiable presence, other villages have been largely consumed by the patterns of twentieth-century development. The turnpike tollgate village of San Domingo, the predominately German village of Georgetown, and the crossroads village of Raspeburg represent historic places with unfamiliar names.

Holcomb considers the legacy of "founding families." The influence of the Gorsuch, Gatch, Keene, Erdmann, and many other families can be found in both community place names and in the actual appearance of communities. The commanding presence of Johns Hopkins's Italian Villa, "Clifton," continues to inspire the imagination. By Hopkins's own description, this "Heaven on Earth" lives on as a premiere site within Baltimore City's park system. "Montebello," the estate of "Railroad King" John Work Garrett, is associated today with a remarkable and handsome municipal water filtration plant.

In this portrait, one sees the patterns of human activity in a not-so-distant past. The role of the church in community building, particularly the social network of the Quakers and the Methodists, defines the character of the earliest communities. Reverence for the generations that came before can be appreciated in the study of twenty historic cemeteries, including B'Nae Israel, Laurel Hill, and Immanuel Lutheran. In contrast, the significance of breweries in the local economy is also emphasized, as it fostered a beer garden culture in the late nineteenth century. Attractions like Hall Springs and Darley Park beckoned City dwellers to enjoy leisure time excursions. Few may know that deep and early roots of the Maryland horse racing enterprise are evident in Northeast Baltimore's history. Mill workers, lamp lighters, and arabbers are also part of the rich texture of this image.

Inevitably, a city flows out. One of the earliest planned suburbs in Baltimore is the 1852 development of Homestead on the old Gorsuch Estate. The wooden cottages built here reflect the architectural aesthetic of Andrew Jackson Downing. Given that wood construction had been outlawed within the City limits, these cottages "across the border" became associated with country-like qualities. Even at this early time, the Homestead suburb was promoted as being beautiful and healthy. The myths of city and country remain the central theme of this portrait.

The advent of the streetcar supported a subsequent building boom. During the 1920s, the streetcar and automobile flourished together, but soon the automobile defined the details of Northeast Baltimore's roads, mainstreets, and homes. The connecting ribbons of roadways bear the influential mark of the Olmsted Plan of 1904. From the Alameda (1914) to Walther Avenue (1931), the concept of extending parks into neighborhoods guided corridor development.

In the early twentieth century, the sylvan aspects of the land fostered belief in the ideals of suburban development. Place names such as "Arcadia" and "Beverly Hills" still support a suburban myth that is grounded in reality. The broad green band of Herring Run Park maintains the connection between neighborhood and nature. To this day, owl, fox, and the elusive Baltimore Oriole are active members of the community. In fact, the contemporary livability of Northeast Baltimore is linked to its high quality architecture found in a natural setting.

Eric L. Holcomb presents a thoughtful portrait of an evolving landscape. It reflects the virtue of careful study, an unrelenting curiosity, and a true affection for a worthy place.

Kathleen G. Kotarba
Executive Director
Baltimore City Commission for Historical & Architectural Preservation

A house in Northeast Baltimore, location unknown. (Photo by James H. Lewis, courtesy of Jack Hennessy)

INTRODUCTION

> History may be servitude,
> History may be freedom. See, now they vanish,
> The faces and places, with the self which, as it could, loved them,
> To become renewed, transfigured, in another pattern...
>
> —T. S. Eliot, *Four Quartets,* "Little Gidding"[1]

THIS BOOK is about patterns, patterns of human existence manifested in the landscape of Northeast Baltimore. Each generation created, redefined, and added to the landscape of previous generations. Today, we have a tightly woven tapestry that captures glimpses of the past—seemingly chaotic and at the same time eloquently whole. This book is about patterns of patterns of patterns. They are embedded into the physical environment, are captured in dusty folders within archives, frozen onto black and white photographs, and treasured in our memories. By studying the streets, collections in archives, and listening to stories of Northeast citizens, this book emerged. Tightly woven within the landscape, Northeast Baltimore's history unfolds in its architecture, streets, monuments, cemeteries, and natural landscapes—carefully, and not so carefully preserved. To study the history of Northeast Baltimore, one must not sit in dusty archives or peruse through books, pamphlets, and letters, but walk the neighborhoods, parks, and cemeteries, drive on its ancient truck roads, and peer into the storefronts. The history is still here! History becomes more than bookish facts; it becomes "a pattern of timeless moments."

T. S. Eliot says it better:

> A people without history
> Is not redeemed from time, for history is a pattern
> Of timeless moments. So, while the light fails

On a winter's afternoon, in a secluded chapel
History is now and England.[2]

Throughout the book I rely heavily on landscape and architectural history. The history of architecture is a history of changing fashions, which ornament the façades, and manipulate the buildings' shape. Buildings relate to other buildings, creating streetscapes, a microscopic human ecology. Neighborhoods emerge, tied to each other by roads, churches, parks, and commerce. All bound and knit together, Northeast Baltimore is a definitive part of the five-county Baltimore Metropolitan region. From porch-bracket to aerial photographs, historical tidbits reveal clues to the past.

Like an archaeologist reading bits of broken pottery and pipe stems, patterns were discovered and placed into pages of this book. Nevertheless, a story of the physical development of Northeast Baltimore would be like a description of a computer without any programs. It would describe its shape, materials, and circuit board, but would never produce a picture on the monitor. Only from human activity—memories captured in diaries, newspapers, letters, local histories, momentos, and manifestos—does the landscape become full of life. One theme winds throughout this book: the relationship of Northeast Baltimore to the city. Northeast Baltimore is the product of mixing the city with the country. Simply put, Northeast Baltimore is the relationship between rural landscapes and urban amenities, rural adjectives and urban nouns, rural solitude and the urban bustle, rural nature and urban culture, and rural simplicity and urban sophistication.

The mixing of city and country is an ageless theme that in every era manifests itself in new forms. Northeast Baltimore neighborhoods evolved out of a rich precedence found in the development of Western Culture.

City and Country: Two Sides of the Same Coin

The city and the country need each other. Without one, the other could not exist. Both are part of an economic social and cultural region. In 1826, Johann Heinrich Von Thunen, a gentleman farmer from Mecklenburg, Germany, published a book called *The Isolated State,* where he described the spatial and economic relationship between city and country.[3] This theory put a city into a wilderness. The city, created for trading purposes, needs the resources of the outlying areas. Von Thunen placed the resources into concentric zones. The first zone surrounding the city must be truck farms selling bulky perishable products. These goods must move quickly, lest they perish. They must be "trucked" to the market frequently. In this rural area, land values are high. More durable goods such as wheat, lumber and wood fill the next zone. Beyond this zone would be open prairies for livestock. It is all part of a human ecosystem. Even though Von Thunen's model places a city in a wilderness and unconnected to other centers of trade, all cities and their hinterlands still follow this model.

Northeast Baltimore was the second ring of Von Thunen's theory. It was part of Baltimore's market system. The land became marked as garden plots averaging one to ten acres in size. Farmhouses, outbuildings, and the crossroad villages decorated the area. In addition, other forces played a role influencing Northeast Baltimore. Wealthy merchants bought large tracts of land and built summer estates. These estates were from one to four hundred acres in size. Finally, towards the end of the nineteenth century, middle-class Baltimoreans were building suburban houses on plots of land from one to ten acres in size. By 1914 the area became suburbanized. Intertwined in these forces were urban and rural aesthetic principles. These principles guided the development of Northeast Baltimore.

Northeast Baltimore's main assets were fertile soil for truck farmers, the "country" ambiance for wealthy merchants, and the close proximity to the city for both. Landscape architects and artists, poets and philosophers, and developers and land speculators meshed these assets into its hybrid: the suburb. If the country and city are dependent upon each other, the suburb is dependent upon both. This hybrid, the suburb, was designed in the picturesque fashion.

The Origins of the Picturesque

By the third quarter of the eighteenth century, glimmers of a changing view of nature crept onto the cultural landscape. Romanticism underpinned the philosophical and poetic argument for the suburban exodus. By the beginning of the nineteenth century, this reactionary movement defined loosely as Romanticism found its poetic voice, captured images upon canvas, and reshaped the garden environment. Romanticism rebelled against the present, the culmination of the scientific method and its industrial technology. It looked back upon the distant past, mostly to the knightly realm of Sir Walter Scott. Romanticism created a mythical utopia where industrial urban centers never existed.

In literature, "Romanticism" began with Wordsworth and Coleridge's *Lyrical Ballads* in 1798. In the preface, Wordsworth argued for a new language and a new subject of poetry rooted in the common man. But most important, Wordsworth explored "the beautiful and permanent forms of nature."[4] In poetry, Wordsworth and Coleridge substituted the subject of urbane culture with peasants in the rural hinterlands communing with nature. Romantic poetry suggested that we become privy to nature's secret by immersing our senses and imagination in nature. Romanticism brought to the outskirts of London an argument for the necessity of nature in our lives. Thus, London's suburban enclaves emphasized the vista and created whole landscapes to please the eye by emphasizing the natural features. This underpinning attitude led the way for a resurgence of the Picturesque Style.

In terms of man's aesthetic relationship with nature, Romanticism reinvigorated two aesthetic ideologies: the Picturesque and the Sublime. Both were ideas passed around in treatises in the eighteenth century. Edmund Burke, in 1756, published his philosophical *Inquiry into the Origin of Our Ideas on the Sublime and the Beautiful*. Burke searched to define beauty and wound up characterizing aspects of artistic design. In other words, he placed qualities upon the definition. "Beauty" is symmetrical, smooth, delicate, and rational, whereas "Sublime" is uncontrolled raw emotional power found in such things as waterfalls, canyons, and mountain ranges. Burke's dichotomy placed the Sublime with its irregular, powerful, and ever-changing aspects on one side of the spectrum, and the Beautiful, a polished, symmetrical, non-changing look on the other. This left room for a middle road. Reverend William Gilpin published in 1768 an essay entitled "Upon Prints," which explored rules and principles of landscape painting. He proposed that certain scenes are "picturesque," i.e., worthy of painting. The picturesque was irregular, rough textured, mysterious, but not overwhelming, awe-filled, or life threatening. The picturesque mood illustrated itself upon the grounds of country estates and weekend villas. The picturesque was the middle road between classicism and the wildness of untamed nature. It was the middle road between the Sublime and the Beautiful, the urbane and the wild. Picturesque landscapes were full of rolling greens and peppered with exotic ruins, Chinese pagodas, and formal gardens of classical antiquity, flora, and fauna. Landscape architects fashioned country estates with such images of distant lands as a means of escape for the rich. It was a way of leaving behind the reality of a burgeoning industrial world. Thus, the picturesque was to the English a revolt from the industrial landscape. Ironically, the folks who bought, built, and fashioned their weekend villas were merchants and industrialists.

Architectural forms followed the suggestion of Wordsworth in searching for morality of the common man, as seen in architect John Nash's village of thatched roofed cottages. More importantly, these villages could not be urban, for urban held little of picturesque nature. Thus, they must be away from urban centers, but close enough to allow the fruits of commerce to pay for such sylvan surroundings. It is this paradox, the necessity of industry to pay for creating picturesque villages, which becomes inherent in the American suburban endeavor.

The American Picturesque Sensibility

Although America was deeply influenced by the English, its aesthetic influences became Americanized. Transcendentalism became the American version of English Romanticism. In 1836, Ralph Waldo Emerson published his essay "Nature," which boldly looked towards the American landscape as the source for an original American culture. In Emerson's view "nature, the land itself, should be the source for articulating and developing an American cultural identity."[5] His essay praised nature in such a way that "the visible heavens and earth sympathize with Jesus."[6] Emerson suggested that we are not men until nature is within our sight, "The tradesmen the attorney comes out of the din and craft of the street and sees the sky and the woods, and is a man again. In their eternal calm, he finds himself."[7] The English Romantics pointed to nature as a source of inspiration, whereas Emerson and fellow transcendentalist Henry David Thoreau sanctified nature. The English Romantics embraced nature as a backlash to their culture, while Americans looked towards nature as central to the creation of an American culture.

"Nature" philosophically attempted to capture the vastness and diversity of the American landscape. Nowhere in the world has one country harbored such a diverse and seemingly infinite landscape. Americans harnessed this vastness and diversity. America greatly expanded its boundaries, commercial and industrial capacities, and tied it all together with canals, roads, and railroads. Eli Whitney created interchangeable musket parts spawning America's industrial revolution. Lowell, Massachusetts was becoming America's Manchester. Balloon-frame construction allowed any farmer to become a carpenter, and built Chicago and San Francisco within a year. Every day, new towns sprung from Midwest boosters—most of which became ghost towns (2,205 alone in the Iowa Territory.[8]) Therefore, when Romanticism approached the American shores, it exploded into energy unrivalled in England or Europe. A comparison of Wordsworth's cogent poetry to the whirl of American poet Whitman concisely illustrates this point.

While the Transcendentalists sought for American identity through an American landscape, another American was busy transforming the land through architecture and landscape design. Andrew Jackson Downing, America's leading mid-nineteenth-century landscape gardener and architectural critic, argued eloquently for the semi-rural lifestyle. His chief writings, *A Treatise on the Theory and Practice of Landscape Gardening* (1841), *Cottage Residences* (1842), and *The Architecture of Country Houses* (1850) insisted on individual homes, picturesque landscape principles, and semi-rural surroundings. Downing helped to impress onto the American landscape the curved street,

Katherine Beecher Stowe's Christian morality marries with Andrew Jackson Downing's picturesque principles in this idealized homestead. (Illustration from Stowe's book, 1869)

park-like residential residences, and quaint cottages decorated in natural details. More than anything Downing's works became the bridge between the philosophy and art of the Transcendentalists and the built environment. Downing sculpted Transcendentalism into a landscaped reality. What is more, he created guidebooks on how to do it.

In Downing's books, architecture became the vehicle for Romanticism. Downing listed the architectural styles in which one with enough money could choose: American Log Cabin, Frame House, English Cottage, Collegiate, Gothic Manor House, French Suburban, Swiss Cottage, Lombard Italian, Tuscan, Greek, Oriental, Moorish, and Castellated. Each architectural style prompted associations and feelings within the viewer. Greek and Roman architecture longed for the classical antiquity, Gothic harkened back to Sir Walter Scott's medieval knight, American Log Cabin to the tall tails of Davy Crocket, English Cottage to Wordsworth's Lake District, Oriental to the fabled Far East.

Baltimore's Picturesque and Suburban Beginnings

In Baltimore, the picturesque principles found firm ground. In 1832, Robert Gilmore hired Alexander Jackson Davis to construct Glen Ellen—a Gothic Villa estate considered the first in the United States. Today the estate is under the water of Loch Raven Reservoir (nevertheless, several architectural details are at the Cloisters Mansion, out Falls Road, in Baltimore).

In October 1838, Greenmount Cemetery Company was chartered to improve sixty acres of land owned by the wealthy merchant Robert Oliver. By July 13, 1839, Greenmount was dedicated by John Pendleton Kennedy:

> Though Scarce an half hours walk from yon living mart
> Where one hundred thousand human beings toil in their noisy crafts,
> Here the deep quiet of the Country reigns, broken by no ruder voice than such as
> Marks the tranquility of rural life
> The voice birds on the branches warbling...[9]

John Pendleton Kennedy painted bucolic sympathies within his poem, not to sell plots for the dead, but to sell Baltimoreans on the significance of creating a Romantic cemetery. The main entrance on the southwest corner of Greenmount Avenue is framed by a gothic-inspired gatehouse (1846, Robert Cary Long, Jr.). The chapel, which sits at the top of the hill and is seen prominently from Guilford and Mt. Royal, looks like a cathedral spire anchored into place with flying buttresses (1856, Niernsee and Neilson). Once inside, paths wind and curve throughout the cemetery, heading up steep hills and meandering around funerary art, stately mature trees, flora, and fauna. Though empty in 1839, Greenmount Cemetery must have shown off its bucolic splendor, the foundation of the picturesque.

Just seven years after the creation of Central Park in New York City, Baltimore followed suit. In 1860 Mayor Swan awarded street space to the horsecar companies. In turn the companies gave five percent of their proceeds towards the creation of Druid Hill. Located two or three miles from the center of town, the park was designed by Howard Daniels, the designer of Cincinnati's Spring Grove Cemetery and landscape architect for Llewelyn Park. During the 1870s over a dozen park structures were built. And by 1894, M.C. Robbins, in the *Garden and Forest* magazine, wrote the following:

> The surface of the park is delightfully diversified. There are shady ravines and smooth hill-slopes, from the summit of which one has a broad outlook upon the picturesque groups of trees, and the shadow-flecked grass between, where flocks of Southdown sheep graze, guarded by collie and shepherd. One charming feature of the wood is the free herd of deer, of which two hundred are permitted to roam at large through its precincts.[10]

Robbins goes on to describe the park as having sixteen miles of winding paths, and several lakes such as a boating lake, a fishing lake, the Ponds of the Three Sisters, and Druid Lake, which was the largest. Throughout the park various buildings and structures of exotic styles litter the landscape. The Park proved to be Maryland's most significant Romantic landscape.

Seven years before the creation of Druid Hill Park, Baltimore received its first railroad suburb. In 1853, just one year after the inception of Llewellyn Park, Mt. Washington was conceived. In 1853 George Gelbach and Reverend Elias Heiner bought three hundred acres at Mount Washington. A visionary entrepreneur, Gelbach launched an advertising campaign in mid-June of 1853:

> The situation of this property is highly salubrious and picturesque; and although it is quite elevated, the land is not abrupt or broken but is very handsomely rounded in knolls and gradually sloping hills presenting numerous fine building sites, the

Druid Hill Park's Wallace Monument as depicted in an early 1900s postcard. (R. Wallace Collection)

ascent to which from the railroad and turnpike with the trains and carriages passing. Many of the sites have a handsome growth of forest trees, affording a delightful shade. The grounds are laid off with fine, broad avenues, promenades, and carriage drives, lakes, waterfalls and fountains.[11]

Spurious at best, Gelbach crammed into his brochure any connotations that would arouse within the reader a warm feeling of bucolic living. Gelbach helped to articulate the suburban ideal, even though Mount Washington never had broad avenues, waterfalls, and lakes. In Gelbach's embellished description, he mixed urban characteristics with country adjectives. Promenades, broad avenues, and fountains are positive urban characteristics while waterfalls, lakes, and forest trees are nice country characteristics. Gelbach pioneered two suburban advances in Baltimore: the idea of year-round living and a planned suburban community for city workers. Gelbach took the lead in Baltimore by creating a community solely for residential use. It was a leap forecasting twentieth-century development.

By 1870 Baltimore was building the quaint suburban villages of detached summer homes. As these residential villages sprung up on the outskirts of Baltimore, geographical and technological realities dictated their location, shape, and further defined the suburban character. The 1870s and 1880s saw the creation of many suburban developments surrounding Baltimore: Walbrook, Irvington, Orangeville, Mount Washington, Catonsville, Homestead, and many others. By 1898 there were over sixty-five subdivisions listed on the Bromely Baltimore County Map. The forces behind Baltimore's suburban development were quietly at work in Northeast Baltimore when, by the turn of the twentieth century, development occurred at a scale unknown anywhere else within the limits of Baltimore.

Northeast Baltimore is a story of relationships between diverse geographical areas. It is a story of the country rubbing against and becoming altered by urban sophistication. It is a story of urban usurpation desperately trying—and in many ways succeeding—to capture, hold, and retain some attributes of the country. The book is presented in three parts: what happened in Northeast Baltimore before Baltimore, when it was overlooking Baltimore, and when it became part of Baltimore. Remarkably within the neighborhoods much of it is still here!

THE CITY AS SUBURB

Rugged topography of the Herring Run north of Argonne Drive still retains its original unspoiled character. (Photo by Robert Wallace)

BEFORE THERE WAS *a* CITY
1659–1781

Northeast Baltimore's history began not with Native American settlements, nor European colonization, but a conscious effort to settle elsewhere. Before 1660 the Baltimore County area was virtually ignored. During the seventeenth century, 100,000-150,000 European settlers immigrated to Maryland and Virginia.[1] By the end of the seventeenth century, Baltimore County, which also comprised Harford County, consisted of 1,700 inhabitants, the least populated territory in the Maryland Colony. Baltimore County only counted for one in twenty Maryland colonists.[2] Two reasons vouch for Baltimore's uninhabited wilderness: topography and Native American politics.

Europeans settling in Maryland and Virginia searched for flat, easily tilled land along navigable rivers. Baltimore County held little of both. Charles Steffens, in his book *From Gentlemen to Townsmen, The Gentry of Baltimore County Maryland, 1660-1776*, described it this way:

> For land hungry Englishmen the navigable rivers and arable lands below the fall line were magnificent gifts from God. But God had been stingy on the northern Western Shore, squeezing the Coastal Plain into a Narrow Strip only a few miles wide... The terrain of Baltimore County falls rapidly toward the bay in a series of terraces, the highest reaching some 500 feet near today's Loch Raven, ten miles north of downtown Baltimore.

Even the first Englishman to lay eyes on Baltimore County described it in a way that would deter colonization. In June 1608, twenty-six years before the two ships, the Ark and the Dove, landed in Southern Maryland and founded St. Mary's City, Captain John Smith ventured from Jamestown in a flat barge to explore the upper Chesapeake. From his barge Smith described the eastern edge of Baltimore County:

4 THE CITY AS SUBURB

A colonial map of the region shows colonial roads, and marks the location of the Kingsberry (Kingsbury) Furnace. (Courtesy Library of Congress. General map of the Middle British Colonies in America. Printed by Lewis Evans in London for Carrington Bowles, 1771. http://memory.loc.gov/cgi-bin)

> The westerne shore by which we sayled, we found all along well watered, but very mountanous, and barren, the vallies very fertill, but extreame thicke of small wood so well as trees, and much frequented with wolves, Beares, Deere, and other wild beasts.[3]

Just north of the Patapsco River he identified the Back, Middle, Gunpowder and Bush Rivers as "four small rivers, three of them issuing from diverse bogges."[4] Smith's description of Baltimore County as being "Mountainous," "barren," and "extreme thick of small wood" were not desired for building plantations. In 1612 his account of the Chesapeake was printed in England to spur immigration to the new colony. Nevertheless, his description of Baltimore County in comparison with other parts of Maryland and Virginia thwarted settlement of the region. Englishmen were settling the New World for its fertile flat lands—fertile flat lands that could expand the economy of the mother country.

Today, the topography of Northeast Baltimore is described in geological terms. Cutting through the center of Baltimore City is the fault line between the Piedmont

Plateau and the Coastal Range. Here, hills rub against and descend into mud flats that slide into the Chesapeake. A walk through Herring Run Park illustrates the dramatic change from the Piedmont Plateau to the Coastal Range. At the eastern end of the Park by Armistead Gardens the land lays flat, and just beyond Pulaski Highway meshes with the water. Walking westward past Belair Road the land begins to protrude upward. Between Belair and Harford roads, hills line the north side of Herring Run. Here, large boulders and stratified rock formations protrude from the bed of the Herring Run. Moving closer to Harford Road, rock formations stick out from the wooded hills of the north side of the stream. Crossing underneath Harford Road, the landscape begins a dramatic push upwards. Directly south of Argonne Drive, the streambed has cut deeply through a rocky and scenic gorge. Tree-strewn cliffs rise over a hundred feet. A view from the Argonne Bridge looks as wild as any mountain stream in the Appalachian Mountains. Like a paintbrush, the Herring Run over centuries has created a natural treasure of two geological regions colliding with one another. Thus, for the first hundred and some odd years of Maryland Colonization, the Piedmont Plateau was avoided.

While the terrain of the Piedmont Plateau deterred European colonization, Native Americans sidestepped the area for political reasons. The area from the Susquehanna down to the Patuxent was a "demilitarized zone" between the Susquehannocks and the Algonquins. As early as 1608, Captain Smith mentioned that the Patapsco Valley was deserted. The Algonquins were a peaceful tribe that intermingled with the early Maryland settlers in Southern Maryland. The Susquehannocks, a warring tribe, used the region of Baltimore County as a hunting ground. George Alsop, a former indentured servant of Lord Baltimore, described in his book, *A Character of the Province of Maryland*, the Susquehannocks as "seven feet tall, deep voiced, and great warriors."[5] This demilitarized zone was far too dangerous for settlement by the Algonquins and Englishmen. Meanwhile, the Susquehannocks comfortably inhabited the area around the Susquehanna River and only ventured south for hunting. For the first sixty years of European settlement only fur traders ventured into Baltimore County to trade with the Susquehannocks.

Nevertheless, land-hungry Europeans incessantly searched for land to increase their riches. By the middle of the seventeenth century, action was taken to settle more of the Maryland Colony.

Native American control of the region had to be usurped before Baltimore County could be created and systematically colonized. A generation after the first Maryland settlement at St. Mary's City, the coupling of armed colonists and ravaging disease pushed the Susquehannocks into submission. Consequently, in 1652 the Maryland

Proprietary Government persuaded the Susquehannocks to sign a peace treaty, which included relinquishing much of their lands.[6] In 1659 or 1660, Baltimore County was established. Originally, Baltimore County included Harford and Cecil counties until 1674, when Cecil County was formed. Not until 1773 did Baltimore County split to create Harford County. With Baltimore County formally opened, conflict between Native Americans and Europeans did not disappear. In 1681, the Maryland Council proposed to raise a group of Rangers for each county to protect frontier settlements against Native Americans. On August 16, 1692, a Council was held at the house of John Larkin of Anne Arundel County where "Captain Thomas Richardson was appointed Chief Ranger for part of Baltimore county namely 'from the Falls of Back River (i.e. Herring Run) upward to the extent of the said country.' Thomas Hooker was appointed Ranger from the falls of Back River to the Patapsco River." The following day the council ordered "that the Rangers appointed to watch and guard the Frontiers of the Province be continued and that Captain Thomas Richardson with twelve men under his Command be appointed to range on the Frontiers of Baltimore County."[7]

Several violent conflicts between Native Americans and colonists were recorded. With the Native American politics turned upside down by European settlement, Native Americans became more nomadic, and resettled where they could best survive. Here, in the old demilitarized zone, the uninhabited land became desirable to small groups of Native Americans and Europeans. One such conflict was with Robert Gorsuch. Living on the Gunpowder River in 1661, he described the incident: "Indians dressed in blue and some in red match coats, killed his wife and plundered his house. About four or five days later they returned and killed five cows, a steer, and some hogs."[8]

Another settler living near Northeast Baltimore, John Taylor, stated that "nine male Indians with one woman came to his house, but being ordered off, they departed, but returned in two weeks and damaged his goods to the value of about one thousand pounds of Tobacco." Another account concerned three settlers on the Middle River, Francis Freeman, Richard Enock, and his wife.[9] On their settlement, they were assaulted and Richard Enock was killed. These accounts are significant, not in telling of the savagery of Native Americans, but for some of the only records to survive. They at best preserve a scant memory of Native American activity in Baltimore County.

Other records also give clues to the Native American inhabitants of this region.[10] In the old county levies (1683-1706) there are references to tobacco credit to settlers who brought skins of wolves that were "of Indian killing." Secondly, after the killing of Richard Enock, "Mr. Francis Watkins went with four of their family to the Indian Cabbin that the Indians belonged to and demanded the murderers, but that the Indians kept him off with their guns presented upon which he raised a file or more of men and went again but the Indians were all gone."[11] These Native Americans were part of the Nanticoke Tribe, which used to inhabit the Eastern Shore. This "cabbin" was located off Deep Creek on the Back River Neck. Off Deep Creek was a smaller branch known as "Indian Fort." These names, which may indicate Native American settlements, were not permanent settlements prior to the English settlement, but Native resettlements that occurred from European colonization usurping the pre-colonial Native American way of life.

Not only did the Rangers play a significant role in the development of Baltimore County by guarding against lawlessness, but also for their efforts at improving the land with roads, buildings, and plantations. The Rangers' records describe a network of Baltimore County Roads. Through a careful analysis of Baltimore County Ranger Captain Oldton's descriptions, William Marye has plotted a conjectural route of the Garrison Road that led from the Patapsco to the Susquehanna. This road, according to Marye, ran through the western part of Baltimore City (today's Garrison Avenue comes closest). The Garrison Road eventually crossed the Old Main Road (U.S. Route 1) in South Baltimore. William Marye suggests that Captain Oldton and his men built a road, a short cut, from the Back River Neck to the old Garrison Road. William Marye states of this shortcut:

> Whatever paths or roads may have existed before 1700 on the land on which Baltimore City is now built, Darley Path and the old main Road which later became known as the Philadelphia Road, are, so far as I am aware, the only ones of which any record exists... If Darley Path, as originally laid out led from the Main Road to "Darley Hall," and there stopped, it could scarcely have been more than two miles in length; but there is a possibility that it penetrated much farther into the forest, and that it may even have "tapped" the road which led from the Garrison to Deer Creek.[12]

Darley Path became the southern portion of Harford Road (from Clifton Park to the head of the Jones Falls), and the first road to penetrate into Northeast Baltimore.

During the seventeenth century, the Back and Middle Rivers connected Northeast Baltimore to the Maryland Colony and England. But at the turn of the eighteenth century, Captain John Oldton connected Darley Hall to Jonestown, creating another entryway into Northeast Baltimore. If Darley Path was a rolling road, most likely Darley Hall was a tobacco plantation. Farmers put axles through their hogshead of tobacco and carted them to the nearest wharf. Settlement in Northeast Baltimore, therefore, began as an outgrowth of the Back River Neck where the Rangers lived, and steadily moved inward. The building of Darley Path helped to shift the settlement pattern from the Back

8 THE CITY AS SUBURB

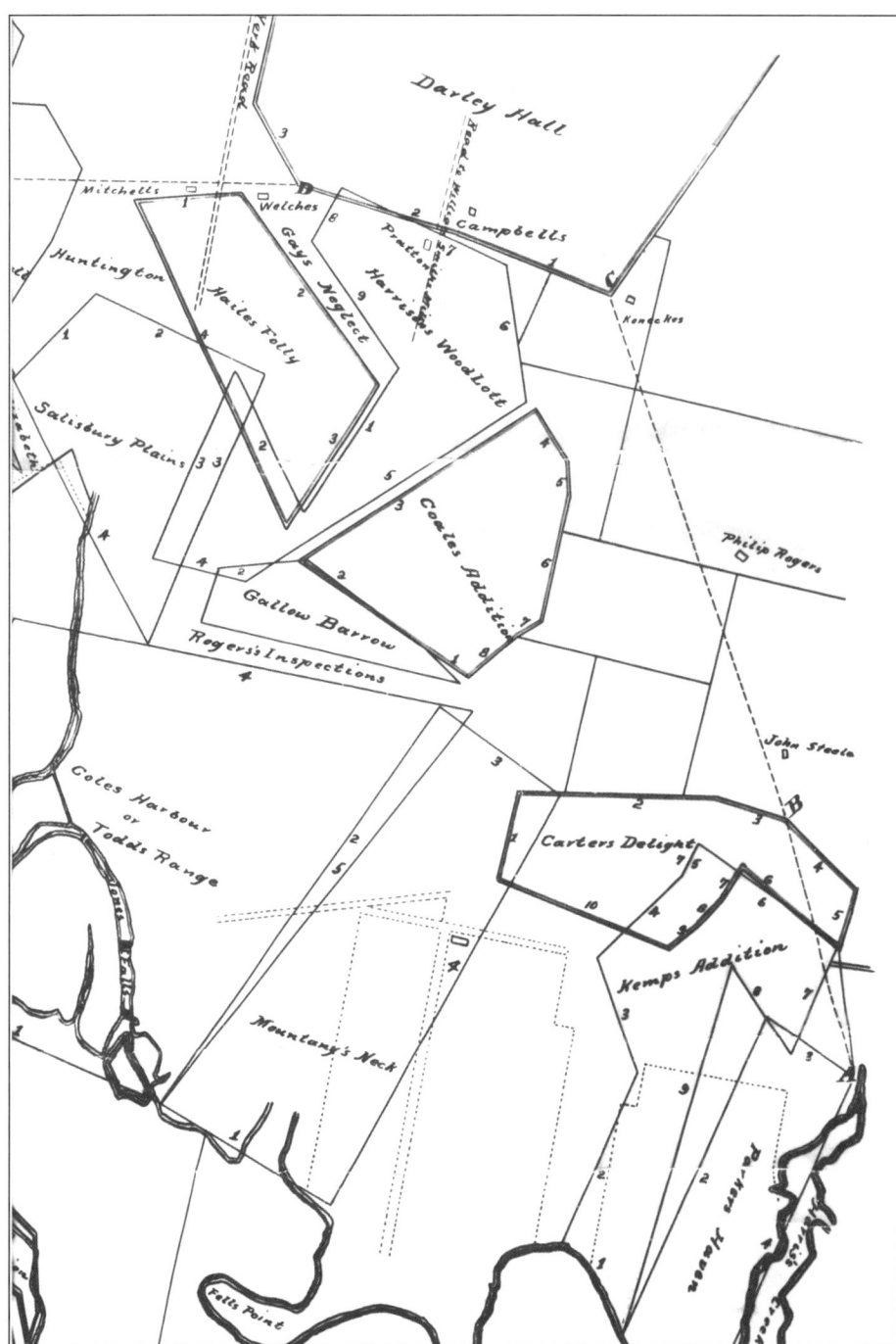

This map, drawn by H. Macubbin, Jr. in 1786, depicts Campbell's estate "Belmont" and Captain Oldton's estate, "Darley Hall." The road passing through Darley Hall, "Road to William Smith's Mill," later became Harford Road in 1792. Lines were added here and throughout the text to frame maps and reproductions. (Courtesy of CHAP)

River Neck to the Baltimore area. Therefore, the creation of Darley Path was the beginning of Northeast Baltimore's complex relationship with Baltimore City. In fact, this relationship was created at least twenty-nine years before the creation of Baltimore Town.

The Rangers also became some of the first land speculators owning several tracts of land. By 1694, Captain Oldton commanded the Baltimore County Rangers. Under his command were the following rangers: Daniell Welsh, Henry King, Thomas Robards, Tobias Stansberry, Josias Bridges, and Moses Edwards. Captain Oldton and all of the Rangers owned land throughout Baltimore County. In a list of taxables taken in June of 1694, all the Rangers were listed as having land on the south side of the Back River. In addition, some of the rangers owned land throughout the County. Henry King patented the land known as Kingsbury in 1698. This tract was located at the mouth of the Herring Run. Tobias Stansbury owned Mount Hayes on the North Side of the Back River. By the 1740s the Stansbury Family owned several lots in downtown Baltimore and other tracts around the Gunpowder Falls. Moses Edwards in 1701 bought "Come by Chance" from John Richardson, which was on the West Side of Jones Falls. Edwards also owned "Edwards Enlargement," now in East Baltimore. Moses Edwards also conveyed land on the Middle River Neck to St. Paul's Parish. And Captain John Oldton owned several tracts of land: Gardeson on the Back River, Pemblicoe where Pimloco racecourse is today, and Darley Hall which, today, is part of Clifton Park. The land holdings of the Rangers resembled the typical pattern of land distribution throughout Baltimore County.

Before 1680 land was granted to settlers on a headright basis. In other words, Lord Baltimore issued land at 50 acres per settler. After 1680 land was sold outright to land investors. Acquiring land was intertwined in a three-fold process. First, a Warrant was issued for a Deputy Surveyor to lay out a number of acres for a specific person. Second, a Certificate of Survey was issued after the Deputy Surveyor stated the exact location and boundaries of the land. And last, the survey was written into a Certificate of Patent, which codified the survey into legal jargon. As one might imagine, describing exact boundaries in the wilderness led to many errors, which produced court battles for decades to come.

This rush of land grabbing in the 1690s populated as well as stunted the growth of the county. A petition delivered to the Governor in 1697 stated "diverse Tracts of Land Appertaining to Severall Gentlemen not residing in this County who take noe Care to Seate the same."[13] Even in the late seventeenth century, absentee landlords plagued Baltimore County!

Northeast Baltimore followed the typical patterns of Baltimore County land development of plantations squeaking out a living from agriculture until 1734, when William Chetwynd began to assemble large tracts of Land for the Principio Iron Company. With the introduction of the iron industry, Northeast Baltimore transformed from a backwater plantation community to an iron furnace plantation encompassing much of Northeast Baltimore. By the end of the land consolidation the Principio Iron Company owned over 4,900 acres in North and Northeast Baltimore Town.[14]

The Principio Iron Company was an English conglomerate made up of British iron masters, merchants, and capitalists. Their interest in Maryland and Virginia colonies began in 1715 when the Principio Company acquired large tracts of land in Cecil County near the mouth of the Susquehanna River. In 1718, the company sent the Colonies' first shipment of pig iron to England. It is not known whether the shipment came from the company's Virginia furnace or the Cecil County furnace. By 1751, the Principio Company's hold on Maryland "outranked all competitors and was the sole proprietor of four furnaces and two forges; Principio Furnace and Forge, Cecil County Maryland, built prior to 1720; Northeast forge, Cecil County Maryland, built about 1720; Accokeek Furnace, Virginia, built about 1725; Kingsbury Furnace, Baltimore County, Maryland, built about 1744; and Lancashire Furnace, Baltimore County, Maryland, purchased 1751 (from Dr. Charles Carroll)."[15] At its height, the Principio Iron Company owned over 30,000 acres in Maryland and Virginia.

Iron had a significant role to play in the creation of Baltimore Town. Baltimore Town was established not only as a sheltered port, but also as a place rich in iron ore. Captain John Smith in his famous 1608 voyage described Whetstone Point, where Federal Hill and Locust Point is today, as a "bole armeniac," after a bright red medicinal substance. The color identified the area as rich in iron ore. Baltimore Town was to be originally laid out on Whetstone Point, but due to the iron deposits, it was moved to current day Central Business District. In 1727 the Principio Company purchased on Whetstone Point "all the iron ore opened and discovered or shut and not yet discovered for the sum of 300 sterling money of Great Britain and 20 current money of Maryland." In addition, the Principio Company in 1724 bought Gorsuch Point (around Canton today) for its iron deposits. At this point, Baltimore's iron ore was shipped to the Northeast forge in Cecil County, but by 1745 these iron deposits fed the furnace at Kingsbury, which was located on both sides of the Herring Run at the intersection of today's Pulaski Highway.

Known history of the Kingsbury tract began in 1698.[16] In 1698 Charles Calvert granted 124 acres to Henry King. By 1724 William and Susanna King, son and daughter-in-law of Henry, sold to Thomas Sheredine not only the original 124 acres of Kingsbury, but also 500 acres of Maiden's Hill. Sometime between 1724 and 1733 Kingsbury was resurveyed and encompassed 473 acres. Most likely, part of Maiden's Hill was incorporated into the Kingsbury tract. In 1733, Samuel Chew and Philip Thomas gave receipt to Thomas Sheredine for the following tracts: 473 acres of Kingsbury resurveyed, 250 acres of Long Point, 500 acres of Mason's Oats, 187 acres of The Plains, 100 acres of Rogers road, and 150 acres of Sheredine's Bottom. Colonel Thomas Sheredine turned around in November of 1734 and sold Kingsbury and Sheredine's Bottom to William Chetwynd of Beddington, County Surrey, and John Whittiwicks of Craden, County Surrey, who represented the Principio Iron Company.

In addition to acquiring ore-rich lands, the Company also needed vast wooded lands for charcoal. For the Kingsbury Furnace, the Principio Company acquired much more land than stated above. In 1735, 3,000 acres called Grindon was conveyed to the Principio Company. In 1741, 50 acres of Wilmot's Neglect was conveyed to the Principio Iron Company. In April of 1743, 1,900 acres of Sheredine's Discovery was conveyed to the Principio Iron Company.[17] The total acreage cannot be tallied from the above land grants, since many of the land patents may have been merged with one another. But it is safe to assume that the Principio Iron Company owned at least 4,900 acres of Northeast Baltimore. This large portion of land was needed to feed the constant furnace of Kingsbury. Iron ore was a short boat ride directly south.

The Kingsbury Iron Furnace made its first batch of pig iron in 1745.[18] By the mid-1750s, Kingsbury Furnace and the Lancashire Furnace (3½ miles northeast of Kingsbury) produced more pig iron than the furnace in Cecil County, which soon closed. Between 1745 and 1750, a duration of fifty-two months, in which blasts would continue for almost a year at a time, the company produced 3,853 tons of pig iron.[19] The furnace ended operations in 1780 when the Maryland General Assembly passed an act to seize and confiscate all British Property within the State.

In 1781 an inventory was taken of the Kingsbury Furnace. From a list of articles sold from the Kingsbury Furnace by the Commission of British Confiscated Property, the furnace resembled a small village plantation with a general store and access to navigable waters. The iron works also had "two grist mills and a vast quantity of merchandise—hardware and textiles." Other merchandise mentioned were two smith's shops each with a full set of tools, eight wagons of varying type, nineteen horses, twenty-five sheep, eighteen cows, nine pigs, seventeen boars, one lot of furniture, blankets, crow bars and several wheel barrows. Other buildings mentioned in the inventory were as follows:

Salt House	Wheelwright's Shop	Beazy's (African American Worker) House
Negro Kitchen	Casting House	Miner's Care
Smith's Shop	Nail Store	Job Key's House
Kitchen	Bridge House	Landing House.[20]

The Herring Run at this time was navigable by flat barges, which bought and sold goods to the local residents. In June 29, 1776, Jesse Hollingsworth of Baltimore picked up 800 cannonballs in his flat barge. The inventory of buildings also mentions a "Landing House," which reaffirms that boats maneuvered up the Herring Run to Kingsbury. Today, any boat carrying goods would be hard pressed to venture up the Herring Run to Pulaski Highway. Most likely by the end of the eighteenth century sediment from wood-harvested lands around the Herring Run filled in the Basin. It is estimated that it took 4 to 6 thousand cords of wood a year to keep an iron furnace burning.[21] This type of environmental degradation of colonial waterways is well documented along the Patapsco near Elkridge. Elkridge during the eighteenth century was a large tobacco port where current-day Rolling Road terminates. Nevertheless, the downfall of Elkridge was the barren land made by the stripping of vegetation. Here sediment choked the Patapsco River halting any ships from sailing to the port.[22] This type of degradation may have happened to the Herring Run.

Other evidence suggests a dramatic change to the environment of the Herring Run. A court case between Robert Long, who owned land adjacent to Sheredine's Bottom, states "Francis Phillips thus took 'forcible Possession' called Sheredine's Bottom and kept the same for 12 (or 2) years which time considerable damage was done, and the said Robert Long commence suit for the recovery of said land in 1770."[23] This damage mentioned most likely was the removal of raw materials, i.e. lumber or iron ore. In addition, twenty-two tenants lived on the lands of the Principio Iron Company. Undoubtedly the land was used for agricultural purposes after the Company stripped the area of wood. These tenant farmers could have grown wheat for the two grist mills at the Kingsbury Furnace Plantation. In 1786 Robert Long of Fells Point bought the Kingsbury Tract of land. He built a large new merchant mill, but soon became insolvent and sold the furnace to General Samuel Smith in 1792. General Samuel Smith never made any iron, and shortly into the nineteenth century sold off the land. Kingsbury Furnace never made any iron ore after 1780, and most likely the silting of the Herring Run was a major factor.

The 1781 inventory identified forty-five slaves living and working at the furnace. Their professions include a wide variety of skills such as miners, watermen, blacksmiths, founders, fillers, wagoneers, spinners, colliers, house workers, cooks, and nurses to the children. Although many of these jobs were unskilled, several noted were highly skilled. Holding such a large percentage of skilled jobs illustrated Kingsbury's dependence on slavery. In fact, slavery drove Baltimore County's iron industry. In 1773, tax appraisers listed eight ironworks in Baltimore County with fifty-two percent of the 432-person workforce as slaves. Nottingham Forge had forty-eight slaves while Kingsbury had forty-five slaves.[24]

In the 1781 inventory, several slave women and children were identified, but most slaves were male. This poses several scenarios on the family life and culture of African-American slaves at Kingsbury. Most likely not all the slaves lived at Kingsbury. In the inventory of buildings, Mr. Beazely's house is identified along with the "Negro kitchen." Other quarters may have existed. Their absence from the inventory may be due to their perceived lack of economic worth. Most likely, the slaves lived on other plantations and were rented out to Kingsbury or lived on lands owned by the white workers of the Furnace. It is evident that African-Americans were a sophisticated and integral force in Maryland's industrial evolution.

The Principio's forty-six-year domination ended in a fury of land grabbing which created a complex gentlemen plantation environment. After Robert Long lost his hold over the land, over a hundred lots (actually large tracts of land) were sold. 404 acres were sold to Daniel Bowly who built Furley Hall. 400 acres were sold to Jacob Herticks, and 140 acres sold to W. Abraham Coffman. In addition, David Harris bought land and built "Mount Deposit." As early as the 1810s, Northeast Baltimore resembled a well-developed farmland.

CREATION of BORDERLAND COMMUNITIES 1780–1852

THE SELLING of the Principio Iron Company land holdings spawned a new era of intense development. Wealthy Baltimore merchants and truck farmers quickly settled the land. The wealthy merchants created summer playgrounds dabbling in hobby agriculture, and the truck farmers tilled the soil.

In the early decades of the nineteenth century, the wealthy merchant created private parks based upon the current fashion of landscape design and architecture. Their vision of Northeast Baltimore was a genuine desire to frame, physically and philosophically, beauty into their lives. Their estates were havens of retreat from Baltimore. From late Autumn to early Spring they resided in their town houses amongst the bustle of a sophisticated social and economic network. Here, they reveled in urbanity. For the summer months the merchants moved their families to the outskirts of the city, but close enough, not more than an hour's commute, to their businesses. These estates were sub-urban, dependent upon the daily activities of the city. Their vision combined urban amenities (townhouses) with country beauty (country estates) and designed both of them according to a rich precedence found in Western culture.

Meanwhile, the truck farmers had an entirely different vision for Northeast Baltimore. For the truck farmer, the city held markets where goods were bought and sold. The location of agricultural land close to the city was essential in order to transport or "truck" quickly their perishables to market. The farm was their livelihood where fashions of the day were thwarted by utilitarian needs. Without a brigade of servants or slaves, nor the economic resources of the Baltimore elite, these farmers struggled to create profitable farms. They overcame depleted fields, rough untilled soil, shortage of labor and supplies, and ill-built backbreaking roads. Nevertheless, through decades of

Opposite: Chevalier D'Anmour, French Consulate and merchant of early nineteenth-century Baltimore, built his home at the northeast corner of North Avenue and Harford Road around 1780.
(Courtesy EPFL Maryland Room)

1801 Hanna & Warner Map of Baltimore and environs. (Courtesy of CHAP Archives)

hard work and improved farming tools and techniques the truck farmers persevered and prospered. Once established they reached out to one another and began creating a borderland community. During the early years their social activities were housed on the farms. Parishes were formed and met in farmhouses, or barns, and finally in churches built on a farmer's land. Finally, churches, schools, post offices, taverns, and general stores were erected in centrally located areas. By the mid-nineteenth century crossroad villages appeared.

Throughout the early decades of the nineteenth century, these two visions coexisted separately within the vast open northeast landscape. But as Northeast Baltimore's population increased, the wealthy merchants and the truck farmers began crossing paths. Many times they were at odds, other times they worked together addressing the pressing needs of a Baltimore borderland region. In some instances, truck farmers rose to the prominence of the Baltimore merchant, other times country estates became important income producing farms. This cross-fertilization incrementally increased throughout the nineteenth century, creating a dynamic tension that slowly shaped Northeast Baltimore. Fundamentally this tension originated from geographic loyalty— the wealthy merchants were Baltimore City residents, while the truck farmers were Baltimore County residents.

Dependence upon Baltimore

Northeast Baltimore could not have developed without Baltimore's rapid rise into a national city that was intricately tied to the global economy. Baltimore provided manufactured goods and farmer's markets for Northeast Baltimore. In addition, the city's financial stability and instability, political activities, and cultural and religious institutions influenced Northeast's development. Nevertheless, it was a reciprocal relationship. Northeast Baltimore supplied the city with food and other natural resources. The hobby farms provided necessary experiments for the improvement of agriculture as well as the necessary wealth for infrastructure improvements.

Baltimore in the 1790s was a bustling pioneer town struggling to find organization during an era of population explosion. Between 1790 and 1860 Baltimore's population rose from a little over 10,000 to more than 210,000 people.[1] This population increase caused great stress on the physical, political, economic, and social networks of Baltimore. In the 1790s Baltimore had approximately three thousand houses (whereas in 1752 Baltimore had twenty-five houses), a chaotically expanding port, and fledgling cultural, religious, and social institutions.[2] In order to feed the growing population, Baltimore "in 1784 created three market houses, each convenient to the waterfront but on rising ground to permit drainage."[3] The market houses soon became local economic centers, which in turn produced embryonic neighborhoods. The first market house was Center or Marsh Market located where Market Place is today. The second market was Hanover or Camden Market located where Camden Yards is today. The third market was in Fells Point where Broadway Market is today. These market houses did not extend beyond the local economy only, but mostly provided the essential nourishment for Baltimore.

Baltimore at this time was a thriving international port providing flour and goods to the Caribbean, Great Britain, Mediterranean, and South America. In order to keep a growing port humming smoothly, the Maryland General Assembly in 1782 created a board of Port Wardens who were charged with surveying the harbor and ensuring that the shipping channels remained clear.[4] In 1797 they created a boundary in which wharves could not extend. Large three-story brick warehouses were built upon the wharves as they extended further out into the harbor. Not only did the demand for waterfront access create wharves over a thousand feet long (Baltimore merchants, Dugan and McElderry, both built 1,600-foot wharves), it also created dry land from the muck of the harbor's first dredging operation! Water Street today marks the shoreline of eighteenth-century Baltimore. In 1797 the public waterway boundary line was crucial in keeping order along the waterfront. The creation of the waterfront as well as the board of port wardens illustrated the thriving economy of Baltimore, the economy that gave reason for Northeast Baltimore to exist as a borderland region.[5]

By 1801 Baltimore boasted several public buildings, three market houses, and fourteen churches. The public buildings noted were the jail, the courthouse, and the Customs House. Private institutions also thrived as cultural centers of Baltimore. The Library Company of Baltimore was organized in 1795, the same year the Customs House was built. In 1786 Hallam and Henry opened a theater at Baltimore and Albemarle Streets. In the 1790s the Assembly Room was built to accommodate the collection of the Library Company and social functions such as balls and receptions. Baltimore also boasted the Indian Queen and Fountain Inn for travelers passing through Baltimore.[6] The religious fervor of Baltimoreans manifested into fourteen churches and ten denominations: Quakers, Presbyterians, German Calvinists, German Reformed Lutherans, German Lutherans, Mennonites, Baptists, Roman Catholics, Episcopalians, and Methodists. The Jewish community also became a strong force in Baltimore.[7]

In addition to the religious, cultural, and social institutions, several financial institutions were established which were absolutely critical in the growth of Baltimore and its borderland regions. Between 1787 and 1795 Baltimore was inundated with financial institutions: The Baltimore Fire Insurance Company, the Baltimore Branch of the Bank of the United States, Bank of Maryland, and the Bank of Baltimore. Also, in 1792 Baltimore Town Commissioners instituted a "house tax" for the purpose of lighting the streets and providing a 'night watch.' The house tax followed some very basic rules: three-story dwellings more than eighteen feet wide and two-story dwellings more that thirty feet wide must pay fifteen shillings a year. Three-story dwellings less than eighteen feet wide and two-story dwellings less than thirty feet wide must pay ten shillings. One-story dwellings must pay five shillings. However, in 1798 the 'house tax' was repealed when authority was given to jurisdictions to provide for direct taxation.[8] This authority greatly expanded Baltimore's ability to tax its citizens and consequently provide for essential internal improvements such as harbor dredging, street building, and police protection.

During the first few decades of the nineteenth century Baltimore continued to expand and flourish as its social, cultural, religious, and economic institutions scrambled to keep pace with the city's sheer vitality. And Baltimore's sheer vitality was the single most influential element that directly and indirectly shaped the city's Northeast borderland region.

The Vision of the Wealthy Merchant

During the 1790s and the first decade of the nineteenth century, many wealthy merchant's estates were built close to Harford, Belair and Philadelphia Roads. Huddling next to Harford Road and directly north of North Avenue were Belmont, Clifton, Montebello, Homestead, and Coldstream. Connected to the city by the Philadelphia Road were Mount Deposit and Clairmont. Further out and tied to the Philadelphia Road by Bowley's Lane was Furley Hall. These estates marked a new level of maturity for Baltimore, a sign that Baltimore was a world-class city guided by a merchant elite.

Wealthy merchants were not just commercial businessmen but participants in a culture-bearing elite. These merchants were educated in the classics, well versed in agriculture, dabbled in inventions, science, and architecture. They controlled the politics of the day, and were officers in the military. They were the builders, financiers, real estate developers and politicians of Baltimore. In addition, they were tied by business to England and Europe, which undoubtedly influenced their tastes. As the economic opportunity arose, they began building their country estates that allowed them yet another outlet for their creativity.

Architecture at the time was considered an expression of one's wealth and social status, of one's unique position in society. To promptly express one's importance, their country estates and townhomes were fashioned in the latest architectural style. After the revolution, wealthy Americans endeavored to create an architecture that embodied the values of the new Republic.

During this period known as the Federal Period the architecture was a refinement of the classical details found in pre-revolutionary America. It was America's version of Britain's Adamesque architecture, and France's Rococo fashions. These classical details ornamented the many components of their estates. Doors were ornamented with fanlights and sidelights. Columns and pilasters (flat square columns that were ornamental and not structural) followed the Classical orders. Windows at this time were ornamented with segmental (semicircular) arches, flat arches or keystones. Windows were constructed of many small glass panes, usually six or nine panes to one window sash. Cornices and rooflines were decorated with dentils and modillions and sometimes topped with a balustrade. The house was symmetrical and geometrically well proportioned, exhibiting organization and order.

These classical details fit nicely into the enthusiasm and philosophy of the young republic. Although the architecture was based upon European patterns, the wealthy merchants were intensely aware that their new Republic differed greatly from the governmental systems of Europe. They wanted to fashion the land and architecture according to classical styles that symbolized the democratic systems of ancient Greece and Rome.

In the early Republic, the dissemination of Federalist architectural details followed several deliberate patterns. First, the wealthy merchant played a significant role in the design. Since the merchants were well read and in many cases well traveled, they designed the house or hand-picked details from design books. Second, the merchant was often in charge of acquiring the building materials. Here, the merchant played the part of a modern-day general contractor. The training of the craftsmen dictated to the merchant what design could be used. Therefore, wherever the craftsmen learned their trade—Ireland, France, England, or Philadelphia—always played a part in the design.

Throughout the colonies, several pattern books came into the hands of craftsmen and merchants alike. In 1794 J. R. Rice and Company advertised the following books on architecture: *The British Architect or the Builder's Treasury; The Practical Builder; Workman's General Assistant;* and *The Town and Country Builder's Assistant*.[9] Also, in 1795, Ambrose Clark and James Keddie of Maryland listed several books for sale: *Nicholson and Paine's Carpenter, Paine's Practical Builder, Builder's Jewel and Repository, Crunden's Designs, Miller's Farm Houses, Shop Front, Principals of Ornament, Sheraton's Ornaments* and *Rawlin's Designs*. Obviously, local merchants and craftsmen had at their fingertips several copies of pattern books, which they inevitably used in the construction of Baltimore.

All the early estates of Northeast Baltimore were designed with Classical details. Some were very simple like Belmont, while others like Montebello were highly original designs. Still others were fashionable farmhouses. In addition, the grounds became cultivated and elaborated upon with decorative plantings. Each estate expressed the character of each merchant, the character of political power, wealth, and elitism. These estates were built with the capital acquired in Baltimore City, unlike the truck farmers whose money was made from the soil of their farms.

The Merchants and Their Estates

General Samuel Smith and Montebello

At the turn of the nineteenth century, General Samuel Smith was the most successful merchant in Baltimore. Between 1796 and 1799, General Samuel Smith built Montebello near the corner of Hillen and Harford roads. His country home was a manifestation of his individuality and success. Montebello in many ways symbolized General Smith's life as a fiercely independent politician, a cunning businessman and a hero in the Revolutionary War and the War of 1812.

In 1752 Sam Smith was born into the wealthy elite. At the age of fourteen he finished his formal education in Baltimore and began working for his father. At nineteen he went to England and worked as a clerk for Mildred Roberts.[10] Almost a year later, between 1772 and 1774, Smith sailed to the ports of France, Spain, and the Mediterranean, forming trade agreements for his father's company. Highly successful in his

Portrait: General Samuel Smith. (Courtesy EPFL Maryland Room)

endeavors, Smith greatly expanded the profits of his father's company. While travelling through the ports of Europe, he acquired a taste for French literature and fine furniture, a taste he kept throughout his life.

Just prior to the Revolutionary War Smith returned to Baltimore, where he stayed until his death. Upon return, his father made him a partner in the family business. When the Revolutionary War broke out, Smith enlisted as a Captain in Colonel Smallwood's regiment. Smith saw much fighting at the Battle of Long Island. Shortly thereafter he went to defend Fort Mifflin on Mud Island located at the mouth of the Schuykill River. While fighting gallantly Smith could not stop the British Fleet, but was bestowed with the title of "Hero of Mud Island."

On leave in Baltimore in 1778 Smith married Margaret Spear and in 1779 he resigned from the Army. Back in business Smith sold food to the Maryland and Virginia militias, a contract that proved profitable. During this time Smith made a small fortune running the British blockades and providing essential food to the Caribbean settlements. Smith became deeply involved in Baltimore affairs. In 1783 he was appointed brigadier general of the Maryland Militia and a warden of the port of Baltimore. In 1790 Smith helped to incorporate the Bank of Maryland. While leading such a fulfilling public life, Smith also engaged in a thriving private life.

In the 1780s the Smith family lived in a large two-story brick mansion on Gay Street near his father's home. Smith had, by 1783, three children; Louis, St. John, and Elizabeth. In all, Smith's wife Margaret gave birth to twelve children, of which six lived to adulthood. In 1785, Robert Hunter attended a dinner party at the Smith's house that he described as follows:

> The party began at 3:00 p.m. in a second-floor drawing Room. There Samuel and Margaret "a genteel and elegant woman" presided over a "most agreeable company." In the early evening the guests were treated to violin music and at 10:00 they were finally led downstairs to the dining room and offered an elegant dinner.[11]

In addition to a thriving social life, the Smiths also attended the First Presbyterian Church, the church his father helped to form. Working diligently at his business, throwing long elegant parties, running the Maryland Militia, and performing civic duties in the young town, Smith lived a happy, fulfilling life in Baltimore. Nevertheless, Smith had yet to venture into his long political career.

Smith's entrance into politics coincided with taking on a new partner, James Buchanan, in his firm, in 1790. That same year Smith entered the Maryland House of Delegates. From this jumping point, in 1792, Smith threw his name into the race for the fifth district congressman. He beat out Baltimore heavy hitters Charles Ridgley and John O'Donnell of Canton. From 1792 to 1833 Smith spent his life as a Representative and a Senator. Smith first entered Congress as a Federalist, but shortly thereafter aligned himself with Jefferson's Republican Party. Smith always defended the views of the merchant class and consistently voted for a strong military. Smith dedicated himself to a life of politics with few disruptions.

During the War of 1812 Smith was in charge of the defense of Baltimore. In 1813 Smith organized the militia, fortified Fort McHenry, and built a line of defense on today's Patterson Park. After the War of 1812, Smith was again a national hero. A contemporary wrote of the general, "Washington saved his country and General Smith saved his City."[12] Nevertheless, as Smith entered into the war, his political career was waning. After the War, his new status as hero thrust him into another nineteen years in political office. His political career was sound enough to carry him through the Baltimore banking scandal of 1819.

This scandal began in 1816 when the Second Bank of the United States was Chartered. James Buchanan, Smith's partner, was appointed President of the Baltimore Branch of the Second Bank of the United States, and a member of the Central Board of Directors in Philadelphia. Buchanan, along with James McCulloch and George Williams, borrowed money from the bank in order to buy stock in the bank, hoping to make a large profit. At the height of their manipulations the three bank officials had illegally spent around three million dollars of the institution's funds. Buchanan allegedly did this using Sam Smith's name without his knowledge. After the 1818 financial panic, when credit was tightened, Buchanan was exposed. However, Smith lost his town house, his country estate, and his firm. Still, he retained his good name in Washington, D.C. and continued as a Maryland Senator for fourteen more years.

In 1833, Smith retired from the senate and returned to Baltimore, but his political career was not over. During the bank riots of 1835, Smith, at eighty-three, marched through the streets demanding order. The rioters fell silent in front of Smith's leadership. Again, Baltimore citizens saw Smith as the savior of the City. At the next mayoral election, the citizens called for the election of General Sam Smith as Mayor. On September 7, Smith was elected to his last political office. In 1838 Smith stepped down as Mayor and on April 22, 1839, he died at the age of 87.

General Sam Smith also contributed to the architecture and landscape of Baltimore. In 1796 he began building his commodious townhouse on the north side of Water Street. Griffith in his *Annals of Baltimore* stated that the house was "erected on a plan furnished by himself (Smith) and executed by Messr. John Scroggs, Robert Stuart and James Mosher, Builders."[13] In addition, during the 1790s Smith bought large tracts of land in and around Baltimore. In 1792 he bought the old Kingsbury Furnace from Robert Long of Fells Point. He also began a several-year endeavor assembling 520 acres for a summer home. Sometime between 1796 and 1799 Smith began construction on Montebello.

Montebello stood as Smith's finest architectural achievement. Smith named the estate after a French military victory at Montebello, Italy (which took place in 1800). Following the rules of Federal Classicism, Montebello emerged as one of America's most original country houses. The house faced southwest towards the center of Baltimore. Approaching it from the front the ground sloped downwards for about two hundred feet until the front lawn evened out by the road. In the back of Montebello, the land was scooped out in an amphitheater fashion giving much light into the ground-

24　THE CITY AS SUBURB

1796 William Birch engraving of the Montebello Estate. (Courtesy EPFL Maryland Room)

level rooms.[14] During Smith's time the view from Montebello reached the inner harbor. A balustraded porch wrapped around the front of the house.

Inside the house one entered a one-story large 'living' room used for social gatherings. In the center of the ceiling was a lantern (a cupola skylight). A marble floor gave a polished feeling reflecting as much light as possible. On each side of the living room was two smaller rooms most likely used as bedrooms. The rear half of the building was two stories high with an above-ground basement. Three oval rooms were positioned in a cross plan with the middle protruding out from the rear facade. The dining room was directly behind the living room and elegantly ornamented. The walls were trimmed with a low-paneled wainscoting and the windows and doors ornamented with pilasters and architraves. The juncture of the walls and ceilings were adorned with a simple dentilled cornice. Fine marble mantels were placed in most rooms. To the right was a "withdrawing" room. On the left was the pantry, and stairs to the second floor. The second floor was segmented into three large bedrooms. The house was lavishly furnished.

Smith's propensity towards French furniture was prevalent throughout the house. He also possessed a rich library. He collected much of the classics written in Greek and

Latin and many French books. He also had books by the great English writers: Locke, Fielding, and Pope. There were two portraits, one of himself and the other of Margaret Spear. He had busts of Thomas Jefferson and Benjamin Franklin. The cellar held a roomy kitchen, a laundry room, and a lavish wine cellar.

There is no attribute for the designer of Montebello, but there are several conjectures. Around 1796, William Birch drew a perspective drawing of Montebello. After laying out the gardens of Riversdale, Birch was described as an architect as well as an artist. Another theory suggests that the builder of Homewood (still in existence on the campus of the Johns Hopkins University) was the builder of Montebello. Many of the interior details of both houses were very similar. Some individuals even believe Sam Smith was the designer and he certainly could have been. Smith was a close friend with Thomas Jefferson (who designed the Virginia Capital, Monticello, and the University of Virginia). In 1801 Thomas Jefferson and Sam Smith roomed at the same boarding house in Washington, D.C. The evenings outside of the political circle certainly would have been filled with chat related to architecture. It is certain that Smith played a significant role in the design. Like all wealthy merchants Smith, too, was interested in the design of the young country.

Montebello also contained outbuildings: stables, smokehouse, barns, and icehouses. In addition there were slave quarters. Not much was written about the surrounding land or the slave population of Montebello. However, the estate was a working farm and slaves were the primary labor force. General Smith's contribution to Baltimore and the nation was prolific; nevertheless, he was not a Baltimore County resident and added little outside of Montebello to the growth of the Northeast Baltimore borderland region. In fact, most merchants during the 1790s and the early 1800s contributed little to the fledgling northeast region.

Henry Thompson and Clifton

Henry Thompson arrived in Baltimore in 1794 at the age of twenty.[15] Born in Yorkshire, England, he immigrated to the United States and began work with his cousin Hugh Thompson, a partner with the prominent merchant Robert Oliver. With such a connection, Henry was welcomed into the Baltimore elite. In 1798, Henry married Ann Lux Bowly, the daughter of Daniel Bowly who owned Furley Hall. Between 1799 and 1801 he purchased the 250 acres that became Clifton.

As a merchant, he set up his counting house on Water Street where he chartered ships that traded goods throughout the world. He traded products as diverse as sugar, salt, ginseng, flour, animals, hardware, and tools. His ports-of-call ranged from Boston and New Orleans to Rio de Janeiro and points in between. In his diary, Mr. Thomp-

Surviving plasterwork in Henry Thompson's former parlor at Clifton Estate. (Author's photo)

son mentions accommodating the captains of his ships at Clifton. He also became involved with many civic endeavors. He was a director for the Harford Road Turnpike, and a Commissioner of Opening Streets for Baltimore Town (which turned into the 1823 Poppleton's plat). He was a director of the Bank of Baltimore, Secretary of the Agricultural Society, and a Captain in the Third Maryland Brigade during the War of 1812.

At Clifton he was involved in gentleman farming. Here, he experimented with agricultural techniques while running a profitable farm. The farm itself was self-sufficient. He raised cattle, sheep, hogs, and fowl. The farm also produced milk and eggs and grew vegetables and grain of all kinds. Most of his agricultural experiments were dedicated to fertilizer. He soaked fields in manure, plaster of paris, and even urine. He had a successful orchard where he grew apples, pears, and a vineyard for grapes. As a functional farm, Clifton had ice-houses, root cellars, barns, smokehouses, and other buildings.

Today, the house that Thompson built survives! Within the mansion rebuilt for Hopkins in 1852, Henry's house sits as the focal point of the Hopkins era house. Completed in 1803, the house was two stories high and two rooms wide, built on the central hall plan. It was built of rough cast stone and more than 23,000 bricks were used to make walls more than a foot thick. In 1812 an addition was built onto the house.

Here, two new rooms flanked the original center hall house.[16] A hallway was built on the west side of the house connecting the two side rooms. Most significantly, Thompson added an octagonal dining room that jutted out from the west façade. Above the dining room was a bedroom and below was the new kitchen. This added greatly to the house, which was a focal point for social gatherings. Distinguished guests included Chief Justice William Wirt, Charles Carroll of Carrollton, and the Ridgely, Smith, Bowly, and Oliver families.

Henry Thompson lived comfortably at Clifton while contributing to the growth of Baltimore. However in 1835, when a depression fell over Baltimore, Thompson lost his estate. In September of 1835 Thompson sold the property to Daniel Cobb. In 1839, a year after Cobb died, the property was sold to Johns Hopkins at public auction. Thus, an estate well groomed by the elite was passed on to one of the young power brokers of Baltimore.

Chevalier D'Anmour and Belmont

Belmont, an estate of twenty-five acres, was built around 1780 by the city's first French Consul, Chevalier D'Anmour. It was located at today's northeast corner of North Avenue and Harford Road. Chevalier D'Anmour first appeared in Baltimore sometime before the Revolutionary War. During the Revolution, he returned to France in support of the American cause. In 1779 he was appointed French Consul General to the United States and moved to Baltimore. Sometime in the 1780s, he built Belmont.

His house, though built of brick, was a simple two-story rectangular box. The front façade is broken up into three bays, with the center bay ornamented with a Federal-style door and a Palladian window adorning the second story. The roofline emphasized the central bay with a low angular pedimented dormer. Accenting the dormer was a semicircular window. There is no architectural attribute to who designed the house, but it was based upon the massing and shape of houses built in Baltimore Town at that time.

In addition to building one the first country estates in Northeast Baltimore, Chevalier D'Anmour also built the first monument to Christopher Columbus in the United States. Francis Beirne writes of D'Anmour's admiration for Christopher Columbus:

> On the occasion of the 300th anniversary of the discovery someone remarked in his presence that it was strange no monument had ever been raised to Christopher Columbus in this country. D'Anmour was impressed and immediately pledged himself to correct the omission. On August 3, 1792, the date of the departure of Columbus from Laos in Spain, the cornerstone was laid. The monument is said to have been completed by August 22. On October 12, 1792, the date of the landing on San Salvador, it was officially dedicated.[17]

Chevalier D'Anmour house; photo for the Historic American Buildings Survey, 1936. (Courtesy EPFL Maryland Room)

Today the monument stands at Heinz Park[18] at the corner of Harford Road and Walther Avenue. The monument is an Egyptian obelisk sitting on a rectangular pedestal with an inscription, "SACRED TO THE MEMORY OF CHRIS. COLUMBUS. OCTOB. XII, MDCCVIIIC."

Chevalier D'Anmour held onto the property until around 1796 when he sold twenty-five acres to Archibald Campbell, the President of the Baltimore Branch of the Bank of the United States. Sometime around 1805 (the year Campbell died), the estate was sold to Baltimore merchant Colonel Thomas Tenant. An ad for the building stated that:

Creation of Borderland Communities 29

> The subscriber offers for sale that handsome elegant Country Seat called Belmont, formerly the residence of Chevalier D'Anmour, beautifully situated within a mile and a half of the City of Baltimore, containing about 50 acres, well enclosed with good post and rail fences, and divided into lots of different sizes. The dwelling house, kitchen, wash house, stables etc. are in good order. There is a handsome grove of lofty oaks and an extensive kitchen garden and orchard well stocked with fruit of the best and choicest kind; likewise a large well constructed ice house, and two pumps (one of which is in the garden) that afford plenty of excellent water.
>
> The situation is healthy and commands a beautiful view of the city and harbor of Baltimore and the river Patapsco. Application should be made to Mr. Archibald Campbell or to James Hindman.[19]

The author of the ad, by carefully choosing what is and what is not described, shed insight into the elements important to the early country estates. First, he mentioned the builder of the estate. This did several things. It placed the estate into a social class. Chevalier D'Anmour, being a part of the social elite, was a recognizable name. In addition, the name of the country seat was also recognizable. Second, he noted the distance to Baltimore. The distance of one and a half miles from Baltimore Town placed Bel-

The interior and exterior of D'Anmour's house reflected the Federal Period's obsession with absolute symmetry; photo for the Historic American Building Survey, 1936. (Courtesy EPFL Maryland Room)

Coldstream Estate in the early twentieth century. (Courtesy EPFL Maryland Room)

mont into commuting distance. Third, the estate was described as being "well enclosed with good post and rail fences." It was not well enclosed for practical farming reasons like separating livestock from fields, but to present an orderly estate. This touched on the Federal period emphasis on symmetry, harmony, and order. Fourth, "a handsome grove of Oak Trees" touched on the potential buyer's desire for shade, order, and symmetry. Shade was the nineteenth century's version of air conditioning. Finally, the ad described the estate as a healthy area with a beautiful view. The estate was far enough from the epidemic-ridden city to be healthy, but close enough to keep an eye on the activities of the city. The estate was owned by the Tenant family until 1842 when it was sold to the hotel owner David Barnum.[20]

William Patterson and Coldstream

Adjacent to Montebello and across the Street from Clifton, stood the old Patterson estate, Coldstream.[21] William Patterson began renting the property several years before he bought it in 1805. Patterson was a well-known revolutionary hero, and an important merchant. Born in Ireland, William Patterson first immigrated to Philadelphia at the age of fourteen. Sometime before 1775 he moved to Baltimore. By 1775 he owned ships and traded gunpowder and arms during the war. He was the first President of the Bank of Maryland in 1790, and an organizer of the Merchant's exchange in 1815. In

1827 he was one of the original directors of the Baltimore and Ohio Railroad and in 1828 a partner in the Canton Company.

Coldstream was a bulky stucco house framed in Federal Period proportions. A bold front portico was built in proportions of a Greek or Roman temple, with Doric columns. It sat on top of the hill overlooking the city. On the northwest side of the house a small two-story appendage popped out of its side. The roof was a pedimented dormer with a semicircular light in the center. The walls were smooth and without bulky ornament. The cornice was plain. Once again the plain simplicity of the ornamentation was a Federal Period attribute that helped to reinforce the simplicity of harmony and order.

David Harris and Mount Deposit

Mount Deposit, the summer home of David Harris, was located three miles out the Old Philadelphia Road, just south of the Herring Run where Armistead Gardens is today. The Harris family was instrumental in creating and sustaining the trade route between Baltimore and Western Maryland and Pennsylvania. As a young adult, David Harris moved to Baltimore, where he quickly rose to the prominent position of Cashier for the Office of Discount and Deposit at the Baltimore Branch of the Bank of the United States. Established within the circles of the financial elite, Harris began building Mount Deposit, an estate he named after the institution that gave him the wealth to build it.[22]

Between 1791 and 1793, Mount Deposit was built. By 1805, when landscape artist Francis Guy painted three views of the estate, Mount Deposit was a sophisticated summer estate. Incredibly, all three views of Mount Deposit still exist. In 1805 David Harris employed Francis Guy to paint two scenes of Mount Deposit; a view from the south and another view from the north. In addition, Francis Guy painted the front façade of the house onto a John and Hugh Finlay designer chair (which is on display in the Baltimore Museum of Fine Arts). These three paintings captured in great detail a still life of Mount Deposit.[23]

Like all country estates at the time, the main house was oriented toward Baltimore Town. Unlike the polished sophistication of Montebello, or the urban form of Belmont, Mount Deposit in its essence was a high-style farmhouse. The house was five bays wide, a full two stories high, and it sat upon an above ground basement accentuated with an arcade of arches. The front façade was broken into three segments. Two bays of windows flanked a two-story recessed portico. The portico was comprised of two levels of porches. Here the essence of the house was revealed. To combat the Maryland summer heat, the porches were recessed, providing shade from the hot sun. Both windows and doors provided necessary circulation to subdue the staunch summer heat and humidity. On the east façade was a one-story appendage, which held the kitchen, pantry, and other utilitarian rooms. The removal of the kitchen from the main living spaces spoke to reducing heat within the main house.

Much like the front façade, the rear façade too catered to summer heat. To provide shade, the roofline of the rear façade projects over the second-story porch. A main staircase positioned in the center of the house connected the second-story porch to the back yard. Two shed dormer windows peeped out of the roofline, suggesting usable attic space as well as ventilation for the uppermost floor of the house. The design of the house, though based upon Federal Period principals, was guided by the necessity of comfort from the summer heat of Maryland.

One of Guy's paintings captured the grounds in front of Mount Deposit. Well landscaped, the grounds were distinctively divided into various uses. First, a whitewashed fence partitioned a three-terraced lawn ornamented with well pruned evergreen trees. The furthermost terrace was spread out into the landscape and included an unknown outbuilding. The front lawn was strictly designed for pomp and circumstance.

Flanking the front lawn, other fields were used for agricultural purposes. On the east side of the lawn ran the main road to the house. This road was flanked by a fence, which ran directly parallel to the front lawn's whitewashed fence. This suggests that the whitewashed fence was primarily ornamental. Moreover, these fields seemed well kept and highly improved. Two figures stand in the east field. They are tentatively identified as David Harris and his neighbor Daniel Bowly. Dressed in fashionable clothes, these two exemplify the role of country gentlemen.

Guy's other painting of the grounds behind the house further brings to light several important attributes of Mount Deposit. The back lawn, too, was sectioned off with a whitewashed fence. The fence that surrounds the grounds immediately in front and behind the house was built with vertical spindles, unlike the fences sectioning off the agricultural fields. Outbuildings, fences with horizontal railings, interspersed trees at random, and cattle identified Mount Deposit as a working farm. Also, slave quarters were strategically placed out of sight, or totally ignored by the painter.

Interestingly, four figures appear in this painting. The main two in the center are again David Harris and Daniel Bowly, and two unidentified women dressed in fashionable attire are huddled around a tree. The buildings in the far left corner possibly depict Fells Point. This suggests the importance of Mount Deposit's relationship with Fells Point, the main harbor of Baltimore Town at the time.

Upon the death of David Harris in 1809, Mount Deposit was inherited by his daughter Molly, who married General Joseph Sterret. Consequently, the Sterrets renamed the property "Surrey." Sometime in the 1820s, the house burned to the ground and was rebuilt in brick.

Daniel Bowly and Furley Hall

In the 1780s, Daniel Bowly purchased 404 acres of the Principio Iron Company's confiscated land and began building Furley Hall. Thereafter, Bowly increased the size of Furley Hall to 793 acres. The estate was located directly north of Herring Run on the east side of Belair Road. From the 1780s to 1847 the Bowly Family controlled Furley Hall. In 1847 Furley Hall was sold to William Corse, who controlled the estate for the rest of the nineteenth century.

Daniel Bowly married his first cousin, Anne Stewart, in 1775, the daughter of Captain Alexander Stewart.[24] Together they had eleven children. As a wealthy merchant he was also town commissioner, State Senator, a Port warden, a founder of the Bank of Maryland, an organizer of Maryland's first agricultural society, a Commissioner for the Baltimore County Turnpike Commission, and highly active in St. Paul's Church. At the time of Daniel Bowly's death in 1807 he owned 2,563 acres in Baltimore County and Baltimore City: 793 acres were Furley Hall, and an additional 450 acres at Bowley's Quarters. He also owned Bowly's Wharf and a town house that stood on the corner of Water and South Streets, then the most fashionable neighborhood in Baltimore. In 1847 the Bowly heirs sold Furley Hall to William Corse, Sr., who at the time was living at his father-in-law's estate Clairmont, which was directly south of the Herring Run.[25]

The house at Furley Hall that Bowly built was a clapboard two-story structure proportioned in the Federal style and topped with a hipped roof. On the rear façade there was a large outdoor porch with rounded columns. The two porch walls were plastered and decorated with a chair rail. The porch acted as an outdoor extension of the house, providing relief from the summer heat, and had the appearance and convenience of an interior room. Henry Chandlee Forman, in his book *Tidewater Maryland Architecture and Gardens*, best described the interior of the house:

> Upon entering the front doorway of Furley, one came into a passageway about nine feet wide, with an easy-rising stairway on the left side of it. To the right was the sitting room or Back Parlor; to the left, the Best Parlor or Great Room, with its delicately-carved white Directoire mantel that had rinceaux, garlands, urns, oval pattarae, and down-tapering pilasters. Flanking the fireplace were semicircular, round-headed alcoves framed with pilasters on pedestals. Set in separate panels, the French wallpaper was in the Pompeian manner, with arabesques.[26]

Above and opposite page: Front and rear views of Mount Deposit. These are cherished views of Old Baltimore painted by Francis Guy circa 1805. (Courtesy EPFL Maryland Room)

The dining room and kitchen were attached to the side of the main house. This wing was portioned in two parts and made of brick covered in stucco. It was built of brick and situated with gables facing the front and rear façade. Unlike Montebello, which was built at one time, Furley Hall was built in three different phases, according to need and pocketbook.

Henry Chandlee Forman meticulously detailed the layout of the grounds, which captured much of the landscaping completed by William Corse, Sr.[27] Nevertheless, the Bowly family most likely built many of the outbuildings. The approach to the house was from the southwest paralleling the front façade. The driveway connected to a cul de sac framing the front lawn. In the middle were large shade trees. On the other side of the house a pathway connected the main house to the barn and another house. Named Bowly's Quarters, it was a small field stone cottage with a hall and parlor downstairs and two bedrooms above. Some believe this was the house that Daniel Bowly lived in before he built the main house. At the end of the pathway sat the large stone barn measuring seventy feet by thirty feet with two-foot-thick stone walls. Other buildings were the springhouse, the bathhouse (which was used as the schoolroom dur-

ing the Civil War), the smokehouse, the outhouse, ice house, and the summer gazebo. Since William Corse was a nurseryman, the estate was filled with many exotic plantings. In front stood two magnolia trees. In the back was a great Cedar of Lebanon, a purple birch, and a Chinese Ginko.[28] Probably the most famous plant was the "Green Rose of Furley," which in 1953 was the title of a novel by Helen Corse Barney, the daughter of Frank Ellis Corse, and most likely the son and grandaughter of William Corse.

The Merchant Vision *en masse*

By 1822 the sum of country estates in Northeast Baltimore created a borderland landscape, an idyllic vision, that was praised and purported throughout the nineteenth century. The components of the picturesque aesthetic were based upon the middle ground between wilderness and urbanity, between ruggedness and polished smoothness, between symmetry and asymmetry. In essence, the picturesque is man's attempt at making nature more beautiful. By dabbling, man can make nature something altogether better than its original form. We do this by adding man's need into the landscape.

In a letter, William Wirt—then Chief Justice of the United States—captured not only the borderland landscape, but also its aesthetic relationship to Baltimore Town. Wirt's letter not only described the earliest view of the northeast borderland landscape, but also was the first description of Northeast Baltimore framed in the picturesque aesthetic. Wirt described a walk he took one spring morning from Baltimore Town to Henry Thompson's house at Clifton:

> Yesterday morning I arose before day. Shaved and dressed by candlelight took my cane and walked to market. There are two market houses, each of them about three or four times as long as ours in Washington. The first I came to was the meat market; the next, which was nearest the basin, was the fish and vegetable market. O! What a quantity of superb beef, mutton, lamb, veal, and all sorts of fowls—hogsheads full of wild ducks, geese, pheasants, partridges; and then on one side of the market-house, leaving only a narrow land between, a line of wagons and carts, groaning under the loads of country productions; these wagons and carts on one side and the market-houses on the other, forming a line as long as from our house to St. John's Church. I must not forget to mention the loads of sweets-cakes of all sorts and fashions that covered the outside tables of the market-houses, and the breakfasts that were cooking everywhere, all around, for the county people who came many miles to market. You may conceive the vast quantity of provisions that must be brought to this market when you are told that sixty thousand people draw their daily supplies from it, which is more than twice as many people as there are in Washington, Georgetown, Alexandria, and Richmond all put together.
>   Well, and so after I walked all round and round and through the market-house, I left it and bent my steps toward the country, and walked two miles and a half out to Mr. Thompson's to breakfast. It had been cloudy and rainy for several days, but the night before had been clear, and although the road was still wet, the morning above head was bright and beautiful. After walking about a mile, I came to the summit of a hill that overlooks the city, and there I stopped for a moment to take a breath and look back on it. The ground had begun to smoke from the warmth of the rising sun, and the city seemed to spread itself out below me to a vast extent—a huge dusky mass, to which there seemed no limit. But towering from above the fog was the Washington Monument (a single beautiful column 160 feet in height, which stands in Howard's Park, and is rendered indescribably striking and interesting from the touching solitude of the scene from which it lifts its head), and several noble steeples of churches interspersed throughout the vast of the city, whose gilded summits were now glittering in the sun. Casting the eye over Baltimore, it lights upon the Chesapeake Bay and after wandering over that flood of waters, it rests upon Fort McHenry and its star-spangled banner. This is the fort where our soldiers gained so much glory in the last war, and the very banner with regard to which Mr. Key's beautiful song of the "Star Spangled Banner"

**Above: Furley Hall Barn.
Left: Old Bowly's Quarters at Furley Hall.**
(Courtesy EPFL Maryland Room)

was written. After feasting my eyes for some time on the rich, diversified and boundless landscape that lay before me, meditating on the future grandeur of this city and the rising glories of the nation, I turned around to resume my walk into the county, when all its soft beauties burst, by surprises upon me. The while I had been looking back on the town, bay, and fort, the sun had risen, and was now so high that its light was pouring full upon hill and valley, field and forest, blazing in bright reflection from all the eastern windows of the hundreds of country-houses that crowned the heights around me, and dancing on all the leaves that waved and wantoned in the morning breeze. No city in the world has a more beautiful country around it than Baltimore in the direction of the west, north, and east. In the direction of Washington it is unimproved, but in the other points all that could have been expected from wealth and fine taste have been accomplished. The grounds, which were originally poor, have been made rich; they lie finely, not flat or tame, or yet abrupt and rugged, but rising and falling in forms of endless diversity, sometimes soft and gentle, at others bold and commanding. This beautifully undulating surface has been improved with great taste, the fields richly covered with grass, the clumps of trees, groves and forests pruned of all dead limbs and all deformities, and flourishing in strong and healthy luxuriance. The sites for the houses are well selected—always upon some eminence, embossed amid beautiful trees, from which their white fronts peep out enchantingly, for the houses are all white, which adds much to the cheerfulness and grace of this unrivaled scenery. I hope one of these days to show it to you in person, and then you will be able to imagine what a delightful ramble I had to Mr. Thompson's yesterday morning. I took them quite by surprise, but it was a most agreeable one, and they were rejoiced to see me. Mr. Thompson inquired most kindly after all in Washington, and giving me a good country breakfast (most delightful butter), brought me back to town in his gig, where we arrived by nine o'clock, an hour before court. Was not this an industrious morning?[29]

Wirt's textbook description of the picturesque landscape continually jumped from descriptions of the built environment and nature. From the outskirts of Baltimore along Harford Road, William Wirt described Baltimore Town. Here, he professed the beauty of the architectural icons that defined early nineteenth-century Baltimore: the Washington Monument, church steeples, Fort McHenry, and the Harbor's ships. After describing the urban form he turned around and described what he saw north of the city. Here Wirt inserted a description of nature, "the sun had risen, and was now so high that its light was pouring full upon hill and valley, field and forest." He then jumped to describing the houses of northeast Baltimore, "blazing in bright reflection from all the eastern windows of the hundreds of country-houses that crowned the heights around me." And back again to nature, he described the sunlight "dancing on all the leaves that waved and wantoned in the morning breeze." Summing up, Wirt masterfully expressed a desired landscape of nature and architecture. His description harmonized the country and urban amenities.

More enlightening, Wirt explained what he considered to be a "rich" landscape:

The grounds, which were originally poor, have been made rich... This beautifully undulating surface has been improved with great taste, the fields richly covered with grass, the clumps of trees, groves and forests pruned of all dead limbs and all deformities, and flourishing in strong and healthy luxuriance.[30]

Wirt's definition of unimproved land is land untouched by man, but moreover untouched by "wealth and fine taste."

Wealth and fine taste necessarily spoke only to the gentlemen farmer, for truck farmers would not have found the time to prune the deformities off of trees or groom untilled fields. Truck farmers were too busy earning a living. Inadvertently, Wirt used "rich" and "wealth" in their connotative and literal sense. Without large sums of money these estates could not have been manicured into a picturesque state.

This analysis of Wirt's letter is incredibly important in that it illuminates one of the strongest intangible forces that shape our landscapes—aesthetic judgement values. Even today, we concur with Wirt. We see a front lawn mowed and trimmed as beautiful, we view well pruned trees and bushes as beautiful. In contrast, unmowed lawns, unpruned and unweeded planting beds are ungainly. We view the Green Spring Valley with delight, while rural farms with trailers are not. The picturesque desire has shaped the landscapes of America into the twenty-first century.

All major cities produced many images of themselves from their borderland regions. Bounded in such books as Nathaniel Parker Willis's two-volume *American Scenery Illustrated* (1840) and William Cullen Bryant's three-volume *Picturesque America; or The Land We Live In* (1874), these images sought vantage points that produced images much like Wirt's description. Always in the foreground were well-manicured estates overlooking an economic center of a town, mill village or city. The view was from a quiet setting, commanding and controlling the bustle of activity. These havens of retreat were places physically—not visually—removed from the activities of the city.

Northeast Baltimore was no different. In addition, the view also had utilitarian purposes. First it allowed, in Northeast Baltimore, merchants to keep a watchful eye on their ships in the harbor. Second, in an age where all the raw sewage of Baltimore drained into the inner basin, filth and disease ran rampant. Today, scientists estimate that it takes nineteen days for tidal action to replenish the water in the Inner Harbor.[31] Fleeing to the hills during summer was a healthy thing to do. The view of a town or city in many ways was a vantage point in the promotion of that city. A picturesque borderland region was a gage for the wealth of a city. This speaks to the symbiotic relationship of city, suburb, and country.

In conclusion, Wirt's letter does more than describe the borderland region with picturesque connotations. By necessity it presented a symbiotic relationship between perception and what is perceived. Wirt provided a description of Northeast Baltimore through the optics of a wealthy merchant well schooled in the fashions of the day. The scene perked his enthusiasm because he perceived the elements in the landscape that verified his vision of what is beautiful. In all, Wirt's description unequivocally proves that the picturesque aesthetic was at work shaping the borderland region as early as 1822.

Tilling the Soil—The Endurance of Truck Farms

Amongst the merchant's estates sat truck farms. The truck farm grew fruits and vegetables as well as produced milk and eggs for the city. They were called truck farms, because the farmer had to quickly move his goods. Thus, he "trucked" his goods to market sometimes on a daily basis.

The daily life of a truck farmer was a grueling operation shaped by labor shortages, farming technology, and sheer grit. At the beginning of the nineteenth century, truck farmers devoted all their effort to growing crops. Their vision of the community was minimized by the harsh realities of farming. Richard Parkinson, an English visitor, provided the best window into the daily life on a truck farm.

In 1798, Richard Parkinson came to the United States to promote an article he wrote on agricultural techniques. After touring the mid-Atlantic Coast, staying mostly at gentleman farms, he decided to rent a farm that was three miles from Baltimore and located on the Old Philadelphia Road known as "Orange Hill." Orange Hill, which Parkinson rented for 300 pounds, encompassed 300 hundred acres with 200 acres of cleared land. The remaining wooded land was used for firewood and fences. Back in England in 1805, he published his account on American farming in two volumes, entitled *Tour in America 1798, 1799, 1800 Exhibiting Sketches of Society & Manners and a Particular Account of the American System of Agriculture*. This book detailed his travels through the mid-Atlantic region as well as the daily life of running Orange Hill in a profitable way. Parkinson was an educated gentleman rubbing elbows with such people as Thomas Jefferson, George Washington, Captain John O'Donnell, and Daniel Bowly II. Nevertheless, on Orange Hill, he and his sons tilled the soil, milked the cows, fertilized the fields, and trucked their goods to market. At Orange Hill he was a truck farmer.

Once settling in Orange Hill, Parkinson quickly surmised his approach to farming. Skeptically he begins his chapter, "Farming on Orange Hill,"

> I thought nothing in the farming line likely to be profitable, except the selling of milk, and what in the country is called truck—which is garden produce, fruits & etc; finding labour so very dear, and scarcely to be had at all, except by the keeping of slaves, which I did not like.

Entering into the dairy business, Parkinson soon realized that he and his children would have to do most of the work:

> I found great trouble in this business: for in two years that I followed it I could never meet with any servant that would milk properly, therefore we obliged to milk the cows and sell the milk ourselves as well as feed the cows and do the greatest part of farming work.

Creation of Borderland Communities 41

At the turn of the nineteenth century, Francis Guy painted many scenes of Baltimore's country estates on John and Hugh Finlay-designed chairs. Today we can see these chairs at the Baltimore Museum of Art.
Above: Montebello.
Below: Mount Deposit.
(Courtesy EPFL Maryland Room)

In the summer, Parkinson rose at two a.m. to milk the cows in order to be in town before the sun rose. Otherwise, milk would sour and the butter would melt. In the winter, he rose by four a.m., milked the cows, and delivered the milk to town before breakfast was served. Parkinson's hard work paid off, for between 1798 and 1800 his was the most sought-after milk in Baltimore Town. Once the cows were "milked out" he sold them to butchers.

Although Parkinson was mainly a dairyman, he diversified into other agricultural pursuits. Parkinson stated of his first duty on the farm:

> My first work on the farm was to dress the meadows; which were called fine; though the greater part of them in England would not have been thought worthy of being called meadow at all, being over run with briars and weeds of different description.

Parkinson grew hay for his own livestock, as well as for sale in Baltimore at nine pounds per ton. After "cleaning and dressing the meadows" Parkinson planted corn, turnips, potato, oats, and timothy seed. He also planted three and one-half acres of buckwheat, had an orchard of peaches and apples, bought sheep, and kept seven hogs. In his garden he grew peas, string beans, tomatoes, squash, pumpkins, cucumbers and other produce for personal consumption as well as the markets in Baltimore.

Parkinson chose not to hold slaves, while most truck farmers at the beginning of the nineteenth century could not afford to. Thus, Parkinson bickered much about labor shortage, a problem faced by many truck farmers. Timing was essential, unless the produce rot in the field or in storage. Restricted by the labor shortage, the farmer planted crops at different times so that they were harvested at different times. This helped deter the need for outside labor.

Nevertheless problems arose. Parkinson described two fiascoes regarding his peaches. When his peaches had ripened on the tree, Parkinson could not find laborers to help pick them. Parkinson and his sons picked the peaches themselves, but didn't have time to bring them to market. Luckily Parkinson found a "black fellow" to sell the peaches in town:

> We were fortunate enough to find a black fellow (who had been one of my mowers) to sell them—this being an employment which they like, viz. Riding to market in a cart drinking whiskey, and cheating you out of part of the money they get for the "truck." He sold as many peaches for us as came to 17 pounds; there would have been little profit upon them if we had hired men to pull them.

It must be noted that no conclusions regarding the "black fellow's" ethics can be drawn. Parkinson's slur is contradicted by his own actions. He not only rehired him to sell their goods at market, but became quite dependent on his labor. It was the "black fellow" that saved Parkinson's peach crop.

His next batch of peaches was another story. Parkinson hired some hands to pick his peaches, but only half were picked. The peaches on the tree were too ripe to sell in Baltimore. Parkinson then stated:

> I mounted my horse and rode to the stills, as there were many small ones within three to four miles of me in the County. The men at the stills were civil enough: they offered to lend me the still, and let me find a man to work it, &c. or they would work it for me; but from the information I obtained I found that my peaches would not more than pay carriage to the stills, they would not pay me for my trouble nor will the peaches pay the farmer, to be given to the hogs.

In the end, these peaches were used to feed his hogs.

The logistics of watering the fields, gardens and livestock created headaches. For the fields, truck farmers relied on rain. For the garden and livestock Parkinson's only source of water was the well near the house. Therefore he fetched twenty to thirty cattle out of all the fields and guided them to the well.

Also, fertilizing the fields was another necessary task. During this time, Parkinson experimented with manure, plaster, and resting of fields. Daniel Bowly summed up the problem, "But that availed nothing: the land was so poor, that without dung its produce was not worth the cultivation, and dung and labour it would not pay for it." Parkinson stated that his "potato fields were dunged with 12,000 bushels of good dung of the cows and horses, made from linseed-cake and Indian corn-stalks." Parkinson proved plaster to be a wonderful fertilizer of turnips but nothing else.

In the late eighteenth century, yellow fever was a major problem—even out in the healthy countryside. In 1798 during the yellow fever epidemic in Baltimore, the mayor ordered all communication with Philadelpia stopped within three miles of the city. Here a visitor stopped by the farm for some rest and food, and inadvertently infected Parkinson's family. For fourteen days his family laid ill, while the only medication was red port. Nevertheless, the family recovered to resume their operations.

Transporting goods to market was a night and day affair. Overloaded wagons and pothole-plagued roads ground the "truck" to a slow crawl. Parkinson described the journey out to the Gittings plantation, around twelve miles from Baltimore on the Harford Road:

> The roads from thence to Baltimore are so bad for carriages as to be a day's work in the winter for a team; and horses are of much more chargeable keeping in England, from the two extremes of heat and cold.

Farmers could only make one trip per day, therefore all goods ready for market had to be precariously transported on overloaded wagons. Markets opened at 2:00 a.m. and farmers carried all they could. Parkinson described the wagon as a peddler's pack:

> A farmer's wagon in America, when she comes into market, is something like a peddler's pack: it consists of butter, eggs, fruits, potatoes, turnips, cucumbers, chickens, ducks, geese, turkeys, wheat flour, Indian flour, buckwheat flour, rye flour, chopped straw &c.[32]

Parkinson left Orange Hill in 1801 and returned to England. He was an English gentleman, and Parkinson's complaints about labor shortages and transportation problems must be put into context. Parkinson was a gentleman whose interest lay in agricultural experimentation. Therefore, Orange Hill was his laboratory. In this sense, Richard Parkinson saw these practical problems as a nuisance. He always compared farming in America to farming in England. English farms by 1800 had hundreds of years of cultivation, labor was rarely a problem, and roads were in much better condition. Parkinson described how hard it was to make a profit in farming, but somehow he found the labor and the time to make a profit. Still, his descriptions of daily farm life provided an accurate picture of Northeast borderland farms.

After Richard Parkinson, Orange Hill, owned by Robert Smith, Esquire—Sam Smith's brother—was rented to other truck farmers. In 1821 Underwood and Whitney took an ad in *The American* touting the dairy business:

> This celebrated establishment has been in operation for upwards of one year, and for pure milk, cleanliness, and its extensive accommodations for one hundred cows—it is believed has not its superior on the continent... The farm is situated about three miles out on the Philadelphia road, and... Mr. Noah Underwood, the late overseer, together with Mr. Joseph Whitney have rented this establishment from Robert Smith, Esquire... their carts are known as the "Orange Farm" and will wait on the public in the morning and evening.[33]

Today, the small village of Orangeville marks the area of Orange Farm.

The incremental development of Northeast's borderland farm region was a slow multi-generational process. During the first decades of the nineteenth century, many truck farms failed. During this time land was bought and sold, rented and re-rented. As some farms went bankrupt, many gentleman estates and prosperous truck farms increased in size. Nevertheless, each generation increased in prosperity as well as size. In turn, the original farmsteads became subdivided among the heirs. Large families were more than the norm; they were a necessity. One way to overcome labor shortage was through large families. Out of the families identified as truck farmers during the first two decades of the nineteenth century, most had families of eight children or more, and some up to twelve children![34]

The Gatch Farm

The earliest known farm family to settle in the area was the Gatch family, arriving in Annapolis on December 26, 1727. In 1737 Godfrey Gatch purchased the family farm located at Belair and White Avenue. Godfrey bought 130 acres of "Sidmore's Last" from Thomas Sligh. Godfrey died in 1759 and his wife Maria lived until 1783, when their son Conduce Gatch inherited the farm. Also arriving with Conduce (their father Godfrey came before them) were his brothers Nicholas and Conron.[35]

During the late eighteenth century, Conduce was assessed for tax purposes as having three horses and twelve black cattle. For a farmer in the eighteenth century to have a herd of cattle and three horses, he was prosperous. The original house was built of stone and situated near Belair Road. From the eight children of Conduce Gatch (all born in the mid-eighteenth century), five of the children stayed in Baltimore County. Within Gardenville throughout the nineteenth century, the Gatch family was an influential clan diversifying their talents and becoming intricately involved in creating their community. The children intermarried other members of influential families throughout the area, the Burgans, Taylors, and Forrestors. Throughout this intricate network, their farms began to prosper and family members found opportunities in other areas.

The Biddison Farm

Another prominent family within the area was the Biddison Family.[36] Abraham Biddison was the founder of the old estate just west of Belair Road directly south of Frankford Avenue. Abraham was born on Swan Creek, which flowed into the Back River. Abraham Biddison married the daughter of Thomas and Elizabeth Burgan whose family held much land on the east side of Belair Road. Their estate was vast enough to leave large sections to their numerous children. The farm was the typical truck farm variety with a healthy orchard and later, in the nineteenth century, a successful dairy.

The Erdman Clan and Their Farms

The Erdman family settled directly north of the Clifton estate on both Harford and Belair roads. In 1816 several Erdman brothers immigrated to Baltimore from Germany.[37] Adam Erdman settled on the site near the Little Flower Church and began working a large farm. Here Adam and his brother tilled the field. The other Erdman brothers chose to settle on Harford Road across the street from the northwest corner of Clifton. A family member in a 1951 *Sun* article stated that Adam would head down to the dock in Baltimore and pick up German immigrants as farmhands. The Erdmans thrived in this area. Erdman Avenue was first cut from Harford Road to Belair Road between 1816 and 1840. Most likely this road was used to communicate between the farms of the Erdman Brothers. Here the Erdman Brothers were influential in forming the village of Georgetown.

William Corse and his Nursery

The most prosperous truck farmer who reached the social position of gentleman farmer was William Corse.[38] William Corse was born on October 7, 1804, near Darlington Harford County. At the age of twenty-two he moved to New York City and apprenticed in the hide and leather business. He returned to Harford County and in 1831 married Deborah Sinclair, the daughter of Robert Sinclair. In 1838 he moved to Clairmont and began helping his father-in-law with his nursery business. Nine years later, William Corse expanded the nursery by buying Furley Hall.

The Community of the Truck Farm

By the 1850s the truck farmers and their families had become prominent Baltimore County citizens who helped shaped the landscape of Northeast Baltimore. During this time another class of farmers settled the area. Many Irish and German immigrants moved out to the Belair and Harford roads and bought or rented small farms of approximately ten acres. On these lots they grew "stoop crops," or vegetables that required bending over to harvest, such as carrots, beans, leeks, celery, and parsley. Many of these families rented stalls in the Belair Market or sold their goods from the back of their wagons.[39]

Labor shortages also forced these farmers to act as good neighbors. During harvest time all farmers would pitch in and help each other to prepare for the winter. Philip Cross, a farmer in northern Baltimore County, described in 1847 a communal husking match:

> About the last of October, the ears were pulled off and hauled in a long pile about 3 feet high and five feet wide, ready for one of the events of the season, the Husking Match. It was generally held after night. All the neighbors were invited. Sometimes the pile was divided by a rail laid across the middle, and two captains were selected, who chose an equal number of huskers, and a race was on. But as a general thing, the corn was not husked very clean, and some farmers would not permit any racing. The jug of old Rye or Rum was frequently passed along the line of huskers, which added to the hilarity of the race. The boys were on hand too, and had a fine time carrying the husks into the fodder where they were stored with pumpkins, and sometimes the cabbage. The fodder house was also a fine place for boys to play on cold winter Sundays.

> After the husking was over, there came the big supper for all. Sometimes the girls of the neighborhood helped prepare the supper, and the young men had the pleasure of seeing them home.
>
> The next day the corn was assorted and put in the corncrib. I personally never had but one fodder house and one husking match, as I always after that cut the corn off at the found and husked it from the shock. After it was the general practice to cut the corn off at the ground, the husking match was not abandoned, but was held in the afternoon and the jug of rye was in the field also.
>
> The women of the household generally had a quilting match in the afternoon, and all the girls of the neighborhood were invited. After sundown, the huskers went into supper, and after supper the young people had a dance, or a play party, which sometimes lasted until the dawn of another day.[40]

Thus, from the security of a working farm, a large extended family of farmers could reach out and begin building a thriving community.

Once the farmhouse was built the local farmer and his family most often exited the front door to either labor his fields, travel to market, or to worship. From the beginning of the smaller farmstead, attending church gathered farm families together. Three distinct denominations left their mark on antebellum Northeast Baltimore: Quakers, Methodists, and Lutherans. These communal religious foundations created prosperous rural villages beyond the parish. Often at first, the parishes met in barns or outbuildings. Later, the parishes built church structures on donated land. The church was the first community building in Northeast Baltimore.

As the sheer number of farms increased, and as intricate social networks were created, the demand for specialized labor arose. The "jack of all trades" farmer soon found it more efficient to devote his energies strictly to farming. This could only be done as members of the community rose to fill the positions of wheelwrights, coopers, lumbermen, carpenters, and blacksmiths. These tradesmen opened shops in centrally located areas within the farming communities. Around these centrally located areas, at crossroads, general stores sprung up supplying everything from a glass of beer to produce, farm supplies, and dry goods. As truck farms persisted and prospered, many families intermarried. Farms of brother and brother, sister and sister, and cousin and cousin laid side by side. Family ties were woven intricately throughout Northeast's complex social network.

The Creation of Religious Institutions:
Quaker, Methodist, and Lutheran Communities

The Quakers were a dominant force in Northeast Baltimore. Their history starts prior to the era of the Principio Iron Works. The first record of a Quaker meeting was "a man's meeting held at Thomas Hooker's residence on the 12 day of the 6th month of 1681."[41] After 1682 Thomas Gorsuch was mentioned in the West River yearly minutes, "If William Stevens could not settle his differences with Thomas Gorsuch, Quarterly Meeting was to be removed from his house."[42] Another reference pinpointed the Quaker meeting at the house of John Wilmore, on the north side of that Patapsco River.[43] The Patapsco Meeting was held in private houses until 1713, when "John Ensor, Planter of Baltimore sold to Richard Taylor, planter, one acre parcel of land,"[44] for the purpose of erecting a meeting house. In 1714, a Quaker petition was presented to the superior court of Baltimore County at Joppa:

> The petition of John Wilmot, Richard Taylor, and Jonathon Hanson, of Patapsco river, in the county aforesaid. Whereas the people called Quakers, have built a Meeting house, to meet together to Love and Worship God, in accordance to his blessed appointment, these are to desire for the body of the People aforesaid. That the aforesaid Meeting House may be recorded, according to the appointment or Parliament, the aforesaid house is built within two miles of Jones Falls, on a parcel of land called, "Darly Hall" and your Petitioners shall as in Dutybound pray which petition of the Quakers aforesaid, be by the Court heard understood and mutually deliberated, is granted & c.[45]

From 1714 to 1781 the Patapsco Meeting was held at Darley Hall and known as "Friendship." In 1781 the meeting was moved to Aisquith Street. Here the meeting was held until 1805 when it moved again to Lombard Street. By 1781 the meetings at Friendship were abandoned.

Out of harm's way from the land grab of the Principio Iron Company, the Quaker meeting house on Harford Road served the wide span of Quakers living north of the Patapsco River. Other meeting houses were formed during the mid-eighteenth century: Gunpowder, Patapsco Forest, Elkridge, and Little Falls. The Quaker community was a tightly closed community suspicious of outsiders. Barbara Mallone described it this way:

> New as a religious group, new as a political presence, new as homesteaders in wilderness where the soil was untilled and the memories of persecution barely buried beneath each day's events, early Friends established closed communities to which admission of new members was at first infrequent even by intermarriage of Friends.[46]

The Quaker community reached far beyond the boundaries of Northeast Baltimore, and in turn, by 1781 Quakers in Northeast Baltimore were part of the larger community, which was centrally located in Baltimore. The Aisquith meeting house was built with 600 seats and at the beginning 244 members were recorded, some of which were Northeast Baltimore residents.

The cemetery and log meeting house on Harford Road was abandoned, but the land was kept in the hands of Quaker stewards. In 1859 the Burial Ground committee minutes "showed that the meeting purchased land adjacent to Friendship in 1859 for $1,408.11."[47] Shortly after 1861 a dwelling was built for the sexton and the grounds were enclosed with an eight-foot stone wall.

Methodism was first introduced into Northeast Baltimore through Philip Gatch, grandson of Conduce Gatch. Philip was born on the old estate in 1751 into the Episcopal Church.[48] Around the age of twenty-one and while living on the estate, Nathan Perigo, a newly converted Methodist preacher, preached on the Gatch estate. Afterwards, Philip Gatch enthusiastically converted his family to Methodism and promptly decided to become a Methodist preacher—the first U.S.-born itinerant preacher in America. In July of 1774 he received his full honors and began his evangelical journey. Philip Gatch infrequently returned home. He first was assigned to the Frederick, Montgomery, and Garret County circuits. Upon several journeys south and east of the estate, Philip's possessive words fell upon deaf ears, whereupon the angry crowd tarred and feathered him. Soon after his work in Maryland he ventured to Virginia and finally in 1798 settled in the borderland region of Cincinnati, becoming a famous preacher and an associate judge of the court of common pleas.

Meanwhile back in Maryland, Philip Gatch's influence was firmly planted. In 1771 or 1772 the Gatch estate was home to Methodist sermons conducted in a barn. Soon the fledgling congregation built a log structure, which finally was replaced by a stone church, forty feet by sixty feet, with balconies built for Negro worshippers. The Gatch Memorial Methodist Church is a direct descendent of the young Philip Gatch's ministry. In 1857, on the site of Gatch's meeting house, a stone chapel was constructed and dedicated by Bishop Waugh and Reverend Thomas Sargent.[49]

Andrew's Chapel was an outgrowth of Gatch's Memorial Church and the conflict over slavery. Twenty-one people seceded from Gatch's Memorial Church to start their own congregation that would approve of slavery. Andrew's Chapel was the first Southern Methodist Church established in Maryland. They first met at the schoolhouse on the corner of Belair Road and Hamilton Avenue. In 1855 the members of the church laid the cornerstone and in 1866 Andrew's Chapel was included on Taylor's circuit. Andrew's Chapel was named after Bishop J.O. Andrew, whose proslavery stance led him to split from the Methodist Church.[50]

Another Methodist Church arose in 1860 when Horatio Whitridge dedicated the Eutaw Methodist Church on land donated by Green's cotton mill. This structure, still standing as a park shelter on the west side of Harford Road, was a one-room structure lighted by kerosene lamps and heated by two coal stoves. The Baltimore circuit, a route that preachers would take to serve rural churches, first serviced the Church. The church never built a parish house for a permanent in-residence preacher. The services of the church consisted of Sunday morning and evening services, afternoon Sunday school, mid-week prayer services, and revival meetings in the autumn of each year.[51]

The Jerusalem Evangelical Lutheran Church, still standing on the Corner of today's Moravia and Belair Roads, was organized in 1841.[52] In 1842 the congregation built a small wooden church. In 1874 a parsonage was built, and in 1875 the corner stone was laid for a brick church for which the Erdmans contributed 500 dollars. Sometime in the twentieth century, the church was remodeled with a Collegiate Gothic-style front façade. The establishment of this church represents a strong German influence in the community as early as 1841.

The Beginnings of the Crossroad Villages

Farm life necessitated a "jack-of-all-trades" mentality. Farms located on stream beds built grist mills, saw mills, and eventually cotton mills. Other trades picked up and mastered around the barnyard included cooper, carpenter, bricklayer, stonemason, wheelwright, blacksmith, locksmith, and moonshiner. As Baltimore grew in population and trade increased, the demand for goods also increased. Thus many Northeast farms may have ventured into household businesses such as quilt making, sewing, cabinetry, furniture making, shoes, leather products, and a sundry of other products. Today, it is an age-old tradition within Baltimore's public markets that amongst the produce vendors we see people selling other items.

By the 1850s there were at least three taverns, two schoolhouses, and two general stores located along the Belair corridor. Along the Harford Road there were at least three taverns, two stores, and three schools strung along the corridor.[53] On both the Harford and Belair Roads these taverns, stores, churches, and schoolhouses were located at crossroads—embryonic farm communities that flourished in the 1850s. In addition to taverns and stores, there were several other buildings located on the early maps that are not identified. Most likely they were blacksmith shops, carriage and carpentry shops, cooper and wheelwright shops.

The only known society created in Northeast Baltimore was the Farmer's and Gardener's Beneficial Society. On December 1, 1849, the following charter members created the society to pay for funeral expenses: John A Betchler, A.G. Erdman, Lorenz Hoffstetter, J.H. Hoffstetter, Charles Hillen, George Kolman, George Ebensein, Jacob Gerst, M. Hoffler, J.H. Koppelman, William Lutz, Tobias Lutz, John Lamley, John

Otto, John Sohn, and William Sauer. For five thousand dollars a Hall was erected.[54]

Within the physical aggregate of these small villages, a social structure was evolving. Within the taverns, folks discussed the issues of the day, traded news, and kept in contact with outside affairs. Churches created space for courting, moral deliverance, and provided necessary help to less fortunate members of the community. Within the Farmer's and Gardener's Beneficial Society, agriculture was discussed and new technology disseminated throughout the region. Blacksmith and carpenter shops and general stores provided an ear to bend and the comfort of one another's company. It was at these institutions that children learned to become "streetwise," to respect the elders, and to run errands for their families. Just several miles out from the bustling city, these rural villages sprung forth, creating close knit environments much like the small towns many miles away from Baltimore's metropolis. Nevertheless, on top of any hill, the farmers could glimpse the thriving city, a beacon they looked towards for their livelihood, culture, and fuel for their dreams.

The Truck Farmer and Wealthy Merchant Together and Apart

Although the visions of the truck farmer and the wealthy merchant were conspicuously different, several issues brought them together. More than any other issue, transportation united Baltimore City and County residents. Well maintained and easily traveled roads were essential to both Baltimore City and its outlying regions. The better the roads the easier and cheaper goods could be transported to local markets and warehouses built on the wharves. The Old Post Road (Old Philadelphia Road), Darley Path that grew into Harford Road, Belair Road, and Bowley's Lane (named after the Bowly family) were the first roads in Northeast Baltimore. As early as 1781, the Old Post Road was first used as a stagecoach and mail route between Philadelphia and Baltimore, a national communication route. Harford and Belair Roads, built by the 1790s, connected Baltimore to the northern reaches of Baltimore and Harford Counties. These roads were essential for shipment of produce for the local markets, and wheat for international trade. Bowley's Lane was first a private road connecting the country estates and farms along the Herring Run to Belair and Old Philadelphia Roads.

By the mid-eighteenth century Baltimore was making headway building roads to its hinterlands in western and northern Maryland—a necessity for Baltimore to continue to economically expand. Thus, in 1787 the Baltimore County Turnpike Company was created. The creation of turnpike companies had to be authorized by the state legislature.[55] Shortly thereafter, Baltimore County constructed the Reisterstown Road and Frederick Road. Between 1787 and 1805 Baltimore County government owned and operated the turnpikes. After 1805, private companies took control.

Conspicuously absent from the Baltimore County turnpike operations were the Old Main Road, Belair Road, and Harford Road. Several reasons may explain the absence of Harford and Belair Roads from being established as an eighteenth-century turnpike. First, the farmland on the northeast side of Baltimore, Harford, and Cecil counties, was close to the water. Farmers in this area could ship their goods to Baltimore on flat barges. Second, the Old Main Road was maintained with state money. And last, the Principio Iron Company's hold on the land prior to the revolution thwarted the development of this area, which inadvertently retarded the growth of the area into a profitable farming region. Politics did not play a part in the absence. Baltimore County had appointed a commission of review that had general supervision over the turnpikes. Two of those commissioners, James Gittings and Daniel Bowly, lived on the Harford and Belair roads. By 1791, the general assembly declared Philadelphia, Belair, and Harford roads as public highways.

The Belair and Harford Roads were built to connect the developing farmland to Baltimore. By 1794, as indicated in Dennis Griffith's map of Maryland, Belair Road connected Baltimore to Kingsville, Belair, Conowingo, Rising Sun, and Newark Delaware. Several landmarks were identified on this map. First is Herring Run. Directly north of Herring Run, Furley Hall was identified. Nothing else was identified in Northeast Baltimore until the crossroads of Joppa Road and finally Perry Hall. Interesting to note, Belair Road at this time was also known as the Perry Hall Road. Harford Road was in existence by 1795 and shown on Dennis Griffith's map. Nevertheless, Richard Parkinson described the road as almost impassable, taking a whole day for a carriage to traverse from the Long Green Valley to Baltimore Town.

In 1805 the legislature passed a law that gave power to three private turnpike companies—The Yorktown Turnpike Company, the Fredericktown Turnpike Company, and the Reisterstown Turnpike Company—to maintain and improve the accessibility of trade routes. Here the state would allow private turnpike companies to build and maintain the roads under the parameters of state regulations. This set a precedent for future turnpike companies. Havre de Grace Turnpike, incorporated in 1814, was the first turnpike company through Northeast Baltimore. However, the company was not allowed to collect tolls until after 1830 or until the road was twenty feet wide and composed of stone, gravel, or other hard substance. The Baltimore and Harford Turnpike Company was established in 1816. The Harford Road Turnpike opened in 1819 from Baltimore to the Gunpowder Falls. Finally, the Baltimore and Jerusalem Turnpike Company was incorporated in 1868.

Illustration of the Jerusalem Evangelical Lutheran Church, constructed in 1875; as depicted in the 1877 Hopkin's Atlas of Baltimore County. (Courtesy Historical Society of Baltimore County)

Horse racing was another enterprise that commingled Baltimore City and County citizens. Horse racing was a very popular sport that crossed class and geographical boundaries. Much like today's sports, horse racing was under the purview of the wealthy merchant's purse. The first mention of horse racing in Baltimore was in 1747, when the Commissioners of Baltimore Town authorized the establishment of an annual fair, which included horse racing.[56] A makeshift racecourse was constructed near today's Pine and Lexington Streets. Horse racing continued at the fairgrounds well until the 1820s.

In 1820 Martin Potter built the first permanent racecourse three miles from the city on the Philadelphia Road just south of the Herring Run, and adjacent to the Old Kingsbury Furnace. Racing was entirely under the management of the race course officers. Two officers who enthusiastically participated in creating the course was John Ridgely of Hampton, and R. Stockton. They were also part owners of the Stockton, Falls & Company stagecoach firm. Baltimore citizens who wanted to spend the day at the races jumped on the stagecoach for transport. Unfortunately, a couple of years later it was abandoned for a location at Canton, known as Potter's Course (named after Martin Potter).

Another little known establishment that brought City and County residents together was the Herring Run House. In the 1808 Whig newspaper of Baltimore, John Carrol submitted this advertisement:

Summer Retreat, or Herring Run House:
The Subscriber begs leave to inform his friends and the public, who study their health, and who delight in an afternoon's excursion—that he has erected a small House adjoining the Herring Run, for the reception of those who may please to honor him with their patronage, as he is determined to keep the best sort of wine and liquors—likewise has provided himself with an excellent cook, for the purpose of serving up Fish in the neatest manner, and suitable to the most delicate palate. Nothing shall be wanting on his part in rendering the place a complete Summer Retreat, to those who may please to honor him with their custom, &c.
—John Carroll.[57]

Here, Baltimore County and City residents would intermingle in democratic fashion, picnicking the day away. Recreation and the desire to escape from the daily grind was shared by both residents and found common ground in such establishments as John Carrol's Herring Run. The House was an early nineteenth-century version of the beer gardens that flourished along the Belair and Harford Roads from the 1850s to the early twentieth century.

Conflict between the visions of the truck farmer and the gentleman agriculturalist was spelled out in several of the farming magazines of the early nineteenth century. Baltimore County Historian John McGrain pointed to an entry in the *American Farmer* that succinctly captured the differing thoughts that fell along class lines. Signed Timothy Clodhopper, this farmer pointed fun at the *American Farmer* magazine and its passion for improving the bloodlines of cattle:

> At one time Alderny's were in fashion, fitted for every purpose; suited to every soil; peculiarly adapted to our climate; to all but our purses. Next came North Devons in turn; their beauty, agility, vigor, and shape had attracted the eye of the 'rich Mr. Coke', and had been honored by mingling in 'Holkam Park' with his Deer. As milkers, we are told they are unrivaled in Norfolk; in America, of course, they could not be surpassed... hand bills, sale bills, and prize cups were shown to prove, that we Yankees could boast of distinction as great, as the famed Breeders of Bulls, on the rich banks of the Tees—that 'long horns, middle horns, and no horns,' must yield to 'short horns' in fame.[58]

In short, prize-winning livestock were nothing but expensive ornaments in a gentleman's farm. Robert Brugger, in his book *Maryland, A Middle Temperament*, succinctly captured the conflicting views:

> Small farmers found the Maryland Agricultural Society little more than another gentleman's club. Working farmers cared nothing for essays on applying manure or speeches about bone meal. Machinery contests at fairs, instead of drawing farmers, developed into promotional affairs.[59]

The Maryland Agricultural Society created rules that thwarted the enrollment of truck farmers in their organization. Robert Smith and Edward Lloyd organized the Maryland Agricultural Society in 1818. The society, geared toward gentleman farmers, met at various showcase farms throughout the State. Almost all members were landholders that made their money from activities other than farming. Throughout the years they held contests in which prizes included silver utensils. Many Baltimore County farms won prizes such as the Hayfields in the Greenspring Valley, the Gittings estate in the Long Green Valley, and the Sinclair Nursery in Northeast Baltimore. Nevertheless, the prizes were restricted to large, prominent farms. McGrain described it this way:

> The committee determined to restrict awards to real dirt farmers because "it would be a misapplication of the funds of the society to give the premium to a crop of corn made on less than ten acres. In fact they wish to give their premiums

56   THE CITY AS SUBURB

1850s Eutaw Methodist Church; from the 1926 Parks Review. In recent years it has been turned into a park pavillion. (Courtesy of CHAP)

to bona fide farmers. If they offered for small patches, people residing in the neighborhood of cities, convenient to livery stables, gardeners, &c. might take all our premiums.[60]

However, the Maryland Agricultural Society, the *American Farmer* and, subsequently, the *American Turf Register* were more than gentleman clubs; they provided essential information to the small farmer. Edward Lloyd advocated crop rotation, and experimented with soil replenishment. These experiments proved useful in the proceeding years. In addition, farm tools and techniques were presented within the society and the magazines. This again proved useful as the first half of the nineteenth century saw an incredible flourishing of patents for farm implements. The *American Farmer* became a huge proponent of the use of guano (centuries-old bird dung found on South American islands). This fertilizer became prized among the farmers who could afford it. Many truck farmers hauled produce to market and guano back to the farm.

These elitist agricultural societies were useful in the progress of the agricultural revolution in Maryland and the United States, although their information was not directly transferred from journal to the middling farmer. More likely, the information was instead transferred by word of mouth in taverns, churches, and blacksmith shops. Small time farmers who relied on the yield of the land found little use for many of the suggestions and articles in the various farm magazines. They stayed away from the prize fairs to work their farms. Their work paid off as borderland farm villages thrived in the second half of the nineteenth century.

ADVERTISEMENTS.

Clairmont and Furley Hall Nursery,
ESTABLISHED 1828.

The largest stock and greatest variety of Fruit and Ornamental Trees, Foreign and Domestic, to be found in the United States—comprising

Apple, Peach and Pear Trees,
(Standard & Dwarf,)
Evergreen and Shade Trees,
All Varieties of Grape Vines,
Currant, Gooseberry, and
Blackberry Bushes,
Strawberry Plants, etc., etc.

TERMS TO SUIT THE TIMES.

☞ Nursery is located on the Bel Air Road, Baltimore County, and can be reached by way of Gay St.

WM. CORSE & SON,
P. O. Box 248, BALTIMORE, and GARDENVILLE.

CHRISTIAN SCHOLL,	JOHN M. HERRMAN,
Bel Air Road,	**WHEELWRIGHT,**
NEAR 1ST TOLL GATE,	GARDENVILLE.
Wheelwright & Blacksmith	All work in Wood promptly and carefully executed.
MANUFACTURER OF	**LEVI S. SLADE,**
Wagons of All Kinds.	**3 MILE HOUSE,**
Repairing and Horse Shoeing promptly attended to.	LIBERTY ROAD, GARRISON.

JOHN L. HARRIS & CO.
MANUFACTURERS OF

FINE HARNESS  **AND SADDLES,**

And other Articles for the Horse,

No. 62 WEST FAYETTE ST., OPPOSITE THE RENNERT HOUSE,

BALTIMORE.

A THRIVING BORDERLAND REGION
1852–1898

During the first half of the nineteenth century, the wealthy merchants weaved architecture, agriculture, and nature into a picturesque setting framed by the burgeoning Baltimore skyline of monuments, church steeples, and ship masts. Concurrently, truck farmers tilled the soil and set a firm foundation for their children's prosperity—a generation that became part of the Baltimore County movers and shakers. From their efforts, farms and crossroad villages grew into thriving communities. During the latter half of the nineteenth century, Northeast Baltimore again shaped itself according to the differing visions of Baltimore County and City residents. Truck farmers actualized their vision of thriving farm villages supported by prosperous truck farms. On the other hand, the vision of the early nineteenth-century elite widened to include the collective vision of middle-class city residents.

Upon the foundation of crossroad farm villages, Northeast Baltimore became Baltimore's premier truck farm region where land was mostly put to agricultural use. In 1881 J. Thomas Scharf, in his *History of Baltimore City and County,* described Northeast Baltimore:

> The quality of the soil is such as to especially favor the cultivation of vegetables and, in a lesser degree of fruits. The land in this region is highly productive, and much of it commands three hundred dollars or more per acre on the rare occasions when it comes into the market.[1]

This description is far different than Richard Parkinson's tale. Nevertheless, seventy-seven years after Parkinson, the truck farmers and wealthy merchants greatly improved the land. Farmland rose in value along with the truck farmer's social status. From the

Opposite: Advertisements from the 1879 Baltimore County Directory indicate a thriving economy.
(Courtesy Historical Society of Baltimore County)

1880s to the turn of the twentieth century, Northeast Baltimore reveled in its status as an agricultural borderland region—the height of Northeast's agricultural era, and Baltimore's richest truck farming region.

Farm Communities and Villages on the Edge of Baltimore

By the late 1870s, five farm villages along the Belair and Harford roads flourished within the farm communities of Gardenville and Lauraville.[2] These two communities stretched along the Harford and Belair roads and wound throughout Northeast's interior along dirt roads. Connecting Harford and Belair roads were Erdman Avenue, Southern Avenue, Hamilton Avenue, and Towson (Taylor) Avenue. Connecting Harford Road to its western area were Grindon Lane, Old Harford Road, and finally Towson (Taylor) Avenue. And connecting Belair Road to its eastern region were Bowley's Lane, Franklin (Frankford) Avenue, Hamilton Avenue, and Kenwood Avenue, which eventually met up with Golden Ring Road. These roads tied the area into two overlapping communities as well as connected them to points in Baltimore County.

In 1877 G. M. Hopkins published an atlas of Baltimore City and County which portrayed in detail the farm communities of Lauraville and Gardenville. Each parcel of land was identified by owner. In his map the boundaries of Lauraville and Gardenville encompassed an area just south of Herring Run and north of Hamilton Avenue. In addition, the 1878, 1880, and 1882 Maryland directories listed Lauraville and Gardenville as the two farm communities in the area. The directories listed families living in relatively the same area that G. M. Hopkins identified as Lauraville and Gardenville. Both the Hopkins map and the Maryland Directory point to Gardenville and Lauraville as two distinct communities. By superimposing the names and occupations from the Maryland directories onto the Hopkins atlas, crossroad centers of trade, or villages, appeared.

Along Belair Road, three villages flourished: Georgetown (Belair-Edison) at Erdman Avenue; Gardenville near today's Southern Avenue; and Raspeburg near Hamilton Avenue. Along Harford Road, two villages flourished—Lauraville between the Herring Run and Grindon Lane, and Tames Lane (Hamilton) situated on current day Hamilton Avenue. These villages were commercial centers for the Lauraville and Gardenville communities.

Opposite (left): From the 1876 Hopkins Atlas of Baltimore City and Environs. (Courtesy EPFL Maryland Room)
For comparison, opposite (right): From the 1898 Bromley Atlas of Baltimore County. (Courtesy of Historical Society Baltimore County)

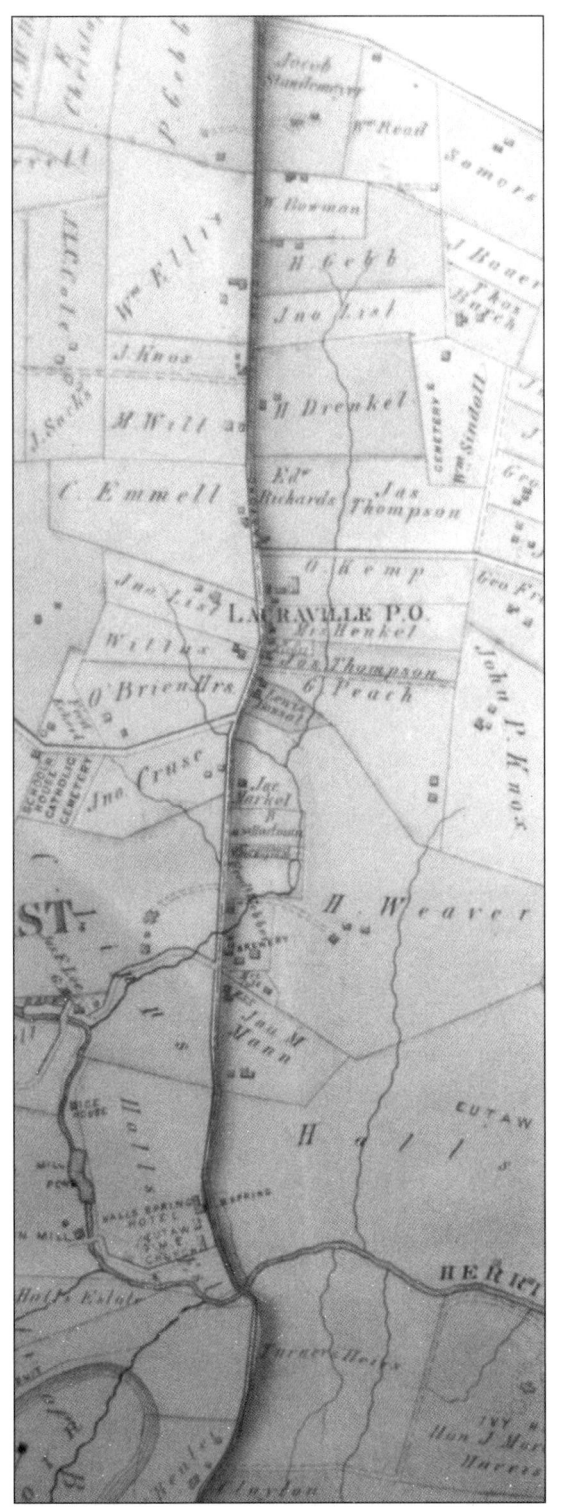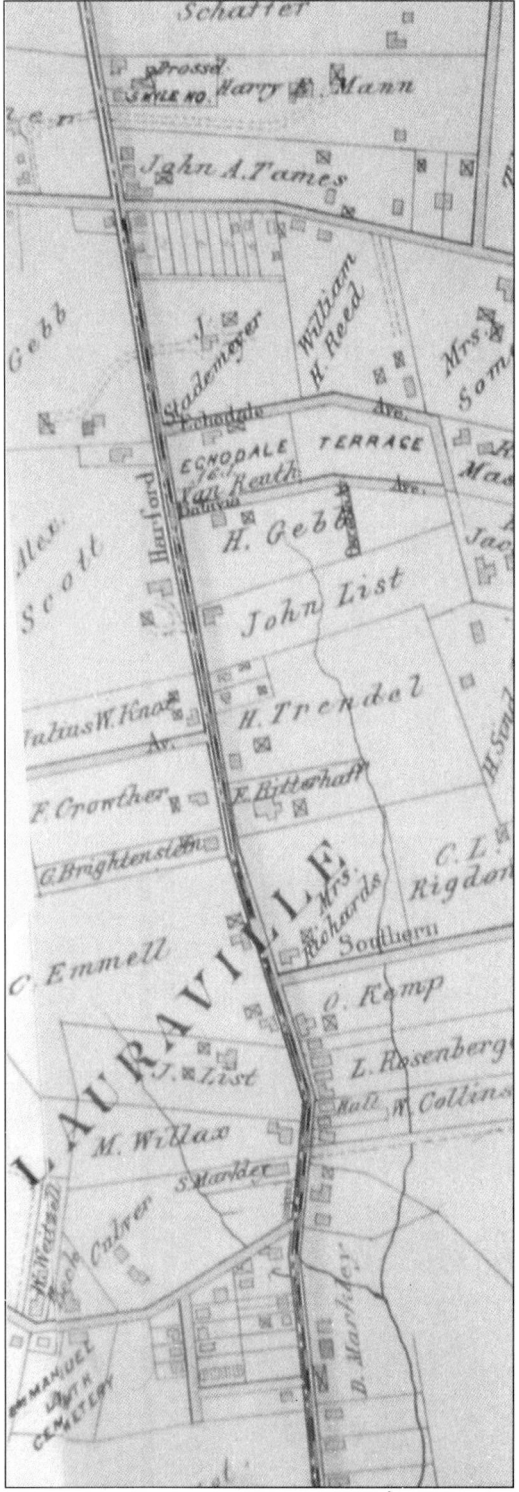

Local Occupations (1880 Maryland Directory)

Lauraville

Population umber of occupations
28
Number of entries   97

Occupation	Count	%
Attorney	1	1%
Blacksmith	4	4%
Brewery	2	2%
Brickmaker	1	1%
Butcher	2	2%
Carpenter	5	5%
Carriage Maker	1	1%
Clerk	2	2%
Cloth Dealer	1	1%
Constable	1	1%
Cooper	1	1%
Farmer	44	45%
Fence Maker	1	1%
Florist	4	4%
General Merchandise	3	3%
Hotel	3	3%
Harnessmaker	1	1%
Horse Dealer	1	1%
Huckster	1	1%
Junk Dealer	2	2%
Justice of the Peace	2	2%
Livery Stable	1	1%
Miller	3	3%
Packer	1	1%
Physician	1	1%
Retired	6	6%
Store and Butcher	1	1%
Wheelwright	1	1%

Gardenville

Population   500
Number of occupations   27
Number of entries   144

Occupation	Count	%
Blacksmith	4	3%
Brewer	3	2%
Bricklayer	1	0.7%
Butcher	7	5%
Carpenter	3	2%
Clerk	1	0.7%
Constable	1	0.7%
Dairy	2	1.4%
Druggist	2	1.4%
Farmer	90	63%
Nursery	1	0.7%
Florist	1	0.7%
General Merchandise	2	1.4%
Groceries	2	1.4%
Justice of the Peace	2	1.4%
Band Leader	1	0.7%
Marble Works	2	1.4%
Miller	1	0.7%
Physician	2	1.4%
Restaurant	2	1.4%
Saloon	4	3%
Shoemaker	3	2%
Store and Saloon	1	0.7%
Tinner	1	0.7%
Tollgate Keeper	1	0.7%
Vinegar Manufacturer	1	0.7%
Wheelwright	4	3%

In addition to agriculture, mills influenced the communities of Gardenville and Lauraville. By the 1880s there were five mills along the Herring Run: Coxon's mill in Gardenville near Bowley's Lane, the Eutaw grist mill between Harford and Belair Roads, Green's cotton mill on the west side of Harford Road, Russell's mill just north of Argonne Drive, and the Ivy mill located where Morgan State University is today. Inevitably these mills created a labor force. Mill hands lived as boarders on farms and in houses on company land within the Herring Run Valley. Although other Baltimore mills created mill towns such as Stone Hill and Dickeyville, no village appeared along the Herring Run. Only Green's Cotton Mill became big enough to build a community structure—the Eutaw Methodist Church. The Coxon, Russell, and Eutaw mills were outgrowths of farms and never became independent economic enterprises.

Breweries also flourished in Northeast Baltimore. Two breweries, the Darley Park Brewery and Weber's Brewery, were located on the Harford Road. Four breweries were located on and near the Belair Road: the Vonderhorst Brewery at North Avenue and Belair Road; the Huebner Brewery (later became Hertlein's brewery) at the 4400 block of Belair Road; Brehm's Brewery on Bowley's Lane, and a small brewery at the west side of Belair Road near today's Brendan Avenue. These breweries played a double role for the area. Attached to all of them were beer gardens that attracted city and county residents alike. In addition, like the truck farms, they supplied the city saloons. There were twenty-nine breweries at ten different locations on the Belair Road and Gay Street corridor. For breweries it was the most strategic location. Belair Road was a direct route from the wheat-growing farm communities in Baltimore and Harford counties, as well as close to malt supply warehouses and the saloons of East Baltimore.

The Communities of Lauraville and Gardenville

The 1882 Maryland directory totaled the population for Lauraville at 500. The directory listed ninety-seven families and twenty-eight different types of occupations. Of the ninety-seven families listed, forty-four were farmers. Seventeen of the twenty-eight occupations catered mostly to the farm community. They entailed such tradesmen as wheelwrights, carpenters, and general store merchandisers. Of the seventeen occupations that catered to Lauraville community, three were professions: an attorney, constable, and Justice of the Peace. Seven occupations—farmer, brewer, butcher, brick maker, florist, miller, and cloth dealer—sold their goods in Baltimore.

Gardenville, with a population of 500, had 144 listed families and twenty-seven different types of occupations listed. Ninety of these families were farmers. Seventeen occupations catered to the local farm community while eleven occupations were dependent upon the Baltimore market. The occupations that served the local farmers were similar to those of Lauraville except a few differences. Gardenville had four saloons, two restaurants, and two marble yards that made gravestones for the local cemeteries.

The listings in the Maryland directories and the Maryland gazetteers are not comprehensive and leave out many landowners as well as tenant farmers and laborers of the area. By criss-crossing the names from the Maryland directories and gazetteers with the names plotted on the Hopkins 1877 map of Baltimore County, there are over forty land tracts not identified by the directories and gazetteers. In addition, many property owners were not identified on the Hopkins map. These discrepancies exist for several reasons. First, many land holdings held by women were not listed in the directory. Secondly, land holdings from absentee landlords or fields rented out to local farmers were not listed. They were not their primary residences. Nevertheless, a close analysis of the names listed and the occupations shed many insights into the area.

Conspicuously absent were farm hands. Nevertheless, the 1880 census manuscripts, which were the census-takers notebooks, shed insight onto other citizens living in Gardenville and Lauraville. Many of the farm families took in boarders. Several of the more prominent families had live-in servants. Boarders were identified as farm laborers, while others were just laborers. They hired themselves out to the various businesses around the area. These laborers were jack-of-all trades, finding work where they could get it. Other boarders were identified as brewery workers. Here in rented

Original gabled roof (above) and later-added front (right) of the John Henry Keene estate. (Author's photos)

rooms of farm families and widows, the labor force of Northeast Baltimore existed. One African-American enclave in Northeast Baltimore was identified near the Ivy Mills. However, many African-Americans were identified in the 1880 census manuscripts as living throughout Northeast Baltimore.

The Farm Villages of Northeast Baltimore
The Village of Lauraville
The Lauraville Village center was located between Herring Run Park and Southern Avenue. The village sprawled out along Harford road until the northern tip entwined with Tames Lane. On the west side of Harford Road, the village dropped into the Herring Run Valley and ended at the Ivy mill complex. To the south it bordered the Herring Run. On its east it mingled with Gardenville where no legitimate boundary was formed. Farmers living between Harford and Belair roads identified themselves with either Lauraville or Gardenville by what road they took to Baltimore and what post office they used. These boundaries were not set in stone and were used generally for postal purposes. The earliest reference of Lauraville was in the 1851 *Maryland Gazetteer*.

Lauraville was named after John Henry Keene's daughter Laura.[3] However, the *Genealogical and Memorial Encyclopedia of the State of Maryland* stated that the village was named for John Henry Keene's estate "Lauraville." John Henry Keene, Sr. was born in 1806 in Talbot County. He married Sally Dorsey Lawrence on September 26, 1831, and died in 1894 at the age of eighty-seven. John was in Northeast Baltimore by 1850; he was listed as retired in the 1880 Maryland Directory. Not much else is known about John Henry Keene, Sr. His large estate shows up on the 1850s map, located directly north of Hamilton Avenue between Harford and Belair Roads. The Old Estate, Lauraville, was sold to J. and W. Erdman between 1877 and 1898. Fantastically it still exists at the southeast corner of Walther and White Road.

John Henry Keene had two sons that became prominent lawyers in Baltimore City.[4] His youngest son, Robert Goldsborough Keene, became a partner with his brother in a prominent law firm. He also joined the Confederate Army during the Civil War, which indicates that the Keene family owned slaves. In his later life he was intricately involved in real estate operations, the most famous being Ocean City. Robert's older brother, John Henry, Jr., studied at Harvard Law school. After retiring from law, he wrote a book, *Justice and Jurisprudence,* and many editorials in the *Sun* paper. Here he professed his ardent Democrat views defending the party and especially his friend, Senator Arthur P. Gorman. John Henry Keene, Jr. lived at 8 West Hamilton Street in his later years with his sisters Laura and Mary Keene. Before moving in with his sisters, he lived in a commodious townhouse he had built at St. Paul and Preston Streets while keeping a summer residence, "Clymarila," in Glencoe, Baltimore County. In 1903 he tore down his townhouse on St. Paul's Street and developed the Earl Court Apartments, still standing today.

John Henry Keene, Jr. was a lively writer with ardent opinions, many of which excoriated modern progress. In 1892 he wrote a letter to Mayor Latrobe, a letter defiling the new electric streetcars:

> This nuisance is not a mere visionary picture, it is a stern reality—a flesh and blood fact with color in its cheeks. It is a system of rapid transit by hissing monsters, often hurled at frightful rates of speed, thumping and bumping at every step. They ascend and descend every grade with Babylonish howls. The air rings with the shrieks of their gongs, and by day and by night, a flesh creeping, saw-mill buzz, with showers of electric sparks, make their struggling, groaning course through the highways of a densely populated city."[5]

Ironically, John Henry Keene, Jr. denounced the streetcars which was the single most technological innovation that would drastically change his boyhood home from a rural retreat to a bustling suburban community. In all, the sons of John Henry Keene, Sr. rose in social status to become two of Baltimore's most interesting socialites.

In 1881, Scharf succinctly described Lauraville as follows:

> The village of Lauraville immediately adjoins Gardenville on the south (more east than south) and extends to the confines of the Johns Hopkins University property at Clifton. It has a population of 197 [incorrect], and, like its neighbor, furnishes the city with quantities of fruits and vegetables and dairy products. For churches and schools the people depend upon those located at Gardenville and on the Belair Road.[6]

Scharf did not mention the Eutaw Methodist Church nor the mills, Weber's Brewery, Hall's Springs Hotel, and several general stores. This omission may be due to Harford Road being the boundary between the ninth and twelfth election districts, thus he didn't write about the area west of Harford Road. Nevertheless, Scharf pointed to the interdependence of Lauraville and Gardenville, an interdependence that is also intertwined by the large extended families that lived in both communities.

Hall's Springs Hotel was located south of the village on the north side of the Herring Run. The hotel existed by 1850. Further evidence suggests that it existed by 1840. It was at Hall's Springs that Henry Raspe (of Raspeburg) was born in 1840. In 1864 an ad for the sale of Hall's Springs Tavern was printed in the *Baltimore Daily Gazette*:

For Sale or Rent
Hall's Springs Tavern and grounds, about twenty five acres. This well-known resort on the Harford Road about three miles from the City is offered for sale or rent.[7]

Eutaw Estate had an interesting relationship with the Hall's Spring's Tavern. In 1861 William Carvel Hall put an ad in the paper to rent his old estate called "Eutaw." Originally it was the estate of William Smith, most likely Sam Smith's uncle. When Carvel Hall bought the estate is unknown. But in 1861 he put an ad in the paper to rent the farm:

The dwelling house at "Eutaw" on the Harford Road 11/2 miles from the city limits, with ice house, spring of remarkably pure water and handsome grounds. Omnibuses pass each way several times a day. [The estate] will be rented for the summer or by the year. William Carvel Hall 58 Exchange Place.

In addition, William Carvel Hall had another house and grounds for rent:

The Hall Springs Hotel—a popular stop for picnickers and truck farmers located in what is now Herring Run Park. (Courtesy EPFL Maryland Room)

About sixty acres of cultivated land with dwelling and stabling at "Eutaw" 1½ miles from the city limits on the Harford Road will be rented low to a responsible tenant.

Hall also had a mill located between Harford and Belair Roads. Here the driveway connected to the Harford road just south of the Herring Run and headed due east. The driveway crossed the Herring Run at the mill dam and headed due east. It was directly north of the millrace. Today, the millrace can still be seen directly north of the asphalt path. Its remnants are now a little gully between the black asphalt path and the dirt path through the woods.

On July 3, 1871, William Bishop, Jr., the proprietor of the hotel, printed the following ad in the *Sun*:

Hall's Springs Hotel
Three miles from the City, on the Harford Turnpike boarders can be accommodated with comfortable rooms. Meals served to transient visitors upon short notice.
The scenery and walks at this place are as interesting and nearly as extensive as Druid Hill Park. The Grand Woods improved by a commodious Pavilion, Swings, Benches, and etc, with the best springs, make it a desirable place for holiday picnics. Cars run between the City Hall and this place every Hour.[8]

Here the ad points to the picturesque setting by comparing it to Druid Hill Park. Also located on the Herring Run north of Hall's Spring's Hotel were several mills. Directly upstream from the Herring Run Hotel was Green's cotton mill. In the *Industries of Maryland* published by the Historical Publishing Company in 1882, the following description was found:

Amon Green & Co., Manufacturers of Cotton Yarn, Carpet Chain, Wrapping twine, Candle Wick, Cotton Bats, Cotton Rope, Knitting Cotton, etc., No. 77 German Street.—There are but two or three manufactures of cotton yarn, carpet chain, wrapping twine etc., in this locality.... Amon and Samuel Green, were the originators of the house nearly forty years ago (1840s), and successfully conducted the business for a number of years, their mills being then located at Hall's Springs. During the war, however, Mr. Samuel Green withdrew from the firm. Soon after this Mr. Amon Green died, and the original mills lay idle for a number of years. They were started again, however, about a year ago under the direct control of the estate of Mr. Green, with Messrs. Samuel H. Green, James T. Green and LP Muller as active partners and managers. A large number of hands are employed at their mills, known as the Columbia, at Hall's Springs, and they turn out about two thousand pounds of their manufactures per day. This firm makes a specialty of carpet warp...[9]

Green's cotton mill. The Green family operated a mill on this site west of Harford Road from the 1840s to the early twentieth century.
(Courtesy EPFL Maryland Room)

Other mills also lined the Herring Run. Directly North of Green's cotton mill stood the Ivy mill, located on the grounds of the current Morgan State University. On Taylor's map of 1857, Russell's mill was located between Green's mill and the Ivy mill. Also, on the Hopkins 1877 map and the 1896 Bromely Baltimore City Atlas, J. Russell's mill and quarry are identified. Some of these mills were industrial extensions of merchant houses of Baltimore City, while some were extensions of prosperous truck farm operations.

For the mills, the Herring Run acted as a source of power as well as a sewer to carry away waste materials. Much like today, Baltimore's industry was located on its periphery. In this sense, the Herring Run conglomeration of mills was a nineteenth-century industrial park of Baltimore. Although no mill village was built, several houses were located on both sides of the Harford Road on the mill lands. Major Howard L. Harker stated that his great grandfather was the grist miller of the Eutaw farm. Unlike Hampden, Mount Washington, and the Mount Vernon Mills, Lauraville was not economically centered on the mills, but on agriculture.

Weber's Brewery was another industry that contributed to both the City and Lauraville's economy. In 1862 Frederick A. Weber, after working for the Albion Brewery at Jones Falls near the old Belvedere Bridge, founded his brewery north of Herring Run.

One year after it was built, on August 11, 1863, the brewery completely burned to the ground. Shortly thereafter, he rebuilt the brewery and added a park and pavilion.

In 1878 Weber produced 2,504 barrels of beer a year.[10] Nevertheless, by the late 1880s the brewery was losing money. In 1886, George Bass became the brewmaster of Weber's Brewery. Finally, in 1889 the Brewery went into receivership, and Weber's stopped all brewing production.

Weber, who learned his trade from his father in Switzerland, didn't upgrade the brewery with modern conveniences such as refrigeration. This never let him achieve the large production needed at that time to sell beer at competitive prices. Instead of a brewery he expanded his beer park with a hotel and a tavern. Weber's Park continued into the 1900s.

Lauraville Village slowly but steadily grew until the early twentieth century. By 1898 houses and businesses on large lots lined Harford Road. By 1900, suburbanization was on Lauraville's horizon. Nevertheless, Lauraville's rural feeling still lingers today.

Tames Lane (the Precursor to Hamilton)

During the 1850s, a small village formed on the Harford Road between Hamilton Avenue and the Old Harford Road. By 1880, Tames Lane grew into a thriving horse and carriage center.[11] The McDonalds had a carpenter shop. Thomas Armstrong was a harness and saddle maker. F. Christopher, a horse dealer, was located off Hamilton Road, where Harvest Farms Grocery is located today. The Hoddinott brothers were blacksmiths, wheelwrights and carriage dealers. Much like the twentieth-century car dealerships and mechanic garages that flocked around each other on the Belair Road, the Old Harford Road village was a center for horse transportation. All these businesses complemented each other, creating the region's horse dealership. In addition, there was a tavern, general store, two hotels, a shoemaker, brick maker, and a post office. By 1890 there was another general store, a butcher, and a physician. Two hotels were located between the Old Harford Road and Hamilton Avenue. A Presbyterian church was located on the Old Harford Road. Robert Moore's estate Glenmore was off the Old Harford Road. He was a cloth dealer.

There was also the five-mile house and a tavern ran by James Baird. One mile up the road was the six-mile house. These houses were nineteenth-century versions of highway rest stops. Here, the farmer trucking his goods to market could rest his horse, quench his thirst, or rent a room for the night.

The first general store was run by John Tames, who was also listed as a butcher. It was from Tames General Store that the village was dubbed Tames Lane. Tames Lane ran from Harford Road to Belair Road. Today it is the eastern portion of Hamilton Avenue. The road was changed to Hamilton Avenue after Caughy Hamilton, who owned the estate of "Fair Oaks," donated property for the road's western extension.

The Hoddinott brothers owned the most successful businesses in this area. From their humble beginnings at Tames Lane, the family in 1870 opened a factory in downtown Baltimore, while keeping their shops near the Old Harford Road. In 1882, the Hoddinott family advertised their business citywide in the *Industries of Maryland 1882* publication. In full the ad ran as follows:

> Hoddinott Bros., Carriage Manufacturers, New Nos. 225 and 227 North Street which is now Guilford Avenue.—A prominent and prosperous firm engaged in the carriage-building trade in the city is that of Hoddinott Bros., who stand in the front rank in this line in Baltimore, the vehicles turned out in this well-ordered establishment being excellent in every feature—in general workmanship, artistic finish, and durability—and as a consequence are in steady and extensive demand. This concern was started in 1870, and the business has been conducted ever since... Messrs. E.C. And J.W. Hoddinott are natives of Baltimore County, but raised in this city, and are well favorably known in the community.[12]

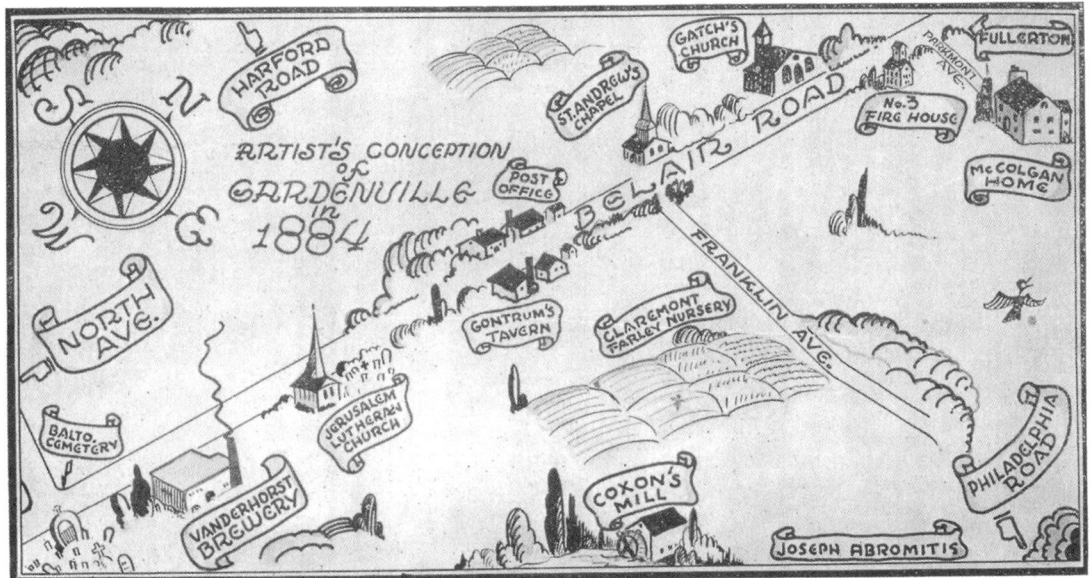

Map drawn for the 1934 *Jubilee Celebration of Saint Anthony's of Padua Church.* (Photo and map courtesy of CHAP)

Right: The Gardenville Band—in existence since the late 1800s. (From 1934 *Jubilee Celebration of St. Anthony's of Padua Church*, courtesy of CHAP)

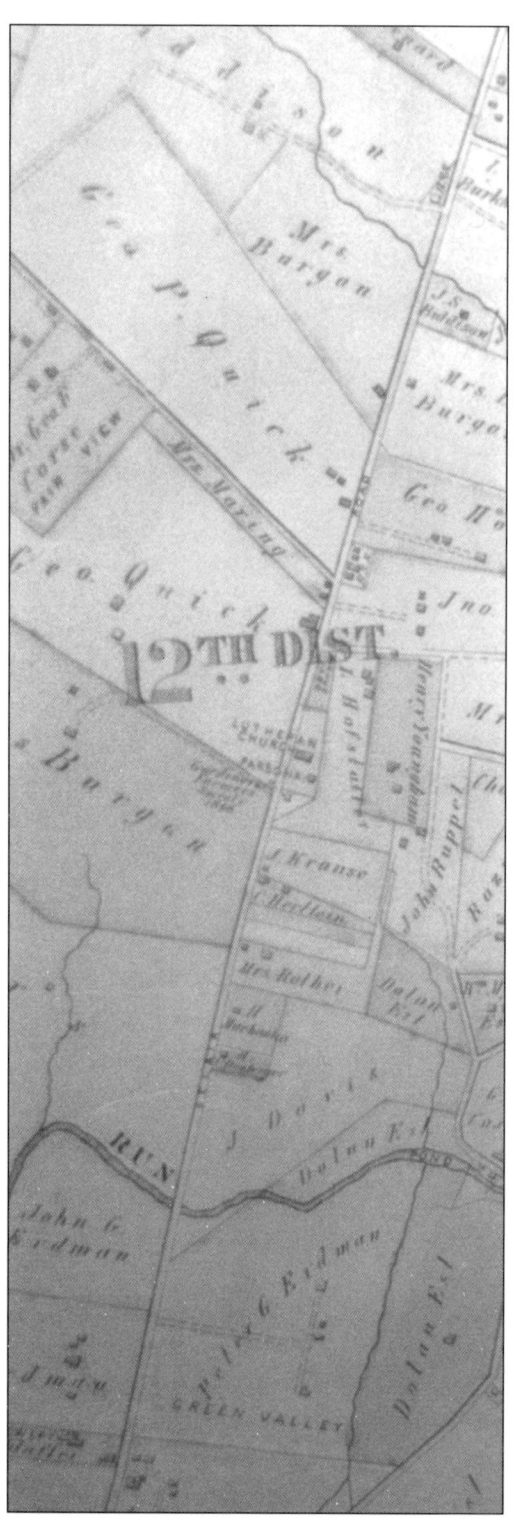

The Hoddinott family had resided and conducted business in Tames Lane since 1851. In 1871 G.W. & Son Blacksmiths and Wheelwrights were listed in the 1871 *Maryland State Gazette*. The Hoddinotts were a prime example of how borderland residents worked their way into the social and economic community of Baltimore City.

The Village of Gardenville

By the 1880s, Gardenville was more developed than Lauraville. Scharf identified a Methodist Episcopal Church (Andrew's Chapel), Lutheran Church (Jerusalem Evangelical Church), three public schools, Farmers' and Gardeners' Beneficial Society, and a Garden Lodge, No. 114 I.O.O.F. The churches were located several blocks north and south on Belair Road. In 1884, St. Anthony's Catholic school was established. Gontrum's Tavern, a post office, druggist, and several general stores were also opened as well as a doctor's office. The Gardener's Hall was located south of the Lutheran Church. Gerard Hopkins's map of 1877 also identified J.H. Harney and Ernest Sack as carpenters, J. Harman Schone as a clerk, Alex McCormick as a florist, John Schone and Son as merchants, and Joseph A. Neumayer as a music teacher. Also, an ad for catsup was published on the map:

Left: From the 1876 Hopkins Atlas of Baltimore City and Environs. (Courtesy EPF Maryland Room) **For comparison, opposite: From the 1898 Bromley Atlas of Baltimore County.** (Courtesy Historical Society of Baltimore County)

**Tomato Catsup, Manufactured by
ALEXANDER McCORMICK, JR.**
I have been making this Superior Catsup for Ten years, and have been supplying the Leading Hotels and Oyster Houses in Baltimore and Washington. Samples sent on application. Warranted to keep for years.
Address Alexander McCormick, Gardenville.
(For sale by gallon or barrel.)[13]

In the 1880 Maryland Directory, Alexander McCormick was listed as a farmer. Undoubtedly, he grew tomatoes.

One brewery dominated Gardenville. In 1852 John N. Huebner opened his brewery across the street from the future site of the Most Holy Redeemer Cemetery.[14] John Huebner first worked in a shoe and boot shop. In 1849–50 he was working as a distiller in Baltimore City. In 1852 Huebner opened his brewery. His brewery was a small crude wooden structure that produced a small amount of beer.

In 1857 Neisendorfer bought the Belair Road brewery from Huebner and ran it for two years. In 1859 Neisendorfer moved his operations to Bowley's Lane into a larger facility. The Belair Road brewery laid idle until 1866 when Gottfried C. Hertlein purchased the property. Hertlein enlarged the brewery, updated its equipment, and dug

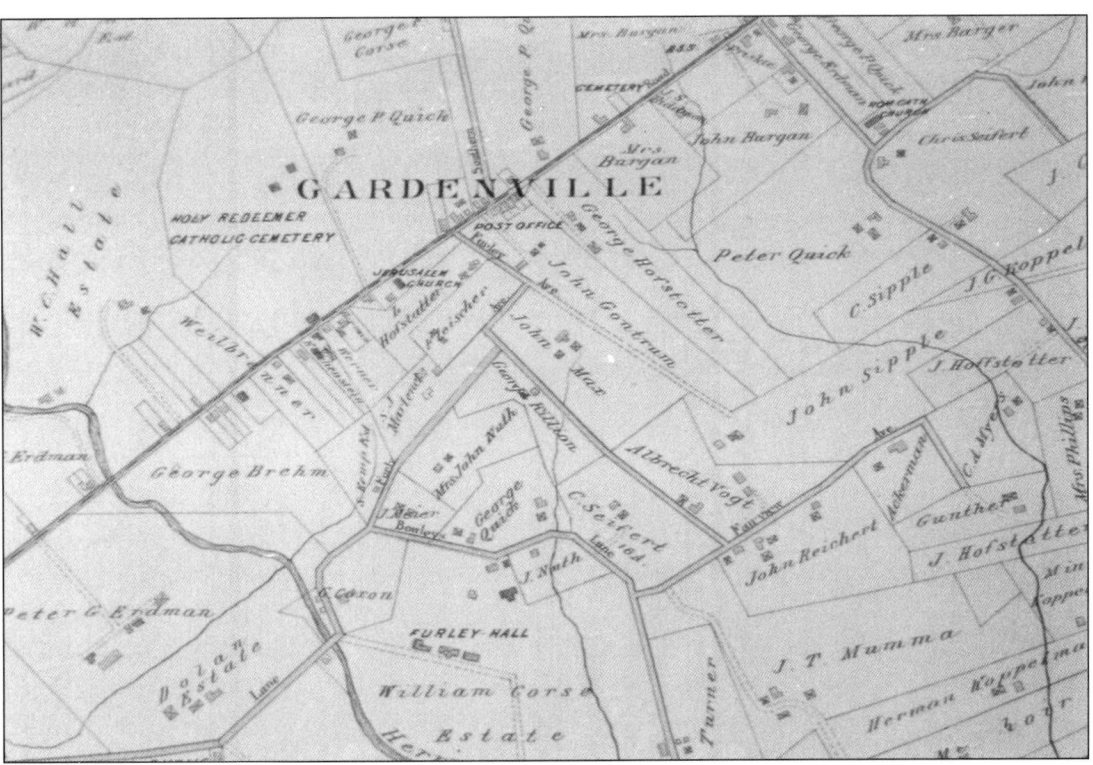

deeper beer cellars. A steam pump was installed to pump water from a spring located on the property. The spring also fed a man-made pond, which was used for ice. In 1878 Otto Woerner took over the brewery and ran it until 1890 when he moved to the city. From the 1890s to 1912, the Herman family owned the property. Here the property was used as a beer garden that had band concerts, movies, and several other family-oriented activities. In 1912 the property was sold to John Seidel who built the current bowling alley. Rumors abound that the beer cellars still exist.

The Village of Georgetown

At the intersection of Erdman Avenue and Belair Road, another crossroads village grew into a thriving center. Scharf wrote of Georgetown:

> On July 15, 1879 a meeting of residents was held to decide the proper name for the community. Centerville and Georgetown were proposed and the latter was selected by a majority of 14 votes. Most of the people are Germans, and for several years they had been in the habit of choosing a burgomaster of the village, a custom which they resolved to continue.[15]

Georgetown was named after three prominent citizens of the area: George Brehm, George Lamley, and George Erdman. The village, however, was thriving as early as the 1850s. In the 1850s there was a tavern, a general store, and a stocking factory. Also by 1855 Neisendorf's brewery opened and in 1853 Old Har Sinai cemetery was established.

Architectural evidence points to several rowhouse structures built in the 1830s and 1840s. Located in the middle of the 3200 block of Belair Road, there is one two-story side-gabled with dormer rowhouse. This rowhouse form was popular in Baltimore from the 1800s to 1830s. Two other rowhouses date to the 1840s. They are two-and-a-half stories high with eyebrow windows near the cornice. These houses are similar to many houses in Fells Point and Federal Hill that were built between 1840s to the mid-1850s. In addition, over a dozen other rowhouses were built in the 1870s and 1880s along the 3200 block of Belair, and on Erdman Avenue just east of Belair. During this time, four alley houses were built behind the rowhouses on Belair Road. They are Northeast's only alley houses.

These rowhouses in Georgetown characterize the village in several ways. First, the village identified itself with the urban form of Baltimore. Second, the rowhouse form produced higher building density, thus higher land values and greater commercial activity. Georgetown either thought of itself as being an up-and-coming commercial center, or as part of the city form. In addition, the location of several industries may have produced the need for housing.

Brehm's Brewery was the largest employer in the area.[16] Formerly the Neisendorfer's Brewery, the place had been taken over shortly after 1866 when Neisendorfer passed away. A few months later Brehm married Niesendorfer's widow. Fire destroyed the frame structure in 1870. The brewery was rebuilt in brick, and furnished with the most modern equipment available. In 1899 the Maryland Brewing Company bought the George Brehm's 'celebrated beer' for $400,000 dollars. Having over extended itself by 1901, the company sold back the brewery to Brehm for $185,000 dollars. Brehm died in 1904. His son Henry took over the family business. Henry erected in July of 1907 a new brewhouse and storage house, designed by Philadelphia architect Kurt Peuckert. Throughout the years of Prohibition, the Brehm's Beverage Company continued by producing sodas and resumed full beer production once Prohibition was repealed. Around 1940, the Burton Brewing Company, after buying the brewery five years earlier, went into receivership. At the end of August of that year the property was bought by the Colonial Mortgage Company, and rowhouse development replaced beer production.

Most interesting is Georgetown's persistent rowhouse form. Georgetown was Northeast's only rowhouse village and today Georgetown is Northeast's largest rowhouse suburb. Early design decisions influenced its later rowhouse suburb form.

The Village of Raspeburg

The village of Raspeburg was an outgrowth of Gardenville and did not become an official village until the opening of the post office in the 1890s. By 1877 John Henry Raspe had a store at the corner of Hamilton and Belair Roads. A school, blacksmith's shop, and carpenter's shop grew around Raspe's store. By the 1880s it resembled many of the other small crossroads villages in the Northeast. Gatch's Methodist Church was just a few blocks up from the store. On the 1898 map, the village of Raspeburg was listed as a village with all the amenities, including a hotel and Gatch's quarry.

In the 1880s, as the story goes, Nicholas Gatch suggested that the little crossroads village be named after John Henry Raspe, for his store. It was a general store that sold everything seemingly needed in a farm community. J. Charles Raspe, the son of John Henry Raspe, recalled:

> It couldn't be helped. There wasn't another store for two miles in any direction and that was a good distance then. So the people in the neighborhood the Gatches, Evanses, Coles, Seitzes and Carters were the big families had to depend on us for goods, and news, too. The store was full of everything needed in a farm community. Near the chunk of stove, among the big barrels of vinegar, syrup and crackers and the plowshares, harness and other farm equipment, the neighbors sat and talked and exchanged the news with John Henry Raspe, who knew more about local happenings than anyone and who was a clearing house for information.[17]

Erdman House, corner of Harford Road and Erdman Avenue. (Author's photo)

During the late 1890s, the postal service decided to put a post office in the village. It was placed in the store and mail was brought to it by streetcar. Raspe died in 1903 just before the major transformation of the village into a neighborhood.

A Few of the Residents of Northeast Baltimore

As Baltimore City's population grew so did the Northeast borderland region. Many of the established families grew to prominence and stamped their activities onto the area. The children of these families were given the same opportunities of the wealthy Baltimore City residents of the early nineteenth century. Many went to college and became doctors, lawyers, bankers, and businessmen. Other children took over their family's farm. Some rose to local and state political offices. In addition, many children branched out into other services for the area, such as quarrying, carpentry, and milling.

During the Civil War, the area was full of divided sympathies. Many of the young men joined the Confederate army while their neighbors joined the Union cause. And in some cases, brother and brother fought on different sides. For example, there are some stained glass windows in Andrew's Chapel made in memory of the Gatch family—despite the chapel's earlier secession. The Quaker contingency quietly went on with their lives peaceably contributing to the Union cause. Despite neighbors choosing sides, not much in Northeast Baltimore was effected by the Civil War.

For the Baltimore County residents, the small villages were tight social networks. Throughout the genealogies of the residents, many of the families intermarried one another, showing that the social network was placed within the villages and small churches, and not in Baltimore City. At the same time, many prominent Baltimore City residents found the area desirous for their country seats. They bought land and built summer homes on a scale less than the wealthy merchants at the beginning of the nineteenth century. Interestingly, this pattern was shown while overlaying the names and occupants of the 1882 Maryland Directory on the 1877 Hopkins map. After most of the land parcels were identified, Baltimore City residents owned many of the areas not identified in the Maryland directory.

- **John Erdman's** family emigrated from Germany to Baltimore County prior to 1803. They settled on the Belair and Harford Roads. The family owned several farms and produce stalls in Baltimore's markets. By the 1880s the Erdman clan not only had a road named after them, but also owned extensive lands throughout the ninth and twelfth districts of Baltimore County. The lineage of John Erdman illustrated the rise of his family to prominence.

    John Erdman, born in 1803, was the son of Peter Erdman. Early on, John learned blacksmithing. However, he was always a farmer. John married Mary Hoddinott of the Hoddinott family of Tamesville. John and Mary had seven sons and one daughter. Three of his children became farmers—Peter G., Gottlieb H., and Charles. Frederick went to Baltimore and sold produce (obviously grown at his brothers' farms). John Jr. became an ice cream and confectionary maker (who probably got his milk from his cousin John W. Erdman). Francis was a butcher who owned stalls in the Belair and Lexington Markets. The daughter married local farmer Jacob Lamley. All of John Erdman's children stayed in the Baltimore region and connected to truck farming. Some of John's children were educated in the local public schools, while others were educated at Schipe's School on Gay Street.

    The grandchildren of John Erdman also continued farming Northeast Baltimore. Peter Erdman, the son of John Erdman, had five sons and five daughters. All the sons were farmers and the daughters all married farmers. In many cases, the third generation of the Baltimore County residents made economic and social inroads into the city. It was the fourth and fifth generation who would grow neighborhoods instead of crops, reaping profits unforeseen in the mid-nineteenth century.

- **John Tames,** the namesake of Tames Lane, was a shoemaker. John first plied his trade in Reisterstown, then Baltimore City. Before 1848 he moved to Harford Road. On Harford Road, he opened a general store. He had three boys and three girls. His sons worked at the general store while his daughters married farmers from Lauraville. The other girl died at 20. In 1887 John Tames died and his business continued under the proprietorship of his sons. In addition, attached to the store, the Tames brothers ran a farm employing three hands.

- **John Otto** lived off of Southern Avenue a few blocks from Harford Road. He first worked as a farm hand until he was able to buy his truck garden. The land was subsequently cleared and improved. Here, the farm buildings were built incrementally as necessity and finances dictated. John married Barbara Sastler and they had four sons and two daughters. Henry, John, and Albert were farmers in Gardenville and Lauraville, while Leonard moved to Virginia. Sophia never married and stayed at the farm on Southern Avenue, and Lizzie Otto married Jacob Krach, a local Lauraville boy. Albert owned a stall in the Lexington market. All were part of the Methodist Episcopal Church South (Andrew's Chapel).

- **Julius W. Knox** was a first-generation-born American (born in 1834). He was educated in Baltimore City. At the age of twenty-seven he married Sophia Reuter. At twenty-eight he moved to his own farm and spent the rest of his life tilling the soil. They had ten children. Louis and William went into the horse-raising business, Charles studied electricity, Teresa became an artist, and Hazel a professional singer.

- **Frederick Neidhart,** a first-generation American, grew up in Waverly. At the age of thirteen, Frederick went to Baltimore and apprenticed as a shoemaker. He remained in Baltimore for ten years. Afterward Frederick moved to the Lauraville area where he plied his trade. He also purchased a farm of eight and a half acres and grew vegetables. He bought his land unimproved, and consequently built "a neat residence, a large barn and other buildings, also planted shade and ornamental trees, thereby greatly increasing the value of the place." On his farm he employed one helper.

- **The Honorable J. Morrison Harris** was the grandson of David Harris of Mount Deposit. J. Morrison Harris had a country estate that comprised the eastern portion of Mayfield and much of today's Herring Run Park. J. Morrison Harris began his career as a clerk in the Citizen's Bank, and thereafter began to study law at the office of David Stewart. After his study he went to Europe for a year and upon his return opened a law office on Courtland Street. In 1881 he married Sidney C. Hall, the daughter of B. W. Hall of the family that owned Eutaw Farms directly north of the Herring Run. In 1853, J. Morrison built his country estate. In 1858 he was elected to the third district in Congress where he served until 1864. Thereafter he ran for Governor and lost by a slim margin.

- **Judge John Gontrum** emigrated from Germany to Baltimore County when he was seven years old. John Gontrum educated himself in night school and at home. He supported himself through school as a truck farmer. In 1849 he bought his first piece of land in the burgeoning town of Gardenville. In 1867 he was elected judge of the Orphan's Court of Baltimore County, serving two terms of four years. He also became a director of the Belair and Jerusalem Turnpike. His residence was described as "commodious and occupies a charming location in the midst of a beautiful yard with large shade trees. The barn is also substantial and large. The groundswork was done by two hired men, with Judge Gontrum as superintendent."[18]

- **George Corse** was born and raised at the Sinclair Nursery already described.[19] After attending medical school he bought a house on Southern Avenue. It was described as follows:

One of the most charming homes in the county. The approach to the house is made through rows of ornamental and shade trees that dot the well-kept lawn and furnish a delightful shelter from the heat of the sun. Passing through the lawn we reach the house, a substantial structure, built in 1883. It stands upon an eminence commanding a fine view of the city as well as much of the twelfth district, and from it can also be seen five counties, Kent, Cecil, Ann Arundel, Howard and Baltimore. As the eye sweeps over the landscape noting with pleasure the fertile fields and thriving towns, one sees also the bay in the distance and the ships sailing into port."[20]

The census manuscripts shed insights into the lives of other Northeast Baltimoreans. Farm hands abounded throughout the region on a regular and seasonal basis. Almost all working farms had boarders living on the homesteads, either in the main house or in other dwellings on the property. William Johnson worked and boarded at Margaret McCormick's Farm. Franklin Schaffler had four boarders at his house, all of whom worked on his farm. Franklin Shaffler also owned and ran a hotel. He was forty years old with seven kids ranging in age from one to twelve. Elizabeth Dayton, at sixty years old, was a servant to Henry and Mary Gebb. In addition to Elizabeth, the Gebbs had four other boarders. One of them, Samuel Matthews, lived in a separate dwelling on the estate with his wife, seven children, and one grandchild. Fifty-five-year-old Jeremiah was a servant to Mary Broom. Several of the craftsmen had apprentices living with them. For example, Christian Sholler, a shoemaker of Georgetown, had William Brown, a nineteen-year-old apprentice, living with his family.

The vast majority of women were identified as 'keeping house.' Nonetheless, keeping house on a farmstead was quite different than housewives of the twentieth century. They were partners with their husbands on the farm, working hand in hand with them. Their domain was considered the house, while the husbands worked outside. The work of the housewife and farmer intertwined daily and in innumerable ways. In addition, many women who were widows continued to run the family farm. Most of these women had boarders or adult children to help run the farm. In true chauvinistic fashion, the Maryland directories and gazetteers did not list many of these farms in their directories.

Many African-Americans lived in Northeast Baltimore. In the 1880 census manuscripts many families and individuals were identified. George Lee, age twenty-two, was a servant for the Franklin family in Gardenville. The Coleman family lived in Gardenville near the Corse Farm. The census manuscripts suggest that the Coleman family owned or rented their own farm. The family consisted of Dennis Coleman, age forty-five, his wife Belinda, five sons, three daughters, and a boarder! Dennis Coleman was identified as a sailor, his oldest son drove a mill wagon (maybe for Coxon's mill), and his other sons worked on the farm. Belinda was identified as keeping house.

Living on or near Samuel Regester's homestead were three generations of the Distance family. The first generation was Thad and Lydia, ages sixty-eight and fifty-four respectively. They had five children still living with them. Two daughters were at home and the son worked on the farm. L.M. and Martha Distance, ages thirty-six and thirty-four, headed the next generation. They had two sons and two daughters. Interestingly, one of the sons was named Samuel R. Distance. Also on the farm were other African-Americans. James Bowly and James Grimes were boarders and worked as farmhands.

Other folks lived within and served the community. Hucksters, junkers, and migrants filtered in and out of the area. Lizette Woodsworth Reese, who lived in Waverly as well as on the Harford Road, wrote eloquently about hucksters of the area:

> If you lived in Waverly [or the Harford Road], and for your health's or your church's sake, ate fish on Friday; or if you had little skill in the concocting of certain succulent dishes, and much faith in those who had that heaven-given faculty; or if you were pinched for time, or else for a holiday; then, when you heard a particular bellowing voice out in the village highway, you ran to your door, ready to exchange your country's silver for the wares which that bellower carried.
> "De-b-b-b-b-le c-r-a-b!
> D-e-b-b-l-e c-r-a-b!
> Hit her in de haid wid a
> D-e-b-b-l-e c-r-a-b!"
> This was not the shriek of escaped devils, or melody with a "dying fall"; or the leaping music of the spheres. It was a good, coarse, honest bawl, an invitation to you to come out and buy yourself a platter full of victuals as comely and fit as were Milton's spread out in the pages of his famous poem. You were good, and coarse and honest. You had a stomach—thank God—as well as a soul. Of germs you had scarcely heard. The invention of some man perhaps? Men, it is true, are the devil. You descended the front steps with a colored plate in your hand. "Come over here, uncle."

Other hucksters drove through the streets selling produce. Again, Reese described the following:

> "Look at them berries, lady. Watch me turn 'em out, on this paper. All sound an' firm lady. Nothing wrong the them berries." And the chorus from the wagon would boom out "Strawberries! Straw-ber-ries! Ten Cent a box! Straw-berries!"

The "huckster" survives today. Arabbers still sell produce from colorful horse driven carts. Baltimore is the only city in the United States with such a living tradition that adds colorful adjectives to the vocabulary of the city streets.

Reese again poetically describes another character of the area, the lamplighter:

> Do you believe in magic? Life is full of it. Coming along the edge of the dusk, up the Harford Road, a short, light ladder in one hand, a blazing torch in the other, the lamplighter was a secret creature, in this world, but not of it, a man out of a very old, old book, filled with sharp wood-cuts of wands and bubbling scarlet pots, and incantations sung in blurred, slow words to the music of broken tunes... The Harford Road was lit from one corner to the other. You looked at the west, and saw that it was as pink as the sprawling cup of a mallow blossom; you looked at the east, and saw that it was a vaguer color. The trees there in the Park (Clifton) had suddenly grown longer. And this golden petaling was going on all over Baltimore. You felt as though you were taking part in some great, strange jeweled affair, which you would forever remember, and yet be slow to talk about.[21]

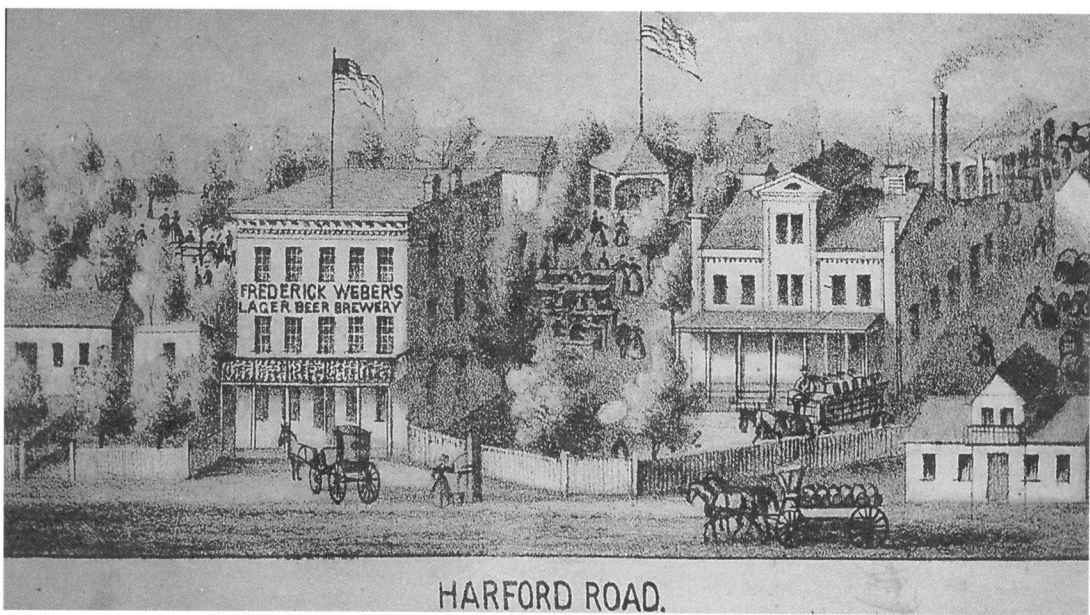

The Gay Street–Belair Road Corridor was home to at least nineteen different breweries. Harford Road had at least four breweries. Weber's Brewery, detail from Sachse's 1869 Bird's Eye View of Baltimore (Courtesy Library of Congress American Memory Website). **Bottom: Brehm's Brewery, detail from the 1869 Sachse Map of Baltimore** (Courtesy Library of Congress American Memory Website). **Opposite: Brehm's Brewery a few years later in 1895** (Courtesy of CHAP Archives).

A Thriving Borderland Region   83

Brehm's Brewery, Belair Avenue, Baltimore.

No matter which way a resident of nineteenth-century Northeast Baltimore turned, the ever-pervasive Baltimore skyline loomed in the background. Shopping excursions, weekly travels to market, or—for the more fortunate—daily excursions to the private academies gave the residents a feeling of being a part of something bigger—the evolving organism of the city. However, the residents did not have to travel to feel the presence of the city, for Baltimore was extending its long tentacles into the region in several ways.

Gontrum family cemetery. (Author's photo)

THE TENTACLES
of the CITY

THE VISION of Baltimore City residents was quite different. The number of great country estates over five hundred acres diminished, were subdivided and became profitable working farms. Smaller country estates increased and two estates blossomed into nationally known havens: Montebello and Clifton. In turn, collective groups of Baltimore City residents were drawn to the open natural setting of the area for the same reason that the wealthy merchants created their havens of retreat. Nevertheless, their uses of the land were quite different.

Open land, valued for itself and its unforeseen possibilities, attracted the attention of Baltimore City. Much like the wealthy merchants, the not-so-rich city residents also found Northeast's open land valuable. Open land offered the same solutions to Baltimorean's "get away fervor" that underlain the creations of the wealthy merchants. This time, though, the physical manifestations were democratized and paid for by an aggregate of citizens. This "get away fervor" found several forms. Homestead became a picturesque neighborhood for middle-class city workers. Cemeteries were fashioned in park-like settings and offered daylong reprieves from the dense urban fabric. Beer gardens and horse racing offered recreational activities for City residents.

In addition, the city's influence was felt in several other ways. In response to the outflow of city residents, the Harford and Hall Spring's Railway formed. Northeast Baltimore not only provided food for the city, but also the land in which to build an intricate water works system for the city. The openness of the land was its most precious asset, whether improved through agriculture, recreational activity, or a clean vista shining off the waters of Lake Montebello and Lake Clifton.

The city tentacles were the impetus for decades-long political debate for control of the area. In 1888 the Maryland State Legislature gave Baltimore City authorization to expand its boundaries to the north and west. The debate for boundary expansion began years earlier and germinated in 1851 when Baltimore County moved its government to Towson. The political struggle between the city and county for open land was about the responsibility of suburbia—the begotten child of urban and rural.

Before 1851 Baltimore City and County shared the cost of several public institutions.[1] By 1851, the City and County residents viewed each other with so much suspicion that the county moved its government to Towson, seven miles north of Baltimore City. The conflict always centered on supplying goods and services in the area between urban and rural—the borderland region. In the belt surrounding Baltimore, the city needed the open land to expand. First, the city bought large tracts of land for parks, almshouses, and land for its water system. Secondly, the borderland region, though politically Baltimore County, began building houses for city workers. This incensed the rural county residents who paid to support these satellite communities of city workers. Nevertheless, as they grew, the county's suburban tax base increased to support itself and eventually the rural hinterlands. However, the suburban communities needed services that the county could not supply—such as water, sewer, police, fire protection, and schools. Thus, suburban areas became the divorced children of Baltimore City and County.

The city, on the other hand, also supplied services, most noticeably police and fire services, to these areas, but received no taxes. This incensed city residents. This battle culminated in 1864 when the county legislators pushed through the State Legislature a law requiring the consent for annexation of the residents directly affected by the shift in boundaries. In 1868 the City Council approved annexation of the 'belt area.' Six years later, the State Legislature approved annexation contingent upon the approval of the suburban residents who at the time were afraid of huge tax increases.

The city campaigned strenuously for annexation, pointing out that annexation meant an ample supply of water, lighting, and police and fire services. In addition, the city offered a tax break of one-half city taxes for ten years. Nevertheless, the industries of Canton and Highlandtown feared city regulations. City regulations, they purported, drove them out of Baltimore. On May 5, 1874, a referendum was held in which the annexation lost by a vote of 1,130 to 575. It took another fourteen years to convince the state legislature to hold another referendum on annexation. This time though, the tax break was lengthened to one-half city taxes for twelve years. In addition, the tax rate on undeveloped land would remain at the current county rate until it was developed. Also, the belt region was broken up into sections—East, North, and South—and would vote separately. With these new incentives, and a huge building boom—between 1874 and 1888 10,000 houses (housing units) in the belt area and 18,000 in Baltimore City proper were built—the annexation finally passed with the exception of the Eastern District.[2]

For more than twenty-four years, the issue of annexation hung over the Northeast borderland region. This issue being alive almost a quarter of a century must have made the residents aware of their special geographic location, a location acute with their own unique issues. The annexation pushed the city line north of Boundary Avenue (North Avenue) to several hundred yards north of Herring Run. The eastern boundary stayed the same, leaving all of Gardenville in the hands of the County. Only the developments along Harford Road were affected.

Stone Etched Upon the Land

Twenty cemeteries were etched on Northeast's landscape. The first cemeteries were, of course, family plots of the hard working farmers. By the 1850s, Baltimore City churches and synagogues began buying the land. Here, droves of citizens would come out the Hall's Springs Railway, or the Belair Road stagecoach line and pay homage to their past loved ones. The trip was a day affair and the families made the best of it by planting flowers, drinking beer, and playing the games provided by the beer gardens. Many of the breweries were strategically located near the cemeteries. Better to bring the customer to you than bring the beer to them. Obviously, they did both. Lastly, several village churches created cemeteries.

Private Family Cemeteries

Gontrum Family Cemetery (mid-nineteenth century). Located at the 4300 block of Furley Avenue between Mannasota and Kavon Avenues, this cemetery was once located on the farm of Judge John Gontrum.

Biddison Family Cemetery (mid-nineteenth century). Still standing amongst the 1920s bungalows, the Biddison Cemetery sits on a small plot no larger than its neighbor's house lots. Here, many of Gardenville's nineteenth century residents are buried—Forresters, Henkels, Burgans, Sindalls, and Barbers. Interesting to note that the two private cemeteries were created by the two families that were related by marriage.[3]

Cemeteries for the Villages

Jerusalem Evangelical Lutheran Cemetery dates to about 1850. However, some stones moved from an earlier cemetery date to the late eighteenth century. This cemetery is one of the few still physically linked to its parent church. The notable families buried here are the Markleys of the Markley Hotel and General Store, Radeckes and Sipples, and the Raspes of Raspeburg. This cemetery and church was the first Lutheran Church in Northeast Baltimore.

Immanuel Lutheran Cemetery Chapel, constructed around 1882 off Grindon Avenue west of Harford Road. (Author's photo)

Immanuel Lutheran Cemetery was organized in 1882. On the grounds is a small Gothic Revival chapel that crowns the cemetery. Here neighborhood residents are buried. The cemetery is linked to the Immanuel Lutheran Church located at Belvedere Road and Loch Raven Boulevard.[4]

Baltimore City Jewish Cemeteries

Baltimore Hebrew Congregation Cemetery. The Baltimore Hebrew congregation is the oldest Jewish congregation in Baltimore. In 1832 three acres were purchased at the site for a cemetery, and in 1866 fifty acres were purchased and another nine acres in 1884. By 1898 this was the largest U.S. Jewish cemetery south of New York.

B'nai Israel Congregation Cemetery. The other famous Jewish cemetery is located at 3701 Southern Avenue and was chartered in 1854. This cemetery served thirty-two congregations of the Jewish Orthodox faith.[5]

Baltimore City Christian Cemeteries

Oak Hill Cemetery, a.k.a. Bohemian Cemetery (1884–present). Established by John Novak, this cemetery was for Bohemians, a non-Catholic movement started in Chicago in 1877.

Most Holy Redeemer Cemetery, a.k.a. St. James formed in 1880 and once connected with the St. James the Less Church in East Baltimore.[6]

Laurel Hill Cemetery (1851–1958). On November 19, 1851, Laurel Hill Cemetery was dedicated as one of Baltimore's premier African-American cemeteries. The cemetery, which embraced twenty-three acres, was created "for the benefit of the colored people of the city and county of Baltimore." From September 1863 to February 1866 the bodies of 230 colored soldiers of the Federal Army were buried at Laurel. In 1886 "some" bodies from Bethel and Sharp Street Church Cemetery were reburied. In 1894 a long procession of local dignitaries, citizens, and the eminent Frederick Douglas marched out the Belair Road to dedicate a monument to Bishop Alex Payne, of the African Methodist Episcopal Church.[7]

In 1911 City roadwork crews dug up the lots of sixty-seven Civil War veterans in order to widen the road. These remains were reinterred at the Loudon Park Cemetery, on Frederick Road. In 1920, the Elmley Street residents began dumping trash into the cemetery. By 1937 the cemetery was in ruins. In 1946 the Belair-Edison Improvement Association was formed with the elimination of Laurel Hill Cemetery as one of its objectives. The new Laurel Cemetery Company in 1952 declared bankruptcy and for 15.68 acres was paid one hundred dollars by the newly formed McKramer Realty Company. By legislative act, signed by Governor Theodore McKeldin, the cemetery was dissolved in 1958. The remaining Civil War soldiers were reburied in Loudon Park and in Johnsville's Freedom District near Eldersburg. Only four to five hundred bodies were recovered from the over three thousand buried. Belair Road Enterprises, Inc. bought the property. Bulldozers for the construction of the shopping center crushed headstones. At present only a supermarket occupies a portion in the shopping center.

Baltimore Hebrew Congregation Cemetery. (Photo by Robert Wallace)

Chapel at Most Holy Redeemer Cemetery—4400 block of Belair Road. (Photo by Robert Wallace)

Communities on the Edge of Baltimore: Homestead and San Domingo

Homestead and San Domingo were not rural farm communities, nor were they neighborhoods of Baltimore. They were sub-urban. However, both differed greatly. Homestead was a community for city workers designed in the latest suburban architectural fashion. On the other hand, San Domingo was suburban purely by its geographic location. San Domingo was the literal edge of Baltimore where urban and rural amenities haphazardly mixed.

The Suburb of Homestead

Homestead was located on the old Gorsuch estate on the west side of Harford Road directly across from Clifton. Around 1852, Robert Gorsuch, Jr. and Edward B. Jackson laid out streets lined with small suburban lots in hopes of creating Baltimore's first suburban development. In 1853-54 they advertised the development in Matchett's *Baltimore City Directory* as such:

> Public attention is invited to this beautiful suburban village, situated on the Harford Road, where eligible building lots 16x90, front on 50 feet streets, and running back to 20 feet alleys, are now selling in fee, without ground rent, or any incumbrance whatever, at prices varying from $75 to $200.

Figure 2.

Public School House No. 4—Ninth Election District.

Located at HOMESTEAD.

Baltimore County Public School, late nineteenth century. (Courtesy of CHAP)

Contrasting urban and suburban architectural forms in Homestead Village. A rural Gothic home attached to an urban rowhouse. (Photo by Robert Wallace)

The situation is one of the most beautiful, most healthy, and most convenient of access in the neighborhood of Baltimore, being immediately contiguous to Clifton Park and Darley Hall. The splendid residences of Johns Hopkins and Dr. Troupe (Darley Hall) on the East; to the estates of the late Wm. Tiffany, Gibson, Taylor and Tinge on the North; to Edward Patterson's and Frisby's on the South, and Huntington Village on the West. It is about 390 feet above tidewater and commands views of the city and bay in the distance.

The property extends from the Harford to the York Turnpike Roads, and is intersected by the Quaker Road or Simonton Lane, and by Greenmount or Jenkins Lane, about 1/4 of a mile above Greenmount Cemetery. A 60 feet wide street, Gorsuch Avenue is now being graded and paved.

A number of Cottages and Countryseats have already been erected, and many other improvements are in contemplation. A beautiful Protestant Episcopal Church is now erected, to which a schoolhouse is attached. The proprietors have also in contemplation, by presenting sites for churches, the accommodation of other religious denominations, and making such other conveniences as a respectable suburban population may require.

A row of rural Gothic-style rowhouses in Homestead Village—another mix of rural and urban architectural attributes. (Photo by Robert Wallace)

> The Surveys for the grand Northern Avenue are laid off within a few hundred feet of the village.
>
> No better investment can therefore be made than by purchasing lots on the "Homestead." The terms of sale viz. by installments, extending over two years, are also so easy as not to preclude any one from buying a portion of this eligible property.[8]

Much like the advertisement used to sell Belmont around 1805, Homestead's advertisement used the same tactics. It was considered beautiful and healthy, 360 feet above sea level. Here one could raise a family away from the unhealthy city (360 feet above the stinking harbor) in the moral "grace" of beauty. However, the height of the village provided a visual link to Baltimore. The ad spoke of being contiguous with five country estates, which provoked two responses. First, the area was identified with prestigious surroundings. The area had a reputation that middle-class folks could buy. Second, the estates added picturesque open spaces that helped to create and preserve the village's suburban ambience.

Nevertheless, the streets of Homestead were laid out in an urban street grid pattern with alleys, and lots on the same scale as many of Baltimore's rowhouse neighborhoods. Economics determined this. In order to provide the middle class with the suburban dream, density was necessary. The smaller the lots, the more the developer could sell. The development was fueled not by an agricultural economy, but the economy of Baltimore. In 1852 there were not many models of a suburban street pattern. Homestead was laid out four years before Olmsted's plan for Central Park.

Architecture played a key role in articulating the suburban ambience. Most of the houses built between 1852 and 1900 were built in wood. Earlier in the century, wood connoted an inexpensive impermanent home. However, by the 1840s the architecture and landscape taste maker, Andrew Jackson Downing, illustrated many wooden "cottages" in his *Cottage Residences*. Wood at the time was the most prevalent building material, a material that was outlawed from use in Baltimore City by 1799. Inadvertently it became associated with country or rural houses. Moreover, wood created a different look, one that was more natural. Clapboard siding was the predominant sheathing material on the houses. By the 1880s, many homes were reshingled or built with cedar shake shingles. Cedar shakes as well as barge board clothed the buildings into a natural looking skin. This material, very different from brick, was not only identified with suburban and rural settings, but also with the suburban aesthetic.

Most of the buildings were designed with several architectural features: gabled dormers, front porches, turrets, towers, and mansard roofs. Many architectural details of many architectural styles made up the Victorian period. First came the Gothic Revival details. They were infused into the Homestead cottages (and elsewhere) as steep pitched roofs, central dormers with pointed windows and vergeboards accenting the eaves, finials, and flowery and vine-like porch and cornice brackets. Next came the Italianate and Second Empire details. The Italianate-placed cupolas on square-like houses became accented with cornices decorated with brackets, modillions, and dentils. Windows were hooded and doors corniced with fancifully carved brackets. The Second Empire added a funky French hat onto the buildings—i.e., a Mansard Roof. And last, the Queen Anne style added decorative trusses, porch supports, big windows, and vertical bands. By the 1880s and 1890s these stylistic details were combined in unique and sometimes gaudy ways.

Another type of housing became prevalent in the area. The duplex, also known as a "semi-detached" house, was a type that shared one party wall with its neighbor. Here, each house, had three walls that emitted light into the interior as well as a side yard. They were designed to look like one house—a rather large house. The duplex provided affordable houses while keeping the suburban look. Like the detached house, duplexes were decorated in the variety of fashions.

The use of the word "cottage" as well as their architectural fashion were deliberate, and aroused specific associations with Baltimore citizens. The cottage and countryseat were defined differently. A country seat at the time was a summer home built on a grander scale than cottages. During the 1840s several architectural critics were gravely concerned about beautifying the outlying areas of cities as well as the country with tasteful houses. They knew of the economic restraints of simple farmers and suburban residents. With this in mind they plied their aesthetics to simple houses and created the "cottage." In Downing's *Architecture of Country Houses* he defined the cottage as a small commodious house.

Although seemingly in the right area, the 1852 suburban scheme never materialized to its full potential. Shortly after its inception and initial burst, the development slowed to a halt until the inception of the Baltimore and Hall's Springs Railway (1870). In 1881 Thomas Scharf wrote of Homestead:

> Homestead is the furthest east of the cluster of villages (in the 9th district), and binds upon the Harford Road. As far back as 1852 a movement was made for the establishment of a suburban village here, there was then no railway communication, however, and the project failed. In 1866 it was revived and became a success. Homestead is charmingly located within a few moment's walk of Lake Clifton, the estate of Horace Abbott, that of the late Thomas Kelso, and President Garrett's "Montebello." It is reached by the Hall's Springs line of horse railway.
> On May 15, 1853, the first services were held in the Homestead Protestant Episcopal Church.[9]

Homestead was Northeast Baltimore's first suburb, and the only one laid out in the nineteenth century. Here the houses were designed with the suburban architectural vocabulary that still can be seen on many of the structures. Nevertheless, it was laid out with urban density on a street grid pattern with alleys. These urban attributes relate to two factors. First, the development was created before many of the United States' full-blown upper-class suburbs. Second, it predates many writings and philosophies purported by such geniuses as Frederick Law Olmsted. It also predates the great parks movement—the movement that shaped Central Park in New York City and Druid Hill Park—that flourished in the 1860s. In this sense Homestead symbolized the beginning stages of the suburban ideal in America, and at its inception relied on urban development patterns. Nonetheless, the suburban character and ambience are felt even today.

Throughout other parts of nineteenth-century Baltimore, many suburban developments flourished, such as Mount Washington, Highland Park (which in the 1890s became Walbrook), Sudbrook, Irvington, Windsor Hills, Roland Park, Catonsville,

Relay, St. Denis, or Halthorpe. Only Homestead briefly brushed Northeast Baltimore. Several reasons partially address the lack of suburbanization in nineteenth-century Northeast Baltimore. First, the tardiness of turnpike development on Harford Road, and especially Belair Road, may be culprits. Second, the railroad connected several areas north, south, and west to the city center. In Northeast Baltimore the railroad just missed northeast on its southeastern edge. This was the railroad suburb of Orangeville. Many nineteenth-century suburbs were tied to rail lines. The land itself revealed another possible reason. The coastal plain was much easier to farm than the Piedmont Range. The highly productive farms of Gardenville just did not lend their land to sale for suburban schemes.

"On the Trail," a sculpture by Edward Berge commemorating the Trail of Tears, has stood in Clifton Park since the early 1900s. (Photo by Robert Wallace)

San Domingo

Located at the corner of North Avenue and Belair Road, San Domingo was a suburb by virtue of being literally at the edge of Baltimore City. Here, the urban "sense of becoming" entwined with the open spaces of the country estates and truck gardens. It was the gateway into the city and out to the farmland of Baltimore County. One would ride past the B&O Railroad tracks and into the city limits of Baltimore. The street name changed, streetcars were prevalent and the view narrowed upon the urban fabric of Baltimore. One would ride into the urban grid pattern that slowly year by year filled up with rowhouses. To the south of the B&O Railroad bridge and within San Domingo rowhouses were built, some unattached but in keeping with the massing and scale of the majority of rowhouses. A few hundred feet north of the bridge, frame dwellings were built surrounded by fields and gardens. Here, the life of Baltimore county residents physically entwined with the residents of Baltimore City.

This village was the end and beginning of the Baltimore and Jerusalem Turnpike, a necessary spot for its tollbooth. This point of entry and exit was a prime spot for nineteenth-century highway travel service industries, taverns, and bars. Blacksmith and carriage repair shops were established. In several ways, the small village acted as a "gas station" rest stop much like the ones found today on our major highways. In addition, the village also attracted two marble yards and a brewery. Today, the area still feels much like it is on the edge, not exactly a part of the urban fabric below North Avenue, but not a part of Belair Edison either. The persistence of place is strong.

The origin of the name "San Domingo" is not known. The earliest known appearance of the name is on Taylor's Map of 1857. One possibility for its name may derive from refugees who immigrated to Baltimore from San Domingo. In 1793, fifty-three ships harboring 1,000 white and 500 black refugees entered Baltimore. Many of the refugees stayed in and around Baltimore, contributing to the population of Baltimore. Whether any of these refugees found a home north of the city on the Belair Road is not known. However, there is significant evidence that the refugees from San Domingo (Haiti) greatly influenced the culture of Baltimore. Another theory along the same lines may be that one of the richer descendants of the San Domingo refugees may have had a country estate within the area of the village. Consequently, when the village arose, it took the name of the estate upon which it was developed.

Nevertheless, the village thrived. John Foote described several establishments and scenes in the village. The tollgate, run by John Sharpe and his wife, was rarely closed. They always trusted the travellers to stop and pay the toll. Most of the traffic was from truck farmers who carried their produce to the city as well as herding cattle, pigs, and sheep to slaughter houses located just south of North Avenue. Across from Sinclair Lane was John Brower's saloon and George Dodd's blacksmith shop. Luken's Tavern was identified as hosting meetings of the San Domingo Democratic Club.

Traffic along Belair Road during the weekdays was full of truck farmers, and brewery wagons from the Brehm and Hertlein breweries. A team of two horses were required to haul the beer to town, while in the winter a team of four horses were required. On the weekends, the traffic flowed north from Baltimore. On Saturdays, Baltimoreans rode the horse car to North Avenue and then rode out Belair on Sam White's stagecoach. They would head for the cemeteries and beer gardens. On Sundays people would come out to the Most Holy Redeemer Cemetery. For kids growing up in the neighborhood, the Coxon's mill held a swimming hole. They would also traipse through farms and wander upon the grounds of Clifton.[10]

Two well-known stone cutter families lived and worked in San Domingo, the

Eagle Brewery, owned by the Von Der Horst family who later became the first owners of the Baltimore Orioles. Detail from the 1869 Sachse Map.
(Courtesy Library of Congress)

Lachenmayer and the Berge families. Lewis Lachenmayer emigrated from Germany in 1848.[11] In Germany he was trained as an architect and upon entering the United States turned to grave stone cutting. In San Domingo, Lewis designed his own house and shop with living quarters on top. Charles Lachenmayer, after taking over the stone cutting business, remodeled the downstairs into an office and showroom. Centerpieces in his house were fancy clocks and bronze sculptures made by Edward Berge, the other stone carver in San Domingo.

Henry Berge, Sr. built a house across the street from the Lachenmayers.[12] Henry and his wife Mary Anne Berge owned a marble yard and granite shop next to their detached rowhouse-type home. It was located at the southwest corner of North Avenue and Milton Streets, one block west of Belair Road, directly south of the Lachenmayer's residence. Here, like Lewis Lachenmayer, Berge fashioned gravestones, mostly for those buried in the Baltimore Cemetery. Henry and Mary Anne were the parents to Edward Berge, who became a famous American sculptor in America and Europe.

Growing up around the etching and carving of gravestones gave Edward his first lessons in sculpture and art appreciation. At the age of twenty in 1896 Edward entered into the first class of the Rinehart School of Art, which was housed at the Maryland Institute College of Art. Edward went to Paris to further his studies and to study under Verlet and Rodin. Throughout his short life (he died in 1924) Edward won several awards and helped to fashion many of Baltimore's parks. The Sea Urchin, designed by Edward Berge and enlarged by his son, Henry, sits in the fountain on the South Square of Mount Vernon Place. He also designed "On the Trail," an Indian sculpture in Clifton Park; Ferdinand C. Latrobe in the median on Broadway Street; General Armistead on the Fort McHenry grounds; General Watson and several others throughout some of Baltimore's parks and cemeteries. He finally died of a heart attack while living in his house at 3024 Harford Road.

San Domingo also contributed to two of Baltimore's favorite pastimes—beer and the Baltimore Orioles.[13] It was through the Vonderhorst Brewery that Baltimore acquired its first professional baseball team. Eagle Brewing Company, located at the northwest corner of Belair Road and North Avenue, was owned and operated by John H. Vonderhorst. In 1866 he, along with Andreas Rupprecht, purchased the oil-cloth mill of Samuel B. Richardson, a five-acre site. By 1880 the brewery complex entailed a five-story Gothic-style brew house, a six-story double malt house, a four-story ice house, which was located over three tiers of deep cellars, a storage building, a cooper shop and a large stable to accommodate thirty-two horses. The grounds of the brewery had a grove of trees and a picnic area where on Sundays and holidays the Germans would gather for picnics and celebrations. VonderHorst named his brewery the Eagle Brewing Company, in part for his name: Horst in German means Eagle's nest. On top of the brewery a large eagle was constructed. The brewery was very successful and each year produced more and more quantities of beer.

John's son Harry became brewmaster around 1874. Between 1875 and 1901, the brewery saw many brewmasters, many of which went into business for themselves as saloon keepers. Carl Peine was brewmaster from 1882 to 1887. In 1887 he opened a saloon at 16 Belair Road, just a couple of blocks north of the brewery. George H. Cremer opened a saloon at 41 Albemarle Street in 1882. Needless to say, the relationship with Eagle Brewing proved profitable for the saloons as well as the brewery. Melchoir Metz opened a saloon at 1700 North Bradford Street. Conrad W. Yuengling, another brewmaster, opened a saloon at 1617 Mulliken Street.

Henry VonderHorst was more famous as the first owner of the Baltimore Orioles, as well as Union Park, which was located at 25th Street near Greenmount Avenue. In 1887 Henry became one of the principal sponsors and owners of a second major league, the American League. At the time the American League was known as the "beer and whiskey league" since breweries and distilleries sponsored most of the teams. Nevertheless, in 1891 the American League dissolved and in 1892 the Baltimore Orioles joined the National League. The Orioles in 1894, 1895, and 1896 won the pennant. In 1897 the Orioles lost the pennant to Boston, most likely due to the greed and excitement of VonderHorst. During the pennant race he allowed 26,000 fans to enter the park, which held only 9,500 fans. The fans in every corner of the ball park interfered with the game. Nevertheless, VonderHorst brought baseball back to Baltimore, on the profits of his brewery, which in turn sold buckets of beer. Henry VonderHorst, along with the Orioles, was transferred to New York, where he died in 1905.

The Park Course Resort and Darley Park

Two other attractions in Northeast Baltimore provided recreation for Baltimore City residents: The Park Course Resort (a racetrack) and Darley Park (a beer garden). Where Armistead Gardens is today there was a horse racing "resort" that had flourished since the 1820s when the Maryland Jockey Club held their annual races. By the 1870s, the course had changed hands several times and was known as the Park Course at Herring Run. On May 25, 1872, the *Baltimore County Union* printed the following article:

> The Trotting Season.—The time for the Spring trotting season of the Maryland Trotting Association, over the Park Course at Herring Run, is rapidly approaching, and it promises to be one of the most interesting that has occurred for years. The association has spared no pains or expense to have the track put in proper condition, and the interest manifest by the owners of horses is greater than ever before. Already there are thirty-one horses in training on the track, and a number of them have made enviable records on the turf. With very few exceptions the horses now in training are owned in Maryland, and it is not yet known how many from other States will contend for the liberal purses to be offered.
>
> Many of the horses will be entered for their first public trial of speed, and the season promises to be one of peculiar interest. For the comfort of visitors to the track during the trotting season every arrangement has been made, and the stands afford a fine view of the entire track. At the hotel kept by Messrs. Shaw and Smith every luxury will be provided for the visitors, and they certainly have the facilities and the knowledge to satisfy to the fullest extent all who stop at the house. The first day's trotting will take place on the 28th inst., and the races will be continued on the 30th and 31st instants. The determined efforts of the association to afford a season of amusement will doubtless be appreciated by the public, for it is said that never before have so many horses been presented on any course in the country, two weeks before the time for the beginning of the contests.[14]

At this time horse racing was one of the nineteenth century's most popular attractions. Here, city residents could come out and enjoy the thrill of watching horse race after horse race. The races broke up the monotony of long six-day workweeks by providing venues where fans could get away from their predictable jobs. Horse racing was much like football and baseball today. It was a game that brought spontaneity to people's lives.

Just north of North Avenue on the Harford Road was the Darley Park Beer Garden and Brewery which began as a small brewery run and owned by George Miller. Miller began his brewery in 1868 on undeveloped land just north of Belmont.[15] In 1871 Conrad and John G. Siegmann purchased the brewery and expanded it. On Klemm's 1872 map the area is marked as Darley Park. When this area was first used as a picnic area has not been determined. Most likely it became a picnic area shortly after the Holy Cross Cemetery was established in 1863. By 1872 Seigman's Beer Garden was known as Darley Park.

During 1872 and 1873, the park was the scene of at least two riots that involved guns. They never happened during the Sunday picnics of cemetery goers. Two articles from the *Baltimore County Union* described the riots. From the *Baltimore County Union,* April 20, 1872:

> **A Free Fight At Darley Park**
> At an early hour this morning a report was received that in a row in Darley Park on the Harford Road, yesterday afternoon between 5:00 and 6:00, two men were dangerously shot, and others severely injured of the nature or extent of the wounds it was impossible to obtain correct and full information.[16]

And on May 17, 1873:

> Riot at Darley Park—On Monday last a picnic of one of the companies of the sixth regiment, Maryland National Guard was held at Darley Park, on the Harford Road. Later in the evening about one hundred and fifty persons attacked the Captain and some of the other officers of the company, when the deputies promptly interfered and rescued the officers, who escaped without injury, and left the park. The rioters then attacked Messrs. Brown, Burke and White, and struck the two former with billies, knocking them down and otherwise abusing them. The deputies then succeeded in reaching the wall of a house in the park, and got into a corner, where they could not be attacked in the rear, drew their pistols and kept the assailants at bay, who finding they could not dislodge them without danger of being shot, left the premises and went to the city...
>
> The peace of Baltimore County has been too frequently disturbed by riotous persons from the City, and it is time that such persons should be taught that acts like these will not be permitted to pass without impunity.[17]

Interesting is the "cut" *Baltimore County Union* tossed at Baltimore City for disturbing the peace (things haven't changed much!).

By 1877 the brewery was under the supervision and ownership of Levi and John Straus. Under the Straus brothers, the Park was well improved with a bowling alley, saloon, shaded grounds, a pavilion, walks, tables, and benches. By 1897 the park mentioned a hotel (obviously for those who couldn't walk home) and the Darley Park bowling club. The park was famous for its German gatherings, for which Mencken mentioned that the park was "outfitted in the stark, Philistine style of the period, with all the tree trunks whitewashed."[18] Vendors circulated about the grounds selling the

German newspaper, the *Wecker*, as well as crab cakes, pretzels, and soft drinks.

Darley Park closed down around 1906 but held private parties in its beer hall, which also doubled as a gymnasium until the area was transformed into a rowhouse community around 1914.

The Hall's Springs Railway and Baltimore Water Works

The streetcar first penetrated Northeast Baltimore in 1870 with the formation of the Hall's Springs Railway. By 1872 the lined reach Darley Park and a year later to Hall's Springs Hotel. The line financially struggled until 1884 when it closed down after a fire destroyed their car barn. It was considered a "jerkwater line" because it wasn't on a main route and its end destination was a rural unpopulous village. Nevertheless, it did connect Hall's Springs and Homestead to the city. In 1885 the line was bought by the City Passenger Railway Company.[19] The line then ran only to Hall's Spring until 1897, when the City Passenger Railway obtained financial control.

As with all major cities certain essential needs must be met: food and its distribution system, streets and transportation, sewage, and water. The northeast borderland region supplied the city with food, and in 1874 it helped to supply the city with water.

Dwelling at the Old Herring Run Water Works—now demolished. (Courtesy of the Peale Museum)

Hobbyists enjoying Lake Montebello sometime prior to the 1920s. The lake was originally built as a reservoir with a 500 million gallon capacity and depths of up to thirty-three feet. (Courtesy EPFL Maryland Room)

Early on in its development, Baltimore acted continually to provide itself with fresh and pure water. In 1800 an act in the Maryland Legislature established a water company in Baltimore. From 1800 to 1852 a private company managed the water system for the city. In 1806 the Baltimore Water Company opened its first system. Here, water was pumped from the Jones Falls through Hemlock log pipes to several distribution points throughout the City. Two reservoirs (outside the City at the time) were created at Cathedral and Pleasant Streets, and several years later at the corner of Charles and Chase Streets.

By 1853 the City of Baltimore bought the water company outright, and the water system became the responsibility of the municipal government. After acquisition, the city began a thirty-five-year building campaign. In 1858 Hampden Reservoir was constructed. Four years later Lake Roland was built. At this point the average consumption was seven to eight million gallons per day. Just two years after Lake Roland,

Panoramic view of the construction of Lake Montebello Filtration Plant around 1911, taken from atop the plant's tower. (Courtesy Library of Congress)

Druid Lake was built as a reservoir. By 1870 many reservoirs were in place and stemmed from the Jones Falls as its primary water source.

However, by 1872, during an extreme drought, city officials became concerned about their water supply and pushed to use the Gunpowder as a complementary source. Thus, in 1874 an ordinance was passed through the City Council to create a permanent water works with the Gunpowder as its main source. Four million dollars was obtained to complete the mission. By 1888—when daily consumption of water averaged between twenty-five to thirty million gallons—the Gunpowder Water Works was complete. In its completion were the following works:

- the creation of Loch Raven with a depth of 4-20 feet, width 100-800 feet, four miles in length and with a holding capacity of 510,000,000 gallons;
- a dam at Loch Raven 800 feet long, thirty feet high, and a spillway 300 feet in width;
- a gatehouse and supply tunnel with a diameter of twelve feet and length of seven miles;
- Lake Montebello with a depth of thirty-three feet and holding capacity of 500,000,000 gallons;
- another conduit tunnel twelve feet in diameter that connected to Lake Clifton;
- the Lake Montebello and Lake Clifton pump houses; and
- forty-inch cast iron pipes as supply mains leading into the city.[20]

In addition to being a part of Baltimore's water lifeline, Lake Montebello was an attractive water haven that greatly enhanced the Herring Run Valley as well as Mayfield, the neighborhood directly to its south. It created lake front property. Today, Montebello is Baltimore's largest lake.

Grandiloquent Country Estates of Johns Hopkins and John Work Garrett

John Work Garrett and Johns Hopkins settled into the area and transformed over 1,900 acres into immense country estates, creating landmark havens of beauty. Johns Hopkins bought Henry Thompson's old estate and transformed it into a Victorian landmark. John Work Garrett bought the old Smith estate from the Tiffany family and Archibald Stirling's estate, combined the properties, and created Baltimore's largest summer retreat. These two country estates defined for Northeast Baltimore, as well as for the city and the nation, eloquence manifest in the poetry of architecture and landscape design.

Johns Hopkins and Clifton

Johns Hopkins's legacy is felt today throughout Baltimore and the world. His endowment of millions of dollars turned into Johns Hopkins University and Hospital, which today is nearly the largest employer in Baltimore City, second only to Baltimore's municipal government. Hopkins's stature and influence was just as large in the mid-nineteenth century. As a wealthy merchant he helped finance the B&O Railroad and financed individual businesses. He bailed out the city during financial straits, and built a standing landmark in Northeast Baltimore.

From a Quaker background, Johns Hopkins was born in 1795, in Anne Arundel County where he spent the first seventeen years of his life. Samuel Hopkins, his father, managed a 500-acre tobacco plantation.[21] In 1807, when Johns was twelve years old, his father freed the slaves. In turn, the Hopkins family—mother, father, and eleven children—began to work the plantation themselves. Joseph Hopkins, Johns's oldest brother, was sent home from a school in Alexandria to work the farm. Johns continued to live on the plantation until 1812. At the age of seventeen, his mother sent him to Baltimore to live with his Uncle Gerard.

At the age of twenty-four Johns Hopkins moved out of his Uncle's house after being denied his first cousin's hand in marriage. During this time marrying first cousins was common, although the practice was on the wane. Johns never got over his cousin Elizabeth, and consequently was a bachelor the rest of his life. In addition Elizabeth never married either. After moving out of his uncle's house he temporarily lived at Beltzoover's Hotel on Baltimore Street. He then moved to one of two houses his father left to him on Franklin and St. Paul streets. Then in 1843, he moved into a house on Lombard Street near Sharp Street with his mother and two sisters. In 1849, after his mother died, he moved to 18 West Saratoga Street, next door to St. Paul's Rectory. While living on Franklin and St. Paul Street he bought Clifton Mansion as his summer home, but did no extensive renovation until 1850.

Hopkins prospered, and by 1847 he was one of the wealthiest merchants in Baltimore. In 1847, at the age of fifty-two, Johns Hopkins became a director of the Baltimore and Ohio Railroad. In 1855 Johns "was elected chairman of the finance committee and became the real directing power behind the throne, with a private holding of between 15,000 and 17,000 shares of the company's stocks." Hopkins's influence within the Baltimore and Ohio Railroad can be glimpsed from his nephew Joseph Hopkins, who wrote of a summer's evening at Clifton:

> I was staying at Clifton, where I spent my summers when a boy, and my cousin Ned Janney, was there too. We knew that Uncle Johns wanted Mr. John Garrett to be president of the Baltimore and Ohio Railroad. There was a great deal of opposition to this among the directors of the road; but I knew that Uncle Johns had determined to put it through and was anxious to see how he would do it. He told Ned and me he was going to have a dinner for the directors of the road and they wanted us to get some frogs for them. We worked hard all one morning and got fifty frogs from the pond at Clifton. The old gentleman was so pleased that he invited us to the dinner. We were very much set up as we knew an important move would be made and we had a great deal of curiosity to see how Uncle Johns would get his way with the opposing directors.
>
> Champagne and other wines flowed freely during the dinner and Jim kept filling our glasses. I never knew exactly what happened, but just about the time that things seemed to be getting interesting Ned and I were quietly taken away from the table.[22]

Johns also became involved with other financial institutions. He was the President of the Merchants' Bank, and a director for the First Nation's Bank, the Mechanics Bank, The Central Bank, the National Union Bank, the Citizens and Farmers Bank, and the Farmers' and Planters' Bank.

Clifton Mansion in a 1932 photograph. (Courtesy EPFL Maryland Room)

On December 24, 1873, Johns Hopkins died quietly in his sleep. Though his life ended, Johns's legacy just began. During the later years of his life he wanted to endow the city with a first-rate hospital and university. The hospital was located where it is today, while the university was to be on the grounds of Clifton. Broadway was supposed to connect the university to the hospital and would become a great promenade named University Boulevard.[23] He endowed eight million dollars to the erection of his two institutions—a buying power that in 1929 equaled well over 100 million dollars today. In order to fulfill his dream, in 1867 he formed two corporations to oversee the hospital and university. Three years later he chose his trustees, all prominent and wealthy men of Baltimore. On January 22, 1876, the university was inaugurated by an address of Thomas Huxley, an imminent scientist of his time and the grandfather of Aldous Huxley, the author of *Brave New World*. The university first opened near the Old Richmond Market on Howard Street, just north of Centre Avenue. The board of trustees decided to open the university in the heart of the city, hoping to accumulate more wealth to construct the campus at Clifton. In the early days Clifton was used as their athletic fields and "a familiar sight was a four horse Hopkins bus filled with football players going out to Clifton for practice."[24] By 1901 the B&O Stock, of which the university owned a great deal, had fallen very low, as the old buildings along Howard Street had become too small. In turn, William Wyman and Mr. Keyser offered to donate land at the current location. Finally, Baltimore City stepped in and offered to buy the grounds of Clifton for one million dollars. With this fate in hand the university was snatched away from the grounds of Clifton. The park, once private and for the luxury of wealthy men, now welcomed all.

Johns Hopkins bought 166 acres of Clifton in 1840. By 1852 the estate was well over 500 acres and Johns transformed the mansion into an Italianate statement of wealth. In 1852 the *Sun* wrote of the estate:

> The central building has been raised one story and has received a considerable addition to the north side, besides the extension of the wings, and the building of a prospect tower on the west, with a wide arcade 109 feet in length, the building measuring 133 feet in extreme length, by 73 feet its greatest depth. From the lodge gate at the Harford Road entrance a well gravelled road winds majestically through the fine trees and lawns of the park to the main entrance of the building, the Port Cochere in the tower affording passage through an arched way into the principal hall, 23 feet high, paved with marble, lighted by four richly stained

Clifton's elegant porte-cochere, date unknown. (Courtesy EPFL Maryland Room)

arched windows, and wainscotted with black walnut, of which the doors and massive stairway are formed...

From the main corridor on the principal floor the first door to the right leads to the parlor, 19 by 28 feet, adjoining which is the breakfast room, 18 feet square, both of which open on the southern arcade, supported by twenty-three arches and pillars. Adjoining the breakfast room are the back stairs, running from the basement to the main chamber, and also the servants' room. Further east are the housekeeping rooms, closets, water fixtures, etc.

Opposite the parlor is the dining room, 18 by 26 feet, which opens on the west to the spacious arcade of five arches, whilst a door on the east conducts to a large salon, which is of elegant proportions and 15 feet high with a semi-circular room on the north 18 feet in diameter. A folding door in the east wall connects the salon with a library 20 feet square which opens on the eastern arcade looking toward the garden and lake.

All the elegant apartments are supplied with elaborately carved Italian marble mantels made in Italy. The main chamber floor and tower contain eight large chambers, bathroom, etc., also a large billiard room 20 by 30 feet opening on a terrace over the bay room and another over the northeastern arcade, decorated by balustrades with pedestals supporting richly ornamented vases. The third floor of the central building has been appropriated for the use of servants containing a number of large rooms.

A convenient stair leads from the second floor of the tower through the various stories of the pavilion, which is supported by twelve arches and surrounded by an iron balcony sustained by ornamental iron brackets. From the pavilion a stair leads to the terrace of the tower affording magnificent and extensive views of the entire city and surrounding country and Patapsco and Gunpowder rivers, the broad expansive Chesapeake whitened by the sail of increasing commerce, besides a bird's-eye view of the extensive grapehouse and orangeries stretching along several hundred feet, the ornamental structures scattered over the whole park with taste and judgement as well as the finely tilled farm grounds beyond...[25]

Twenty-one years later, the *Maryland Farmer* wrote extensively about Clifton. In comparison with the *Sun*'s 1852 article, the Clifton grounds were highlighted in the *Maryland Farmer* article. The *Maryland Farmer* in 1872 produced a column entitled "Evening Rides about the City." In the November issue, the writer proceeded up Harford Road to inspect the country estates of Johns Hopkins and John Work Garrett. The article stated the following about Clifton:

The dwelling is commodious but by no means pretentious. The estate contains almost five hundred acres, and lies beautifully rolling; a portion is in crop, and another portion in grass, but most of it is in wood and ornamental grounds, that are very tastefully laid out in drives and walks, and ornamented with flower beds,

The Gothic-style gardener's cottage at Clifton was constructed around 1852. (Courtesy EPFL Maryland Room)

rare trees and fine fruits; statuary, bridges, lake and fountains, with a large and elegant gothic summer house, two stories high, embowered in trees and vines and flowers. An air of quiet and repose, of independent stillness with a sort of hush of security so pervades this lovely spot that the very birds and squirrels seem domestic, as if they felt they had a protector, with none to make them afraid. It is in some respects more enchanting than Druid Hill and must have cost an immense sum of money to have brought it to its present state of beauty. The grapery is extensive, but it does not appear to have done well this year. The Conservatory is very extensive, as also are forcing and propagating houses. We saw some very large Japonica trees, curious variegated leafed vines and plants from Mexico and Australia; rare and remarkable plants from South America, some of which had the color and feeling of the richest velvet; large masses of geraniums and canna; fine specimens of Acacias, showing the general appearance of the Acacia forests of Australia. A large number of the rarest evergreens are found in this arboreta, and are placed with great judgement and taste, but, in some instances too close to

Lush rose gardens at Clifton. (Courtesy EPFL Maryland Room)

> other trees to allow the full development of their beauty and grandeur. The evergreens form a marked feature of the place. We never have met with, in the national or private conservatories and green houses, some of the specimen of plants which are to be found in this collection, which seems to be rather choice, than extensive. We tasted some of the delicious dwarf pears while viewing the loaded shelves of the fruit room, and were satisfied with the aromatic melting pulp...[26]

Clifton became the epitome of Victorian fancy—a collection of exotic architecture, art, fauna and flora arranged on the landscape to produce for the few (Johns Hopkins's family and friends) a real fantasy world seemingly ages and worlds away from the harsh realities of Baltimore City. In the words of Hopkins he was trying to make Clifton "a heaven on earth." In this sense it was built for the same purposes as Druid Hill Park—a natural retreat where God's handiwork meshed with man's creativity to provide respite for people to recreate themselves. It is interesting to note that today, we

112 THE CITY AS SUBURB

The greenhouse at Clifton. (Courtesy EPFL Maryland Room)

don't view our parks or our backyards as places of exotic retreat (the lazy boy in front of the television accomplishes that). Nevertheless, we still cherish the world of the exotic and have built a huge tourism industry shuttling people around the world to tropical paradises, luxury liners, and far reaches of wilderness. And in many ways Disney World is another substitute for nineteenth-century romantic parks, but this time the main street and urban attributes of the Disney parks have become the exotic!

The architecture and landscape of Clifton were metaphors built in stone and sown in soil. By mid-century, the Italianate style was flourishing in America. The onslaught of the Italianate style manifested several changing themes in American history. Just as the Federal Period reflected the values of the young democratic system of government, the Italianate style reflected the dynamic and creative energy of the Italian Renaissance. It reflected the change in emphasis from sustaining and perpetuating democracy to those whose mercantile reigns shaped and controlled the Industrial Revolution. In this sense, America changed its mythic utopias. Instead of shaping the architecture like the ancient Greeks and Romans, the nineteenth-century tastemakers began associating themselves with the Italian Renaissance amongst other mythic utopias such as medieval England, the American frontier, or the Far East.

Downing, in his "Architecture of Country Houses," stated the following of the Italianate villa:

As a rural style, expressing country life, the Italian is inferior to pointed and high-roofed modes. It is not so essentially country-like in character, it is however remarkable for expressing the elegant culture and variety of accomplishment of the retired citizen or man of the world, and as it is capable of the most varied and irregular as well as very simple outlines, it is also very significant of the multiform tastes, habits, and want of modern civilization. On the whole, then we should say that the Italian style is one that expresses not wholly the spirit of country life nor of town life, but something between both, and which is a mingling of both.[27]

In the mid-nineteenth century within the suburbs of Baltimore, the Italian villa flourished, and Clifton was Baltimore's, if not the country's, best example.

Two other architectural pieces complimented the mansion: the gardener's cottage and the Roman gateway. The gardener's cottage was built between the late 1840s and early 1850s. Here, the cottage exactly resembled in shape, massing, and details Alexander Jackson Davis's gardener's cottage at Blithewood, a sketch of which was published in Andrew Jackson Downing's *Theory and Practice of Landscape Gardening Adapted to North America*. The gardener's cottage was built in the rural Gothic style. Here the style seemed fitting. The cottage was accented by a steep pitched roof and a central dormer over the door. The arches pointing towards the sky were ornamented with elaborate vergeboard (the decorative eaves). Here, the gardener lived in a house that accented his "divine" work.

Entering upon the grounds one travelled through the old Roman gateway. Again the architecture affected the visitor. Outside on Harford Road , the gatehouse marked the area where one would leave the rural scenery of Baltimore and enter into another "world." Here, the gatehouse, styled in Roman massing and detailing, complimented the Italian styling of the mansion. It was a doorway out of Baltimore.

The grounds were littered with many statues, a greenhouse conservatory, imported plants and trees, and a boating lake, all connected to each other with winding walks and drives. Mown lawns were prevalent as well as well tilled fields. Hopkins's hobby was not agriculture, but the capturing of the exotic. Together, the estate was a whole picture, a landscape painting created in reality that produced at every turn another sentiment. In this sense, the estate was like television with all its hundred channels that capture and transport us to another world. Incredibly, Clifton Park still exists.

John Work Garrett and Montebello

In 1871, John Work Garrett bought the old Smith estate from the Tiffany family. In 1842, when Margaret Smith died, the Smith estate was comprised of 473 acres. Shortly after 1842 John Spear Smith, son of Sam and Margaret Smith, sold the property to

William Tiffany, a wealthy merchant. The Tiffany family held onto the property until 1871, when William Tiffany died.[28]

This acquisition added to the immense size of Garrett's estate. He now had a country estate of approximately 1,400 acres. By 1872 Garrett had Upper Montebello renovated, the grounds landscaped, and a haven of magnificence created. John Work Garrett never lived in the old Smith Mansion. His son Thomas Harrison used the estate until Evergreen off of York Road was completed. After Garrett died in 1883, Mary Garrett used the property for various activities such as athletic fields for Bryn Mawr School. In the 1910s some of the property was donated to Morgan State University, and most of the properties sold to developers.

John Work Garrett was born in Baltimore on July 31, 1820, into a wealthy family. His father, Robert Garrett, born in Lisbon, Ireland, emigrated to the U.S. with his mother and brothers at the age of seven.[29] Again, like many of Baltimore's wealthy of the early nineteenth century, Robert Garrett settled with his mother and family in Cumberland, Pennsylvania, which at the time was the western frontier. In 1820 Robert moved to Baltimore, bringing with him knowledge of western trading along with faithful contacts. Shortly thereafter he began a wholesale grocery produce and commission business. From his success Robert Garrett opened a banking facility which in several decades grew to prominence.

John Work Garrett was educated first in Baltimore and then Lafayette College until 1834. Not graduating, he came home and joined his father's business, which was subsequently renamed Robert Garrett and Sons. Under the tutelage of John Work Garrett, the company grew substantially. They became the American agency of George Peabody and Company of London. He was one of the early go-getters of the B&O Railroad and acquired large amounts of stock. In 1858, with the influence of Johns Hopkins, John Work Garrett was named President of the B&O Railroad, a title he kept for twenty-six years, until his death in 1884. During his presidency John guided the institution through financial struggles, sometimes bailing out the railroad with his own money. During the Civil War, John provided railroad services for Union activities. Garrett also connected the B&O Railroad to European Steamship Lines, formed the Baltimore and Ohio Telegraph Company, and laid the Atlantic telegraph cable.

In his private life he was a member of the Associated Reformed Church, and the husband of Rachel Ann Harrison. Together they had four children. Mary Garrett was the benefactor of Bryn Mawr School, and a large contributor to Johns Hopkins Hospital, to which she donated large sums of money on the condition of admitting women to the program. Robert Garrett was the president of the B&O Railroad and builder of the Garrett Jacobs Mansion on Mount Vernon Place. Thomas Harrison Garrett was

A print of J.W. Garrett's "Montebello" in J. Thomas Scharf's *History of Baltimore City and County.* (1881)

the owner of Evergreen Mansion and partner in the family business until his untimely death at thirty-eight. Nobody talks about Henry S. Garrett.

Garrett's estate had two mansions: Montebello and Upper Montebello. Upper Montebello, the house used by Garrett, was first owned by Archibald Stirling.[30] Named Snowden, Stirling first owned the property in 1852. In 1861 Stirling hired Baltimore Architect Edmund Lind for the sum of $1,500. Again in 1865 Lind worked on the structure for the sum of $6,389. From a sketch on Taylor's 1857 map and a lithograph in Scharf's history, Lind's alterations can be seen. The original structure was a simple square-shaped house with appendages jutting out from the side façades. The façades had a smooth-looking surface created by a stucco finish. The cornice was accented by simple dentils and slightly protruded from the plane of the front façade. Simple pediments topped the windows. A double-hipped roof was accented by brick-patterned chimneys. By 1881, the house took on a quite different appearance. Lind refashioned the mansion with the latest architectural details.

Here the stucco façade was covered with narrow, tightly knitted clapboard siding. A wraparound porch was added with scroll sawn brackets, and railing. Bay windows were added as well as a bold deep-eaved Italianate cornice. Here dentils were replaced with modillions. To create a natural look, hanging vines were planted to grow up along the porch brackets. Again the aesthetics of Andrew Jackson Downing were prevalent on the changes of the house. Most notably was the change from a stucco façade to a clapboard siding. This affirms the association that wooden houses were natural and rural, while (by law) urban houses were brick, stucco, or stone.

John Work Garrett's hold over Northeast Baltimore lay in the bigness of his claim. 1,400 acres was consolidated along the Herring Run Valley just west of the Harford Road. In quantity John Work Garrett one-upped Hopkins. He had two mansions, three times the land, a private racetrack with a racing stable, and as many fanciful plants and statuary. In 1872 the *Maryland Farmer* described Montebello after leaving Clifton:

> Leaving through the elegant entrance gateway we went on the Hillen Road for a mile along the large estate of J. W. Garrett, Esq., one of the railroad kings, but whose many official duties involved by his gigantic enterprises, do not preclude his finding time to indulge his rural taste and dolce far niente at his elegant suburban retreat, as we discovered on inspection of his beautiful grounds, although it is a new place and time has not allowed its full beauties to be developed. He too was absent, but his gardener, Mr. McKensie, seemed to take a pride in showing us all that we had time to see, missing however, owing to the lateness of the hour, the pheasant-preserves, and an inspection of the fine stock. The green house, grapery and propagating house are all under one cover, and while it presents an artistic and beautiful appearance is said to combine more of the late improvements as to form, mode of heating and supplying the water, etc., than any such building in the country. We found many rare plants in the conservatory, which has a tank or cistern in the center of the building, supplied by the rains falling on the roof, and thus furnishes the water for heating the whole building. The grapery was in perfect order and had fine specimens of European grapes. Among the flourishing vines we noticed the chasselas, black Hamburgh, splendid white Tokay, with immense bunches of large fruit—magnificent Gros. Cromier Du Cantel—some bunches no doubt would weigh pounds, with single grapes that would scarce get in the little mouth's of beauty, and made us think of the grapes discovered by the spies in the land of Eschol. There too, was a good specimen of the Santa Crus grape, which is a very late ripener. The lemon trees were loaded, with very large fruit. Before the grape house on the terrace was a wide border of flowers, with masses of splendid double Portulacca placed at irregular intervals among other taller flowers. Below the terrace was a large vase filled with blooming plants, surrounded with neatly laid out flower beds differing in shape and filled with flowers tastefully arranged as to colors and size. In the distance was the orchard of dwarf fruits. But we cannot describe all we saw, or speak of what the plan developed to be effected in time. The tout ensemble was highly pleasant to look upon and made

us think how much mental pleasure was often generated by intermarried refine tastes and solid capital. Can moneyed men apply a portion of their large capital to a better, more rational more humanizing purpose than adorning their homesteads with beautiful flowers and trees and useful birds and fruits?[31]

After the death of John Work Garrett, the property was inherited by Mary Garrett who lived on the property well into the twentieth century. Garrett's estate may have been the largest in size that was built in the limits of Baltimore City and maybe the country.

Three generations of flourishing truck farms gave way to the encroaching city. Instead of growing produce for the city, truck farmers changed tunes and ventured into real estate. Their land, once rich for truck farms, became rich for suburban development. Lizette Woodsworth Reese, a Baltimore poet who grew up in Waverly and also lived on the Harford Road, poetically summed up the change that occurred in the early twentieth century:

> "Are there wars and rumors of wars?" said the orchard to me. "They shall cease. Are you young? You shall grow old. Are you sad, distracted, hurrying east and west, at the beck of every wind that whistles? You shall rest. Are you Old? You shall renew your youth. The tree falls; the house is pulled down. Cousins, and doctors, and gypsy folk go." Said the orchard to me, "but the Pattern of them, the thing which means loveliness, or loyalty, or romance, forever endures."[32]

Garrett's famous stables—used as a gymnasium for Bryn Mawr school prior to its demolition.
(Courtesy EPFL Maryland Room)

The Gardenville Athletic Club's baseball team in the early 1900s. (Photo by James H. Lewis, courtesy of Jack Hennessy)

DEMOCRATIZING *the* SUBURBAN DREAM

T HINGS CHANGED. Change collapsed the visions of the wealthy Baltimore merchant and truck farmer into a new era never before conceived. In a matter of eighteen years Northeast Baltimore went from farms surrounding crossroads villages to a suburban region bustling with dozens of neighborhoods. The change was phenomenal. In 1898, only 279 dwellings were located in Northeast Baltimore. By 1940 there stood 14,343 dwelling units—a 5,100 percent increase. The growth was steady:[1]

1781–1899: 279 dwelling units were built
1900–1919: 2,841 dwelling units were built
1920–1929: 7,715 dwelling units were built
1930–1939: 3,508 dwelling units were built

During this time, the number of housing developments jumped from one (Homestead) to over sixty.[2] The number of neighborhood associations went from one to over a dozen. Farm villages were engulfed as Belair and Harford Roads grew into two elongated mainstreets with nine nodes of dense development. This dramatic change was placed into motion by forces far beyond the power and control of the old farm villages.

Throughout the nineteenth century, Northeast Baltimore had a reciprocal and complementary relationship with Baltimore City. However, with the onslaught of twentieth-century forces, Northeast Baltimore's relationship with the city ended—Northeast became part of the city. Here, the land was transformed into neighborhood sectors of the city, part of the expanding economy, culture, and society of Baltimore. However, the new neighborhoods significantly differed from the older Baltimore rowhouse communities. Northeast's rural attributes were folded into the shape and design of the new communities. This process followed calculated subscriptions of mixing rural attributes with urban amenities.

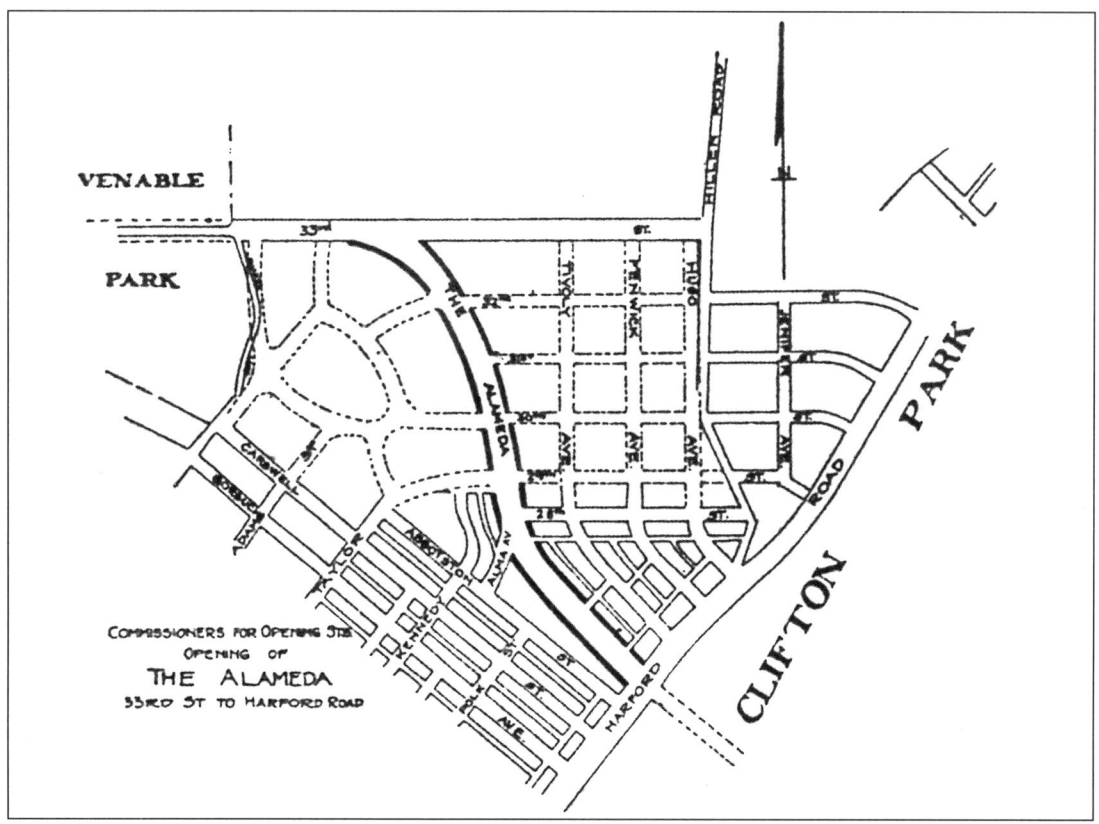

Street plan for The Alameda and surrounding neighborhoods. (Baltimore Municipal Journal—1914)

Progress in three broad areas changed Northeast Baltimore: technological innovation, new systems of organization, and a national suburban ideology. Technology touched the very core of society from transforming housework with electronic gadgetry, to weaving regions together with modern roads, trolley tracks, phone wires, and streetlights. Radio, movie houses, and the telephone transformed the way Baltimoreans interacted with each other. House construction and design changed. Technology even transformed gardens, parks, and front lawns! These modern innovations gave Baltimoreans the ability to transform farmland into neighborhoods seemingly overnight.

New systems of organization were created to disseminate and guide change into the region. All stakeholders in suburban development sought, fought, and developed new ways of doing business. In every case, these new ways were quicker and more efficient, resulting in increased production. Real estate, building, and financial institutions created new programs of lending, new ways to move capital, and factory-like systems to erect whole new neighborhoods. In turn, the Baltimore Municipal Government created new regulations and new avenues of support. Baltimore City implemented comprehensive systems to guide road, sewer, and lighting development. Baltimore introduced comprehensive zoning, planning, and housing policies. The state and federal governments jumped in with financial support for mass-development programs.

The nation's suburban ideology colored the landscape of Northeast Baltimore. The suburban aesthetics fueled the American Dream of owning a detached house on one's own plot of land. Architects and designers pushed this ideal with revival styles and building types. In addition, a global building type was introduced to Northeast's landscape—the bungalow. The picturesque that guided the design on country estates became democratized and was pushed onto small plots of land that lined the ubiquitous suburban street. In all, suburban residential architecture and neighborhood planning strove to abandon the associations with urban living. It was a revolt by Baltimoreans from Baltimore, trying desperately to create country living for urban residents. Although Northeast Baltimore was painted with a national palette of suburban colors, its manifestation was original.

Technological innovation, new systems of organization and the twentieth-century suburban ideal complimented each other and were always conscious co-creators of the vast honeycomb of neighborhoods. Technology created the ability to accelerate change. New systems of organization implemented this change, and the national suburban ideology designed, marketed, and sold a new way of life. Nevertheless, change did not come easily, and there was a fight. This fight was best illustrated in Baltimore's annexation.

Annexation

Although annexation occurred in 1918, major efforts began as early as 1912. The Baltimore Merchants and Manufacturers Association took the first step. They became dismayed that Baltimore's size and population statistics dropped to seventh place. Baltimore was behind Pittsburgh. Size and population, argued the Merchants and Manufacturers Association, determined the dynamism that attracted large companies to a city. The quickest way to increase population was to increase size.

A 1912 bill introduced into the state legislature suggested increasing the size of the city from thirty-two to almost 150 square miles. The bill also suggested sectioning off the city into boroughs. This scheme was too big and too politically controversial and the bill never made it out of committee. Suburbanites within the potential annexed area feared increased property taxes. In turn, city residents feared subsidizing the suburbanites. Nevertheless, for the next six years, politicians and reformists as well as ardent anti-annexationists continually debated and fought for and against annexation.

The debate teetered back and forth from property taxes to urban amenities. Final-

Norman Avenue connecting Clifton to Herring Run.
(Baltimore Municipal Journal—1914)

NORMAN AVE., LOOKING SOUTH FROM MAYFIELD AVE., CEMENT CONCRETE

ly, as subdivisions proliferated, concern for basic urban amenities turned the table. Between 1898 and 1918 thirty-four subdivisions were laid out in Northeast Baltimore. Change was not just coming; it already arrived. Farms were subdivided, houses were erected, and a murmur of concern festered in neighborhood meetings. These new subdivisions needed a predictable supply of safe water, a comprehensive sewer system, electricity, and good roads. As more and more neighborhoods arrived into the annexed area, residents feared contaminated wells, leaking septic tanks, and a county government unable to supply electricity and good roads. In addition, most of the new suburbanites came from the city—folks who survived the city's tax rate. In the end, one fact tipped the scales—Baltimore City could deliver the needed urban amenities. Developers and residents alike were unsure about the county.

In 1918 Baltimore City was expanded to 91.93 square miles, almost tripling its size.[3] The bill was passed with substantial property tax breaks for the annexed area of Baltimore. Current as well as newly constructed properties would pay sixty percent of their property taxes in 1919, with a two-percent increase until the full amount was to be paid in 1939. The promise of a widely efficient municipality partnering in large-scale developments thrilled developers, eased the minds of newly formed neighborhood associations and set the political allegiance of Northeast Baltimore. Moreover, it also changed the way as well as the pace that Northeast Baltimore was developed.

Transportation Technology and Its New System of Organization

Transportation wound its way through Northeast Baltimore on two concurrent tracts. The expansion of the streetcar system led the way. However, by the 1910s, automobile technology found new ways of making inexpensive vehicles as well as new ways of creating roads, thoroughfares, and highways. During the 1920s both the automobile and the streetcar flourished together. The introduction of the streetcars spawned the early development of Northeast Baltimore, while the automobile in the 1910s and 1920s transformed the very shape of Northeast's roads, mainstreets, lot shapes, and even houses.

The Development of Streetcars

With the expansion of the streetcar, Baltimoreans found more freedom of where they could live and work. Before streetcars, most residential development occurred in a radius of two miles from work. With the advent of the horsecar railway, the radius of residential development expanded another mile,[4] but most of Northeast Baltimore was still out of the range of suburbanization. It was the electrification of the Harford Road streetcar and the building of the Belair Road electric streetcar that formed the foundation of the streetcar bedroom communities.

In 1885 the City Passenger Railway bought the Halls Springs' horsecar railway. Nine years later they electrified the line. For three more years the line ran only to Hall's Springs. In 1897 the City Passenger Railway obtained financial control of the Harford Road Turnpike and a year later extended it to Hamilton. In 1904 City Passenger Railway completed the Harford Road line that terminated at Joppa Road.

Belair Road received streetcars significantly later. The story began north of the City where the Baltimore and Ohio Railroad crossed the Gunpowder Falls.[5] The Baltimore and Loreley Electric Railway was incorporated shortly before 1896 as part of a scheme to harness the Gunpowder River as a source of electricity for Baltimore. This railway line quickly obtained trackage rights on the Baltimore and Jerusalem Turnpike (Belair Road) in order to connect Gunpowder River with the City. The scheme failed and in 1896 the Central Railway bought the trackage rights and re-christened the name to the Baltimore Gardenville and Belair Electric Railway. In 1898 the City Pas-

Harford Road north of Darley Avenue, circa 1911. (Courtesy EPFL Maryland Room)

senger Railway bought the Central Railway line and began laying tracks. In 1903 the streetcar reached Overlea.

Streetcar route extensions played a major role in suburban development. To justify the extension of jerkwater lines, there had to be a market for riders. Nevertheless, the streetcar companies knew that their efforts would spawn development, which in turn would create a market. This "chicken or the egg" dilemma fueled the incorporation of many small railway companies and suburban development schemes such as the Hall's Springs Railway, and the Baltimore and Loreley Electric Railway. All these enterprises struggled for profit, failed, and finally merged with larger, financially stable streetcar enterprises. Between June of 1897 and January of 1898, Baltimore saw the passing of small streetcar companies as they merged into three major corporations: the Baltimore Consolidated Railroad Company, The Baltimore City Passenger Railway Company, and The Baltimore and Northern Electric Railway. With the deep pockets of a major corporation, extended streetcar routes could patiently wait for new riders.

Interestingly, Harford Road received a horsecar trolley, twenty-eight years before Belair Road. The reason is tied to geology and land use persistence. Unlike Harford

Road, Belair Road was strictly a 'trucking road' for farmers. The coastal plain in all its tillable flatness lay east of Belair Road. This was "Gardenville." And one cannot haul their perishable goods to market on the horsecar. Thus, the land was more valuable as truck farms than suburban retreats. Consciously or unconsciously, Gardenville's land-use persistence delayed suburban growth.

In addition, Harford Road throughout the nineteenth century was more developed than Belair Road. On the 1857 Taylor's map approximately fifty-two names are located along Harford Road and only twenty-six names on Belair Road. The 1876 Hopkins map shows significantly more small plots lining Harford Road than Belair Road—small plots indicating suburban residences. In 1876 there were twenty identified businesses along Harford Road and only eleven along Belair Road. Although there were slight differences in the numbers, Harford Road physically looked more developed. North of North Avenue, Harford Road had eleven street crossings while Belair Road had only seven. With this in mind, Harford Road began suburbanization several years earlier than Belair Road, which is one major reason for the current difference in neighborhoods between Harford and Belair Roads.

Streetcars served Harford Road until June 19, 1956 and Belair Road until August 31, 1958.[6] However, during the sixty-year tenure of the electric streetcar, the automobile rose in popularity. In 1938, approximately 1,300,000 daily trips were made in Baltimore City. More than half of the trips were made on streetcars and buses. This resulted in 350,000 to 400,000 daily trips of automobiles moving in and out of the central business district.[7] In 1944, with the increase of population, the streetcar actually gained ridership, while automobile trips stayed the same. After the war, with the help of General Motors, Firestone, and Standard Oil, the automobile and buses replaced the streetcar. As early as 1938, the automobile captured at least thirty-three percent of all movement into the city.

The Rise of the Automobile

An old city, growing by the coalescence of numerous ancestral villages, the irregular and discontinuous street plan of Baltimore is the despair of the stranger and the daily inconvenience of its own citizens. The City lies in the path of one of the heaviest highway traffic streams in the country, and by millions of travelers who have moved with that stream the difficulties of the Baltimore passage are well remembered...

The old residential section of the City clustered closely about the central business section, which has grown little since the last fifty years. But, since 1900, the more well-to-do families that formerly lived in the older section have moved in

large numbers to outlying suburban areas, some of which have been included within revised limits of the growing City. The old homes, vacated by this movement, have descended to the less well to do, and by stages large areas have finally reached a critical state of decay.
—Thomas H. MacDonald, United States Bureau of Public Roads, "Toll Roads and Free Roads," 1938[8]

With great fanfare, the automobile arrived on the scene. In 1900 the United States registered only 8,000 automobiles. By 1910, the number rose to 468,000 and by 1920 it exponentially jumped to 8,000,000. In 1930 it rose to 23,000,000 cars.[9] In the Baltimore region, the increase in automobiles proportionately jumped. Baltimore's first auto show in 1906 invited the city's 700 auto owners. By 1910 Baltimore boasted 4,000 registered automobiles. Seven years later the number jumped to 55,000 automobiles and 4,000 trucks (7.3 percent of the national automobile owners). And in 1940 there were 175,000 cars in the Baltimore area.[10] This incredible rise of automobile ownership directly correlated with Henry Ford's inexpensive manufacturing of cars, as well as financial institutions creating nationwide programs for car loans.

In reaction to this phenomenal increase, federal, state, and local governments jumped on board the automobile craze by creating roads. The Federal Bureau of Roads designated Kingsville (a few miles out the Belair Road) a pioneer for road-building experiments. The state of Maryland as well acted progressively to improve roads. In 1898 the Geological Survey Commission created a "Report on Road Construction." A year later the state formed the Highway Division within the Geological Survey. In 1904 the state acted financially, supplying fifty percent state aid to any local jurisdiction that built roads. Two years later, the State Highway Division fully financed the creation of the Baltimore Washington Parkway. In 1908 the newly formed State Roads Commission passed legislation for a seven-year road-building campaign. By 1911, Harford Road was improved and Belair road shortly thereafter. Federal legislation was passed in 1916 and 1921 to help finance road building.

Road Development 1898–1918

Beyond the 1888 city boundaries, and beyond the Herring Run, Baltimore County municipal government provided minimal municipal services. The developers themselves were responsible for digging wells, septic tanks, grading and paving roads, and constructing storm drains and sidewalks. In addition, the new suburban towns of Hamilton, Lauraville, and Overlea provided their own volunteer fire service. With the help of the State Roads Commission, in 1910 Baltimore County began widening and paving Harford and Belair Roads.[11] In order for the State Road Commission to control road

Democratizing the Suburban Dream 127

Horse & carriage were frequently used until the 1920s. (Photo by James H. Lewis, courtesy of Jack Hennessy)

expansion, the turnpike companies were bought. In 1906 the city courts ordered the removal of the tollgate at Harford and The Alameda. In 1910, 16.9 miles of Harford Road were sold to the State Roads Commission.[12] By 1914, Harford Road was improved and widened. In 1926 after annexation, the road was widened again which removed many front lawns, front porches and several buildings.

During this time, the subdivisions were multiplying and by 1915 there were thirty-four subdivisions within the area. Not one of these subdivisions was complete or "built-out." All the subdivisions were directly tied to the trolley lines and the improvement of the Harford and Belair Roads. Concurrently, within the 1888 city-annexed land, Baltimore City began a comprehensive road building campaign.

As early as 1898 Baltimore City created and recreated the first efforts to develop and improve the roads. Improvements in Northeast Baltimore were restricted to south of the Herring Run until the annexation of 1918. In 1888 the city prompted a topographical survey of the annexed area. In 1898 an annex physical improvement plan was passed. Between 1904 and 1907 the Annex Improvement Commission was created, which allocated seven million dollars in loans for the improvement of roads in the annexed area.[13] In order to pay for the improvements, the city pushed legislation through the state, enabling the city to increase property taxes in the annexed area. The City created a system that categorized land as urban, suburban, and rural. Each category was based upon the amount of urban amenities within the area. Attached to each category were different property tax rates. By 1910 the proceeds from property tax revenue in the annexed area exceeded the debt service of the loans.[14] The annexation improvements proved to be a positive investment.

Extensive work was conducted in this area, as roads in web-like patterns expanded a mile or so north of North Avenue. The Annexation Improvement Commission organized this effort, and the city struck a deal with many developers in which cost-sharing for improvements prevailed. In 1914, the Commission paved seventeen miles of roads, twice as much as the year before. Most of the road development was done in conjunction with the building of new subdivisions. Here, the developer would pay for fifty percent of the road costs. In addition, most developers donated the land for roads, thus saving city funds.

By 1910, when the State Roads Commission committed dollars to road improvements, the city was already working within a statewide network. The first effort, of course, was to improve the old toll roads. The process of improving the Harford and Belair Roads was a multi-step time-taxing process. More time was devoted to legal acquisition of property than actual design and construction of the road. Even if the road already existed, the process of condemnation was tortuously long. Several public notices, an accurate assessment of the 'condemned' property, and sufficient time to contest the assessment value were all part of the process. The Belair Road widening project, for example, was held up in the courts for almost two years. Before the development of Northeast Baltimore could be unfolded, Harford and Belair Roads had to be widened.

With the Harford and Belair Roads widened, the city pursued other plans for physical improvements. According to the 1904 Olmsted firm's Comprehensive Park Plan of Baltimore City, several boulevards were to be created in order to connect many of Baltimore's parks together. These streets were designed to fit into a "suburban like setting." In 1914, The Alameda was one such improvement:

> The street or boulevard will be a park-like roadway which will serve to connect the new Thirty-third Street by a winding way and on the most approved lines of city planning with Harford Road, and will not only open up a large area of unimproved territory, but will also be another link connecting the parks with the city.
>
> The name "Alameda" designates the character of the street. This is of Spanish origin and is used in the southwestern United States to mean a shady way or walk planted with "Alamos" or cottonwoods.[15]

The Alameda exemplified the new twentieth-century city planning principles and practices. The Olmsted firm's plan stated that "the parkway is ordinarily designed to serve either as means of approach to a large park or as a connection between large parks." Olmsted goes further and suggests that boulevards should be extensions of the park in order to bring the 're-creative' natural settings to the people. Here, the parkways (in which boulevards are one design) must be free of as many of the annoyances of city streets (streetcars, grade crossings, and urban ambience) as possible. The Alameda did not lead the people to Clifton only, but physically brought Clifton to the neighborhood. Moreover, it was Northeast's first road project that did not lead to downtown Baltimore. It connected 33rd Street to Clifton Park. The Olmsted firm introduced the first road plan in Baltimore that deliberately avoided connecting the outlying regions of Baltimore to downtown. The 'sub' in suburbia was slowly usurping 'urbia'.

In addition, the name, The Alameda, deliberately de-emphasized Baltimore. Much like the Clifton Estate that hearkened back to the sixteenth-century hills of Italy, The Alameda associated itself not with Baltimore, but with the southwest United States, which at the time was very popular. The housing development along The Alameda also desperately tried to separate itself from Baltimore. Today, instead of romanticizing the road as a place to stroll, we romanticize the automobile.

The Great Flood of August 1911 destroyed the Harford Road Bridge (lower right) in the midst of construction. (Courtesy EPFL Maryland Room)

Herring Run Field House. (Courtesy of the Peale Museum)

North of North Avenue and directly south of Clifton Park, Broadway was another effort of stitching the city together with boulevards. Broadway, which was laid out around 1850, was not constructed north of Gay Street until 1876, three years after the death of Johns Hopkins. Undoubtedly, the announcement of Johns Hopkins's plan to build a university at Clifton fueled the construction of Broadway northward from Gay Street. Nevertheless, several obstacles were in the way, such as the Holy Cross Cemetery and Darley Park. From 1876 to 1914, Broadway ended at North Avenue. In 1914, the city made plans to extend the boulevard, but this time, the boulevard was to meet Harford Road and 25th Street—not Clifton Park.[16] The original intent was thwarted. This extension tied Harford Road, 25th Street, and Fells Point together. Thus, this road system created a bypass of downtown Baltimore. By the end of the 1910s not all roads led to Baltimore. After 1918, the City greatly increased their efforts at road development.

Road Development after the 1918 Annexation

After the annexation, Northeast Baltimore saw its road system transformed into an intricate and integral network tying subdivisions to downtown, industrial parks in East Baltimore, and other subdivisions. Road development began under the authority of various city agencies and ended under the authority of the Department of Public Works. The city's road campaign first focused on arterial roads, then turned its attention towards building lateral roads. As automobile travel increased on the arterial and lateral roads, fundamental shifts in relationship to the roads began to take place.

Shortly after the annexation, Baltimore City quickly put into place a comprehensive planning process for the annexed land. A City Plan Committee, appointed by the City Board of Estimates, was created (which replaced the Commission on City Plan, authorized by the state legislature in 1910 for the unsuccessful 1912 annexation effort). First, the City Plan Committee created the "Major Street Plan" for Baltimore City. With the streets planned, other planning issues needed to be coordinated. This new system manifested into large bureaucratic (although very efficient) departments and commissions. In 1925, Baltimore City created the Department of Public Works, which in turn created two new departments that dealt with road construction: the Bureau of Highways, and the Bureau of Plans and Surveys. The Commission for Open-

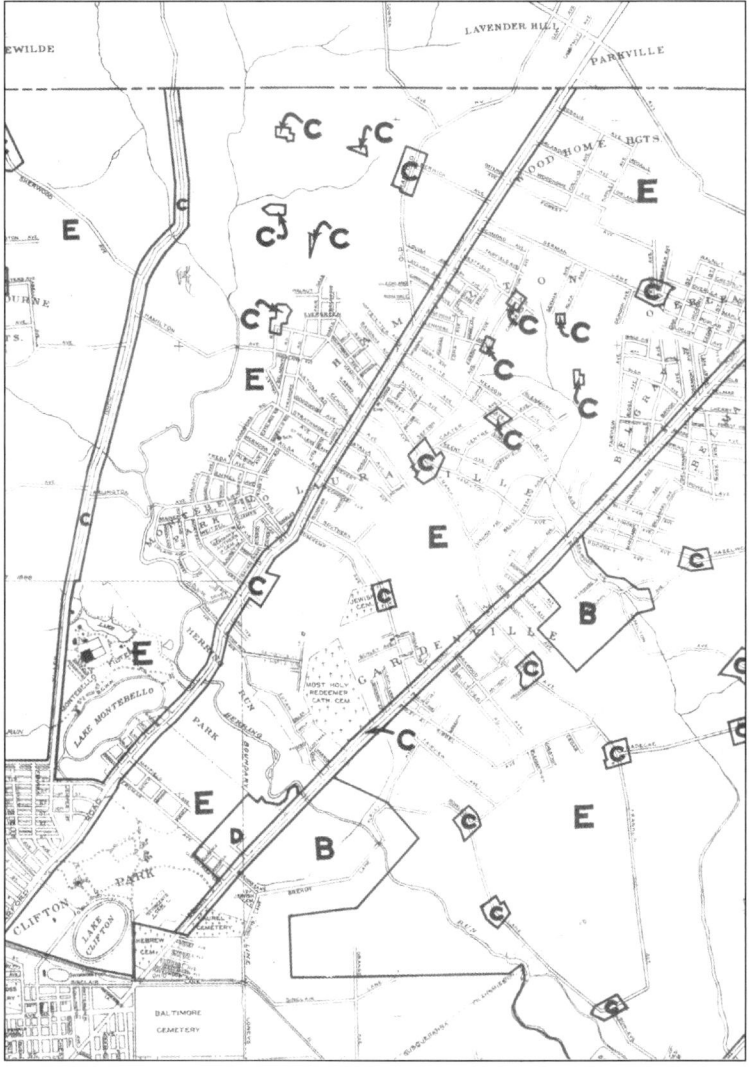

Detail from the 1926 Zoning Ordinance Map shows relative density along the Hillen, Harford, and Belair Road corridors. "B" and "C" areas are the most dense, where sixty to seventy-five percent of the lot could be built upon. "D" areas could be fifty to sixty-five percent built, and "E" areas thirty to forty percent. (Courtesy of CHAP)

ing Streets, which was integrally part of Baltimore's Government since the eighteenth century, realigned itself with the Department of Public Works in order to operate more efficiently. In short, these two bureaus were guided under the "Major Street Plan." This extensive reorganization of city agencies were a direct response to the vast suburban development in the annexed area.

The extensive efforts and components that went into improving and opening streets seemed mind boggling. Property acquisition for roads was a twenty-step process that oftentimes took longer than the actual construction of the road. The road plans had to be filed, then surveyed and written into a bill. The bill was then ushered to the appropriate committee and subsequent agencies for comment and review. Public postings were needed as well as public hearings. Once the bill survived the reviews, it needed to be resurveyed. Afterwards, the condemned property (i.e. the property taken from owners) had to be assessed. Then the owners needed to be compensated. Any appeals triggered a whole new process. Finally an ordinance was passed, property owners were compensated and the city acquired the title. Most of the new roads and all existing road widening projects had to filter through the above twenty-step process.

With a process in place, the City first focused on arterial roads. Baltimore's truck roads became more than a communication and conduit to agricultural lands; they became gateways into the city. On November 15, 1929, highways engineer Nathan L. Smith wrote in the *Municipal Journal* these telling words:

> The impression which a visitor to any city gets as he enters its limits is probably influenced as much by the character of the highways over which he has to travel as by any other cause and, with this in mind, the department of Public Works cooperating with the State Roads Commission had undertaken and made a great deal of progress toward placing Baltimore's entrances in first-class shape.[17]

To impress a visitor, highway engineers thought that wider and smoother were better. Wider meant less congestion, and safer and faster roads. A wide, well-paved road was just one way cities marketed themselves to industry. Nevertheless, wider was not necessarily better for those living and working on and off Harford and Belair Roads. At first, wider roads meant increased economic activity on the main streets, but in the long run too much widening added to the neighborhoods' deterioration.

Along with widening roads, engineers built boulevards. This time though, boulevards were built for automobiles and not pedestrians. Throughout Baltimore's history, the boulevard manifested itself in three periods: the formal boulevard, the park extension, and the automobile boulevard. In 1854, Baltimore City laid out Eutaw Place, America's first Parisian-style boulevard.[18] The boulevard was built as a communal

Fire engine at the Southern Avenue Fire House. (Photo by James H. Lewis, courtesy of Jack Hennessy)

front lawn, a developer's perk to sell house lots. It was built for evening park strollers and newspaper readers. The next wave of boulevards came via the Olmsted Plan of 1903. Here, as illustrated by The Alameda, the boulevard was to extend and connect the parks of Baltimore together. Thus, streets like The Alameda, Norman Avenue, 33rd Street, and Gwynns Falls Parkway were built. However, in the mid-1920s, boulevards changed their emphasis, use, and design, and now catered to the automobile. Walther Avenue was Northeast Baltimore's first automobile boulevard.

In 1924 Baltimore City passed an ordinance authorizing the opening of Walther Avenue. In 1931 Walther Avenue was opened from the Harford Road Bridge to Frankford Avenue. Walther Avenue became Northeast's first all-automobile arterial road. It was built based upon ideas purported by the Olmsted brothers' 1926 report:

> Boulevards should be for light traffic only, trucking being provided for on other roads. The Boulevards are primarily streets, but they should be treated with ample planting strips and trees so that they are attractive in appearance and passage over them is pleasant. Some run radially, carrying principally the traffic of people between their homes and their work; some run circumferentially, connecting outlying area with outlying areas.[19]

This definition emphasized traffic and motorists, unlike the 1904 plan which emphasized pedestrians and park connections. The beautification of the street was no longer for pedestrians, but for motorists "so that they are attractive in appearance and passage over them is pleasant." Its function was to transport motorists to someplace else. Nevertheless, Walther Avenue was designed with a medium strip, thoughtful plantings, and an eye for aesthetics. After WWII Walther Avenue was extended to intersect with Northern Parkway, but this time engineers eliminated the medium strip.

The same year Walther Avenue was finished, another automobile boulevard was being built. The significance of this boulevard was where it led as well as its name. Edison Highway was built for working-class motorists to get to work at the industrial sites in East Baltimore and Baltimore County. In 1931 Edison Highway was constructed on the old roadbed of Lonely's Lane. The city allowed E. J. Gallager, a prolific land developer, to rename the highway. While listening to the radio, Gallager heard that Edison died. The life contributions of Edison astonished Gallager, who suggested to the city officials that the road be named after him.[20] Moreover, this is the first road named as a highway. Edison Highway was the key to the success of Belair Edison's rowhouse neighborhood in the same way streetcar suburbs were dependent upon streetcar lines.

Out of all of Baltimore's boulevards, Loch Raven was supposed to be the most magnificent. In 1924, Loch Raven Boulevard was planned to be 200 feet wide and ramble north from 33rd Street to the city's seven-thousand-acre Loch Raven Reservoir. The plan also envisioned pushing Loch Raven Boulevard northward to connect with Pretty Boy Reservoir. If built, it would have been the largest boulevard in the region. It would have contended in size and fortitude with the Baltimore Washington Parkway.

The 200-foot-wide boulevard was to be partitioned off into three distinct areas. Streetcars would inhabit the middle lane. Trees would divide the streetcars from the north and southbound express lanes, which again were separated from local traffic lanes. Schools, community centers, and other public buildings would bump off from the boulevard and connect with the residential areas. Thus, six rows of trees would line five lanes of traffic.

This plan for Loch Raven Boulevard captured the optimism of city planners. Journalist Clark Hobbes wrote of the plan:

> Thus in theory, Loch Raven Boulevard is something more than a City Street or a State Highway. It takes on a character essentially different from the familiar commercial thoroughfare whose function is to connect centers of population. It is already linked with the park system for it gives access by junction with The Alameda, to the formal entrance to Clifton Park, is close by Herring Run Park and the grounds of the Montebello Filtration Plant, and touches the Mount Pleas-

ant golf course. Primarily an amenity, it suggests escape to the open beauty of wooded hills and watered valleys and pleasant farmland.

These things being true, it is reasonable to expect Loch Raven Boulevard to be developed in a fashion consistent with its function. It might be expected to provide a park-like approach to its park-like terminus in the planning of which natural beauty is cherished and haphazard real estate promotion is discouraged.[21]

In all, the Loch Raven Boulevard did not reach its end terminus. In 1924 the property owners (the heirs to the Garrett, Taylor, and Abell estates) and local land developers fought the city and its condemnation powers. Without the property owner's support, the city couldn't afford the acquisition costs. The City Plan Committee, though they envisioned the boulevard as 200 feet in 1924, could only "induce" the landowners to contribute 120 feet (the extra eighty feet were considered worth developing). The 120-foot boulevard was finally built by the Public Works Administration in 1936. Today, the boulevard terminates at I-695 in a warped four-leaf clover far short of its original muster.

Arterial roadways were (and still are) the umbilical cords to the young subdivisions in Northeast Baltimore and Baltimore County. Northeast's arterials changed shape design and meaning as the automobile grew to importance. From toll roads for farmers to non-descript passageways for coffee-stained grouchy commuters, the arterials changed as they widened. As the emphasis on movement on Harford and Belair roads increased, the roads became less identified with the Northeast communities. The Harford and Belair Roads were widened twice in the first half of the twentieth century (1911 and 1926). Ultimately the roads were widened one more time in the 1950s, when the trolley tracks were eliminated. The 1950s traffic engineers thought of the arterials only as pipelines for commuters.

Once the arterial roads were improved, the city began connecting Baltimore's suburbs together. Today, there are only six "lateral" roads that move from Northeast Baltimore to North Baltimore: 25th Street, 33rd Street, Argonne Drive, Coldspring, Echodale, and Northern Parkway. Unlike arterials that terminated in Baltimore City, laterals ended in neighborhood mainstreets. These laterals symbolize in concrete and asphalt the importance of Baltimore's burgeoning suburbs. Interestingly, the beltway signifies the importance of avoiding Baltimore.

Northern Parkway began first, in 1926, though it was not finished until the 1970s. By 1929, Cold Spring Lane became the second planned lateral road. It spanned from Liberty Heights to the Old Philadelphia Road via Moravia Road. In 1935 Echodale Road was constructed. And finally Argonne came on line after the Argonne Bridge was built over the Herring Run in the late 1940s. With the lateral boulevards in place, more of the interior section of Northeast was accessible for development.

As new lateral roads were being developed, the older nineteenth-century lateral roads were being transformed and engulfed into Baltimore's modern road network. For example, Erdman Avenue once tied Lauraville and Gardenville together, but by 1946 it became a bypass for commuters. The following *Sun* article, published on November 18, 1946, illustrated how older roads and roads in general grew from local connectors for neighborhood residents into bypasses for autoists:

> **Signs Lacking, Autoists Miss Good Highway. Artery, Erdman Avenue, Used only by those Familiar with it**
>
> While Erdman Avenue is being widely used by local motorists as a bypass route—to avoid the congested eastern and downtown sections of the city—the motoring public generally doesn't make maximum use of this traffic artery because it is so poorly marked, a check yesterday disclosed.
>
> The street saves time for motorists who live in the northern suburbs of the City and the metropolitan area and who work in the eastern industrial section of the City or in the rapidly growing industrial areas on the City's eastern fringe such as Dundalk, Sparrows Point and Middle River.
>
> **HELP FOR COLONISTS, TOO**
>
> Also it saves time for many Baltimoreans, who in the summer months take up temporary residence in the waterfront colonies scattered through Baltimore and Harford counties and who work for industries and commercial enterprises scattered in North Baltimore and the adjoining county communities.
>
> By and large these regular travelers are familiar with the route, but many out-of-town motorists, even though they are bent on business or on social calls in the northern part of the metropolitan area, do not know of the route because it is so poorly marked...
>
> **AVENUE "NOT ALONE"**
>
> But the lack of markers is not common to Erdman Avenue only. Motorists won't be attracted to use Monument Street or Orleans Street to avoid downtown traffic. Markers are inconspicuous or lacking altogether.[22]

This article signified the growing emphasis of roads as links to places and not places themselves. In the article there is no mention of the residents—only out-of-towners, and the "motoring" public. The road is only referred to as a bypass and connector. The article also referred to an altogether new group of people: the "motoring public" or "commuters." This is another shift away from geographical identity. This emphasis changed from geographical groups to task-oriented ones. Ironically, as the significance of roads shifted to "autoists," the roads took on more importance in identifying the neighborhoods. As a result, many neighborhoods were named and renamed according to the roads within and around them.

The neighborhood of Georgetown was named after community residents in the village enclave. However, by 1931 the name was wiped out and replaced by Belair Edison—crossroads of the neighborhood. It doesn't stop there! Today, there are twenty-four neighborhoods listed on the mayor's website. These twenty-four neighborhoods make up three larger areas: Belair-Edison, Cedonia Area, and Hamilton. Two of the three areas are named strictly for the roads.

Moreover, thirteen out of twenty-four Northeast neighborhoods are named after the prominent roads in or surrounding their neighborhoods. In many cases, these neighborhoods changed their names. Neighborhoods named or renamed after streets are as follows:
- Georgetown was renamed Belair-Edison;
- Gardenville was renamed Frankford;
- Waltherson was named after Walther Avenue;
- Hamilton and Hamilton Park were renamed Glenham Belford;
- Eutaw Heights was renamed Belair Parkside;
- Woodhome Heights was renamed Woodring;
- North Harford Road was named after Harford Road;
- Rosemont Avenue was named after Rosemont Avenue;
- Cedonia was named after Cedonia Road.

Out of the five farm villages in nineteenth-century Northeast Baltimore, only Lauraville retains its name. When roads were the physical backbones of neighborhoods, the residents chose to name their communities after prominent residents, economic reasons for existing, or cultural associations. But as the roads redefined life, they also became the barriers demarcating the neighborhood boundaries.

Roads themselves changed, multiplied and widened. They also changed the visual ambience of Northeast Baltimore. With roads came street lights, and Baltimore City pioneered their use. In 1784, oil lamps first illuminated Baltimore.[23] Only the main streets in the city were sporadically lit. Nevertheless, from a ship moored in the harbor, the town could be seen in its iridescent glow. In 1816 the system of lighting changed from oil lamps to gas. It was the first city in the country to light its streets by gas. In 1816 an ordinance was passed to allow for Peale's new lighting system to be planted upon the streets. It was not until 1881 that electric arc lights were introduced. Well into the twentieth century, street lighting remained geographically confined to the inner city. In 1898 the city passed three ordinances to remove the overhead wires and put in an underground conduit system for electric lights. Still, the Northeast area was out of reach of night lighting.

With the rise in automobile use, street lighting became a safety issue. The September 20, 1929 edition of the *Baltimore Municipal Journal* argued for a comprehensive street lighting plan:

> The greater use of vehicular traffic on city streets has made it necessary to improve street lighting, in order to facilitate rapid transit and safety to citizens after sundown. The old standard of street lighting, such as the arc light 60 candle power bracket lamp on wood poles and the gas lamps, have been found inadequate for use on the main thoroughfares. Because of the demand for improved lighting, a modern street lighting program has been approved by Mr. C.F. Goob, Chief Engineer, and is now being carried out by the Bureau of Mechanical Electrical Service.[24]

This historic wooden lamp post—note the mortise and tenon craftsmanship—still stands across the street from Safeway on the Harford Road. (Author's photo)

The necessity of making sure that motorists saw streetcars and pedestrians drastically changed the look of the land. One of the first priorities of the new street lighting campaign was the illumination of Belair Road. In 1929 Belair Road became the longest street illumined with modern Novalux fixtures with 600 candlepower bulbs.[25] Approximately eleven miles of the Gay Street/Belair Road corridor were lit. Concurrently, Harford Road was receiving the same treatment from Glenmore Avenue to the city line and from 25th Street to Herring Run. This effort was comprehensively organized, and literally brought light into the night. This continual advance of streetlights was just one more component in the city's role in building subdivisions. The 1920s subdivisions were being built with roads, street lighting, electricity, sidewalks, storm drains, and sewers.

By 1926, after the second widening of Belair and Harford Roads, the automobile gained control of the roads. Instead of the road letting us see the surrounding countryside, much like William Wirt walking along Harford Road in 1822, we began to focus our attention upon where the roads led us. The road stopped being a destination, an Alemada, or a Loch Raven, but a means to connect home and work, home and consumer products. Ironically, as cars drastically expanded the range of daily travel, it also severed neighborhood from neighborhood, and increased the number of places we did not want to be. We had more freedom to go more places, but also more places we desired to pass through.

After World War II, especially with the passage of the 1956 Highway Act, the system of roads exponentially increased the average miles traveled by Americans. The post-World War II highway construction directly impacted only the east side of Northeast Baltimore. Nevertheless, Northeast Baltimore became entangled in the huge juggle and shift of population that the roads created, maintained, and signified.

By the end of World War II highway building became a precise science. All reports submitted to the Commission on City Plan were thoroughly researched and sophisticatedly presented with large sums of data. Traffic counts, curb cuts, stop lights, street lights, signs, and the Maryland Highway Patrol were outgrowths of this new sophisticated organism. This budding tentacled organism had one primary goal: allowing more and more automobiles to roam freely over the Maryland landscape. In the end, the emphasis on traffic not only changed the actual streetscape of Northeast's thoroughfares, but also changed the everyday lives of all Americans.

The Infrastructure of Sewer and Water

The infrastructure of sewer and water were essential for the full-scale development of Northeast Baltimore. Before the annexation of 1918, houses were built with septic tanks. Unfortunately, too many septic tanks in a neighborhood could literally spoil the fresh air of the country. After the annexation, Baltimore City ardently pushed their brand new sewage infrastructure out into the new hinterlands. In order to push such expensive infrastructure in Northeast Baltimore, money had to be found. In 1924, Mayor Jackson addressed the citizens of Baltimore regarding the importance of passing a bond bill known as the sewer loan. This bill was passed and ten million dollars were set aside to purchase private sewers and extend sewers to new areas.

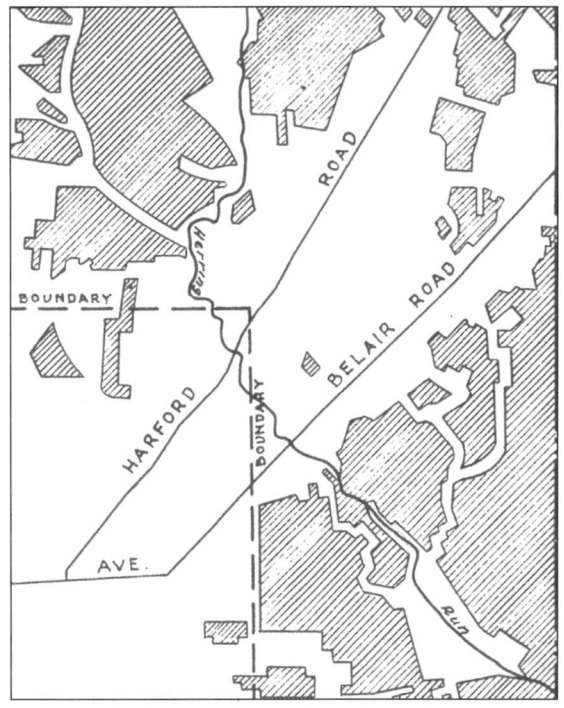

A December 1941 map shows unsewered areas in grey. (Courtesy EPFL Maryland Room)

Baltimore, unlike most major U.S. cities, put off engineering a comprehensive sewer system until the first decade of the twentieth century. Baltimore relied on the "natural system of disposing of sewage," which ultimately meant dumping waste in the Inner Harbor:

> The streams, the surface gutters, the private lines, and cesspool seepages all finally dumped their burdens into the harbor, with the predictable result that in spring and summer that body of water was afloat with rotted garbage and the flotsam and jetsam of urban wastes, smelling like a billion pole cats.[26]

By the 1890s the wealthy could neither turn their noses elsewhere nor retreat to their country estates. Several municipally minded organizations such as the Municipal Arts Society, the Reform League, and the Merchants and Manufacturers Association took action and began a comprehensive political campaign. In 1893 Mendes Cohen, a civil engineer and a director of the Municipal Arts Society, became chairman of the newly created Sewage Commission.[27] In 1905 Cohen and his Commission proposed a comprehensive sewage system. Finally, with ardent support from many civil-minded organizations between 1906 and 1915, Baltimore completed the country's most up-to-date sewage system.

By 1929, the Bureau of Sewers built many mainline sewers and storm drains in the annexed area.[28] The Arcadia Improvement Association, like all Northeast associations, lobbied for the expansion of the sewer system into their neighborhood. The Arcadia Improvement Association history stated the following regarding sewers and storm drains:

> Sanitary sewers were also sorely needed, and these were secured through the untiring efforts of our officers and committees.
>
> Then followed the delicate problem of inducing the property owners to make house connections. This was handled diplomatically and the desired results were accomplished with a very minimum of friction because of the hearty cooperation of the residents. No other improvement has added more to the welfare of our

community, and too much credit cannot be given to those public-spirited citizens who cheerfully deeded a portion of their property to the City of Baltimore for a right-of-way.[29]

In many neighborhoods, such problems were the impetus to creating neighborhood associations. It was these growing pains that brought residents together to lobby at City Hall.

Also during this time, many small streams in Northeast Baltimore were funneled through pipes and buried. This freed up additional land for development as well as control of flooding. For example, Moore's Run was piped into a six-foot, six-inch drainpipe from White Avenue to the northern city boundary line. This allowed ultimate control over much of Northeast Baltimore land. With the burying of Moore's Run, over a dozen subdivisions from the southeast corner to the northwest corner of Northeast Baltimore were built. The sewer and storm drain system throughout Baltimore was a product of twentieth-century city planning in conjunction with civic-minded citizens who made sure their homes were serviced properly.

Other Aspects of Baltimore City Planning

Baltimore's plans for the annexed must be reasonable and practical. Views of those in the localities to be affected will be given first consideration.
The 62 miles of land and water added to the City by the Act of 1918 should be carefully planned in order that its development may be along lines best adapted for its future use. This may be expressed in a sentence:
A Community Should Have That City Plan Which Is Best Suited To Its Particular Needs.
—James H. Preston, Mayor.

The governmental body in charge of "planning" grew directly out of the Topographical Survey Commission of Baltimore. Prior to 1910, Baltimore City planning was regulated to street layout and park plans. In 1910, the Commission on City Plan was created. Authorized by the state legislature, the Commission on City Plan presented recommendations for the location of a street and park system, public buildings, monuments, and airports. They also coordinated with other city departments concerning traffic studies, railroad systems and facilities, the development of piers, wharves and shipping facilities. From 1910 to 1918 the Commission on City Plan began its arduous task of expanding its role. In 1918 the duties of the Commission on City Plan were taken over by the City Plan Committee, which was authorized by the Board of Estimates (i.e., given money).

From 1918 to 1932 the Committee met continuously, and the city accomplished much during this time: implementation of the Major Street Plan; passage of a comprehensive zoning ordinance; publication of a park plan; and continued creation and enhancement of Baltimore's industrial sites. By 1932, the city saw it fit to expand the authority and role of city planning.[30] In this year, the city revived the original Commission on City Plan with nine commissioners representing various professions, and even paid a small salary to its president. By 1933, the State passed legislation supporting the creation of a Comprehensive City Plan. By this time, however, much of Northeast Baltimore was already scrawled into its permanent form.

As Baltimore grew in the early 1920s, the municipal government looked for legal ways to control and guide its growth. A street plan was in place as well as mechanisms to complete the water and sewer systems. Nevertheless, the "use" of land was not regulated. In 1923, Baltimore City created its first comprehensive zoning ordinances, which chopped up the city into "zones."[31] Zoning designated land use as well as density and types of development. It separated types of development by restricting the percentage of the building lot a structure can cover. In the inner city, the buildings were allowed to cover almost ninety percent of the lot. This percentage decreased further from the city center.

In more ways than one, the new concept of city planning, aided by its comrade the zoning board, wrote into law the decentralization of Baltimore. All major cities ardently fell under the spell of the "decentralists." Zoning, with its ability to regulate lot size, building mass, land use, and density changed the shape of all major cities. Zoning prevented Northeast Baltimore from becoming another urban grid rowhouse community. Zoning mostly supported detached dwellings and duplexes. Most houses had to have a side yard. Zoning, therefore, was the basis of uniform neighborhoods, whereupon uniformity would maintain their profit margin. Zoning, more than any other law, shaped the look of Northeast Baltimore. Today, by driving through much of Northeast Baltimore, one can 'read' the effects of the 1923 zoning law by identifying clusters of building types, and uses.

Zoning also separated industry, business, and residential neighborhoods. Most of Northeast Baltimore was zoned residential. Industry was mostly confined to the southeast corner of the area near Herring Run and Pulaski Highway. In addition, Harford and Belair Roads were zoned differently. Belair Road was zoned for heavier industrial use.

The Creation of Northeast's Parks

During the first decade of the twentieth century, Baltimore's parks changed. As early as the 1820s, with the creation of Patterson Park and Mt. Vernon Place, parks were strictly designed as artistic respites from the urban environment. In 1904, the Olmsted Plan emphasized artistic beauty as well as exercise, athletic fields, and playgrounds. In 1906 the Playground and Recreation Association of America was formed. This organization advocated the creation of athletic fields, playgrounds, swimming pools, and golf courses as an integral part in creating positive social values.[32] Philosopher's walks, boating ponds, and exotic trees did not have the same positive affects on Baltimoreans as did a good game of tennis, golf, or baseball. Northeast Baltimore during the first two decades of the twentieth century mixed picturesque retreats with golf courses, tennis courts, swimming pools, and baseball fields. Herring Run Valley, Clifton, Moore's Run, and Mount Pleasant all mingled recreation with natural beauty. Both the athlete and the artist commingled.[33]

Herring Run Park

Two hundred years after the Principio Iron Company laid barren the land for lumber, the Herring Run had grown back beautifully.

By 1908 the city had acquired vast acres of the Herring Run Valley between and bordering Belair and Harford Roads. In 1926 the Olmsted Firm drew up another plan which launched the city into anther buying spree. In addition to outrightly purchasing land, the city used its zoning and municipal powers to influence developers to donate park land in return for permitting development. Frank Novak donated much of the land for Herring Run east of Belair Road.

Today, Herring Run Park is used much like it was during the nineteenth century. Boy Scouts camped while the residents filled water jugs at the famous spring. The Eutaw Methodist Church was turned into a park pavilion, and several other buildings were erected for recreational purposes. Along with the park as a place of picturesque retreat, it was also used for sporting events. Even today, dog walkers, picnickers, cyclists, joggers, and soccer and baseball teams thrive on the open space. A 1913 *Sun* article captured many sentiments of the Herring Run:

> **Go out Walking!** It is the fever of the moment—it is the breath of summer—the song of May.
> And yet walking is not an American exercise. We play baseball and tennis with the thermometer high up in the nineties, but ask us to walk after the middle of May and we signal wildly for a streetcar or an automobile, as our means permit.

> To do 10 miles a day is to the average American an impossible feat, and so it turns out that many Baltimoreans know nothing of the rural beauties that surround them.
>
> It is the intention of the Sunday Sun to print a series of pictures of the walks in the neighborhood of the city showing their loveliest spots, and so we come at once by right of pre-eminence to what many people consider the loveliest of them all—Herring Run.
>
> **The Old Mill Wheel Is Only a Reminder**—Immediately after leaving the bridge you come to an old moss grown mill, its wheel forever stilled, and then you walk through a narrow passage as wild as though it were a part of some untrodden wilderness. Carpeted with ferns it is, and roofed with the intertwined branches of trees. Here and there a white wall of dogwood appears, and the pink of the Judas tree lends decoration. Alongside rambles the sleepy stream, here teased into some semblance of activity by the stones in its pathway, there lying low and dark in a great shadow-flecked pool.
>
> The old swimming pool is in a shady spot and deep and cool, with slippery, moss-covered rocks beside it. And if you're young and innocent and a boy—which is to say if you are a supremely happy creature—you take off your clothes and in you go. Down your spine a delicious shiver finds its way, and then another and another, and after a plunge or so you draw yourself out and lie outstretched upon one of the warm flat rocks to dry. No Turkish towel could more delightfully perform that task, and almost immediately you are fit, unwillingly, to put on your shirt as a sop to propriety.
>
> After this big pool there are many smaller ones, also shaded also lines with the soft green of ferns and set off in the spring with white bloodroot and blue anomomes. It is rumored that there are fish in these pools—mullet and sunfish and such things, but the fishermen do not flock to them and the finny things have grown lazy in their cool seclusion.
>
> There are precipices along the banks of Herring Run—not like those of the great canons of the Western States, but steep banks a hundred feet high or more, and in some places the stream forests that it is only a little run for the pleasure and benefit of those who walked and dashed along it at a great pace, making waterfalls of itself, giving itself airs and whitecaps for the benefit of the beholder. And then there are places where it is a sluggish thing, the little tinkle from which would put the direst insomniac to sleep in a jiffy did he but yield himself to its influence.[34]

In addition to recreational uses of parkland, Baltimore's Herring Run also had a utilitarian use as the terminus of Northeast's storm drain system. All storm drains to the north of the Herring Run ultimately dumped into the stream.

Democratizing the Suburban Dream 145

Horse-mowers like this one kept the landscaping neat in Clifton Park in 1916. (Courtesy EPFL Maryland Room)

Clifton Park

The city's purchase of Clifton Park proved to be a wise decision. In 1901 the Johns Hopkins University board of trustees sold Clifton Park to Baltimore City for one million dollars. Clifton Park became a magnet for recreational activity as the 273-acre park acquired a band stand, swimming pool, tennis courts, athletic fields, and an eighteen-hole golf course. In 1916 the golf course opened, and tee-off was free of charge. More than any other amenity at Clifton, the golf course became the most popular. In 1929, the *Municipal Journal* published the following article:

> **Plan to Make Clifton Park Public Golf Course, Country's Model**
>
> Within the next two weeks final work on the Clifton Park Golf Course, which will transform the 18 holes into one of the best municipal playing grounds in the east, will get under way. This work includes the construction of a house for the ticket seller and starter at the first tee, the covering of the section of seats where caddies await their turn to escort players, and construction of a driving cage and practice putting green...
>
> That the course at Clifton Park measures up favorably with the best in other cities, was disclosed by Alex Morrison, internationally known golf expert. Mr. Morrison appeared at a local playhouse here some months ago, to exhibit his

Clifton Park Golf Course as seen shortly after its opening in 1916.

Baseball fields at Clifton Park in the 1920s.

Clifton Park tennis courts. (Photos above and opposite courtesy EPFL Maryland Room)

skill. During the week he was invited to play the Clifton Park course and accepted. After completing a round he stated he was agreeably surprised at the fine condition of the links.

This course, he said, is one of the best owned and conducted by any municipality in the country on which I have played. Park courses should be constructed with the idea that they are not built for professionals. Those who use the parks, in the main, are beginners at the game, and it is not well to make the courses too hard for them. "With the addition of very few hazards this Clifton Park course could be made better, but even as it is, it is a splendid playing field."

Clifton Park has its appeal, not only to male golfers, but to feminine lovers of the sport as well and they are to be found there daily in large numbers.[35]

Along with the famous Clifton Park golf course, the Clifton Park swimming pool in 1930 was the largest in the country. In 1934 Baltimore had seven swimming pools, five golf courses, twelve tennis courts lighted for night time play, ninety-four total tennis courts, thirty regulation baseball diamonds, and fourteen major parks totalling 3,260 acres.[36] Together, Clifton and Herring Run parks totaled 845.55 acres of land in Northeast Baltimore. Adding Mount Pleasant Golf Course, the total rises to 1,107 acres.[37] The foresight of the Baltimore Municipal Art Society and the creative Parks Commission, Northeast Baltimore was blessed with over a thousand acres of well used parkland.

Innovations in Real Estate Development

The real estate industry reacted to the technological improvements and the municipal activities by reshaping their development strategies. Their object, of course, was to develop more land at a quicker pace. Thus, modern advertising practices proliferated and real estate developers became much more involved in all aspects of the neighborhood development.

Three distinct development practices were used in Northeast Baltimore.[38] The oldest procedure consisted of an individual purchasing a lot and hiring an architect or builder to design and construct a house. By the first decade of the twentieth century, large tracts were subdivided into building lots and were sold to individual owners. These lots huddled close to Harford and Belair Roads. All houses built in this manner were for wealthy residents who had a strong role in the design and erection of the house. This practice still goes on today.

The second development practice consisted of one developer buying a large tract of land, laying out the lots, surveying, and grading the roads. Then the developer would put the subdivision on the market to attract private individuals and small-time builders. Individuals would build their house, while smaller builders would buy three

HAMILTON REAL ESTATE CO., INC.

B. K. PURDUM, President

DEVELOPERS AND BROKERS

SPECIALIZING IN HAMILTON PROPERTY

Modern Homes For Sale or Rent

Well Located Building Lots With Paved Streets, Sewers, Gas, Water

5510 Harford Road, - - - - - Baltimore, Md.

TELEPHONES, HAMILTON 0585-0586

Developer's advertisement pre-World War I. (Courtesy of CHAP Archives)

or four lots and build houses according to general specifications, which were placed in the deed. Many times the developer would play broker to the builders and the individuals as well as market and promote the subdivision. Thus, a potential buyer would ride the streetcar out to the development site, and have a choice of either buying a lot, a house, or buying a lot and having a house built.

The last kind of development practice was all-in-one developer. The speculator was the designer, builder, and seller wrapped into one. The speculator built whole neighborhoods and was the precursor to today's Rylan Homes. The all-in-one developer in Northeast Baltimore originally concentrated on rowhouse developments. After World War II, these kinds of developers bought large tracts and built all types of subdivisions: rowhouses, apartment complexes, and ranch-style housing.

During the 1890s and early 1900s, most development occurred building lot by building lot. Today, most of these houses can be seen close to the Harford and Belair roads. During the 1910s and 1920s, many of the large landowners became intricately involved in real estate. The new practice was to subdivide the land and sell to builders. Throughout the streets of Lauraville, Gardenville, Mayfield, Hamilton, and Raspeburg, two, three, and sometimes four identical houses are seen on the same block. The same builder built these pairs or trios. Literally one can count the number of builders who developed a streetscape.

Financial Institutions Providing the Capital

As it took large sums of money to build the infrastructure of Northeast Baltimore, it also took large sums of money for real estate developers to build their subdivisions. In order to distribute the capital to finance the building of neighborhoods, financial systems had to be created. Many forms of financing mechanisms were created and recreated to supply the developers with sufficient funds to build.

From the latter half of the nineteenth century until the early 1930s, Baltimore created a sophisticated network of building and loan institutions. Sherry Olson notes that "by 1899, one thousand building and loan associations were incorporated in which 250 were active."[39] These small building and loan associations were often started by such institutions as churches, ethnic associations, craft guilds, and union halls. They typically had fifty to 100 shareholders and made loans of $100 to $1,500. During the 1910s, developers created many of the building and loans associations. For example, E. J. Gallagher, prominent rowhouse developer, was also the president of St. James Savings and Loan Association. By 1934, at least twenty-five building and loan associations were located in Northeast Baltimore. Several of the building and loan associations

Built in 1929, the Harford Road Building Association still stands at 4534½ Harford Road. (Author's photo)

included the following:[40] Belair Road Building and Loan Association, Inc., located a 6003 Belair Road; Belmar Permanent Building and Loan Association, located at Belair Road and Belmar Avenue; Beverly Hills Building and Loan Association, located at 4547 Harford Road; George Brehm Perpetual Building and Loan Association, located at 2740 Belair Road; Grindon Building and Loan Association, Inc., located at 4621 Harford Road; Hamilton Permanent Building and Loan Association, located at 5510 Harford Road; Raspeburg Building and Loan Association; and Woodlea Building and Loan Association.

Many of these were within the areas of development and set up by the developers. With financing in an office next to the new subdivision, potential buyers were literally a few steps closer to buying a suburban home. As developers advertised for their open house, young couples would ride the street cars out to the new subdivision, look at the area, and then, if they desired, apply for a loan.

Between 1928 and 1933, home construction in the U.S. dropped ninety-five percent.[41] In order to jump-start a stagnant industry, the National Home Builders Association lobbied the federal government for help. In 1932 the federal government signed into law the Federal Home Loan Bank Act, which established credit to mortgage lenders. This law subsequently became known as the Federal Housing Act of 1934. The creation of federally insured savings banks was the slow demise of the small-time building and loans associations of the early twentieth century.

New Ways of Construction: Innovations of Building Technology and Techniques

In a symbiotic relationship with the new systems of neighborhood development the builders created new technology and techniques. New tools, building materials and uniform standards were created. In addition, builders and designers integrated new mechanical systems into the home. Heating, plumbing, and electrical systems as well as refrigerators, lights, bathrooms, washers, dryers, and kitchen gadgetry substantially impacted home life. Lewis Mumford pointed out that in 1800 ninety percent of the cost of a house went to building the actual structure. However, by 1920, approximately fifty percent of the cost of a house went strictly to the mechanical systems.[42] The building industry reorganized itself to meet the twentieth century.

During the latter half of the nineteenth century, the building industry reinvented itself through literally hundreds of inventions. Steam-powered lumber mills greatly accelerated the production of molding, doors, window frames, studs, joists, sheathing, and rafters. In addition, building ornamentation became accessible to a larger audience. Factory-made building materials and standardization of size and material became the norm. Building material innovation occurred at all levels of construction as well as in the materials themselves: wood, cement, brick and stone, glass, and metal products. In turn, the house builder spent less time producing the individual components that went into the house, and began installing the factory-made materials. In many ways carpenters and masons adopted assembly-like techniques.

The building industry as well as the federal government saw fit to standardize building practices. During World War I Herbert Hoover created the National Bureau of Standards. This new agency tested and experimented with such things as fire-retardant materials (asbestos, for example) and waterproofing. The Division of Building and Housing was created in 1921. In 1923 the federal government created the Bureau of Home Economics and an Advisory Committee on Building Code. The goals, in the words of Gwendolyn Wright, were "mass production and year-round, rather than seasonal, construction. Results included the first standard grading scales for building materials and set uniform construction details."[43] One example was the standardization of the concrete block. In 1924 the concrete block industry, organized under the

Front cover of a developer's brochure from the early twentieth century. (Courtesy UB Archives Gallagher Collection)

Democratizing the Suburban Dream 153

direction of the Concrete Block Manufacturers Association, agreed upon the size of an 8x8x16-inch block.[44]

Portable power tools became the norm on construction sites. The electric power drill was introduced as early as the 1920s.[45] By 1930 Black and Decker was selling portable drills and saws. By the end of World War II hand power tools were the norm for many carpenters. In addition, heavy machinery such as bulldozers, flat bed trucks, and cement mixers became more and more prevalent on the job site. All this technology helped to speed up construction time and proportionately reduced costs. As construction time was reduced, labor costs were reduced and individual pay increased. Labor costs began to be as important as the cost of materials.

Construction innovation went hand in hand with changes in house design and marketing. With the standardization of building materials, the mail order housing and pattern book industry proliferated throughout the country as designs were shipped throughout the country. By 1910, a small-time builder could buy blue prints through the mail for as little as ten dollars. Large manufacturers took the mail order business one step further and began selling kit houses through the mail. Sears and Roebucks, Gordan Van Time, Montgomery Ward, and a dozen other companies shipped by rail thousands of pre-packaged houses (along with building instructions). Sears, for example, identified each building material with notches that referred to pages in the instruction book. Many of the designs were published in newspapers and popular magazines at the time. Here, an owner could pick and choose his/her ornamentation, house size, and shape.

Without the factory-made building components, Northeast Baltimore could not have grown so quickly. Nevertheless, underlying the factory-built system of house construction was the ability to transport the materials to the construction site. Here, the truck and rail transportation were essential. Without a compre-

"The Number 3 Fireless Cooker" along with hundreds of other appliances helped to revolutionize the suburban kitchen. (Courtesy UB Archives Gallagher Collection)

hensive road system and the proliferation of trucks, the suburbs could not have been built. Standardization and comprehensive communication and transportation networks helped to create a national and international debate regarding home design and neighborhood ambience. Upon the factory assembly line, the iron rail, and the flatbeds of trucks, the suburban ideology was transformed and disseminated throughout the country.

Twentieth-Century Suburban Ideology Manifested in Architecture

Twentieth-century dynamism seized the nineteenth-century suburban ideology and created one of America's most unique and original neighborhood—the city/suburb. The city/suburb was different than other streetcar, railroad, or early automobile suburbs by one fact: they were suburbs financed, regulated, and built as part of the city. The municipal government's regulatory, financial, and infrastructure mechanisms created suburbia's city manifestations. Baltimore took the urban neighborhood and reclothed it in suburbia's garb.

The city/suburban house was quite different from the nineteenth-century farmhouse, summer home, or rowhome. Unlike its urban cousin, the suburban house became an unattached three-dimensional form that was pulled back from the street. Here the side façades became design elements in the streetscape. However, unlike its farm cousin, the suburban house had a relationship with the street and its accompanying houses. And unlike the wealthier summer estate that arranged the driveway according to the siting of the house, the suburban home was sited according to the street layout. This created a streetscape of houses of many shapes and sizes geometrically aligned and sitting in their own little lawn-gardens. These streetscapes formed neighborhoods that nestled next to working farms, woods or parks. The juxtaposition of suburbs next to undeveloped land added greatly to the ambience of living in the country, but a neighborhood built by the city in keeping with nature.

Nature—as it was for Downing—was a prime directive in city/suburbia's development. These highly compacted neighborhoods (around ten houses to the acre) struggled to create a park-like setting. Unlike the farmhouse that is placed into nature, the suburban developers switched the process and placed nature amongst the houses. The subdivision was stripped of nature down to dirt. Hills were leveled and gullies were filled. Lots were laid out, streets graded, and houses erected. Nature was introduced back into the subdivision. Finally, lawns and trees were planted and gardens were dug. This time, though, nature became man's bidding.

The prime ornament of the city/suburb was the house. Between 1898 and 1940 there were four forms of detached houses in Northeast Baltimore. First came the I-house, which was a carry-over from the nineteenth century. With suburban development, three new house forms were introduced to the area: the cottage, the bungalow, and the foursquare. The cottage rose out of the nineteenth-century suburban architecture. The foursquare, an American creation, became the middle-class man's Georgian house. And most interesting was the bungalow, truly the first international house type. House types reveled in various architectural ornaments and styles. Architectural detailing and compatible house size created commodious and unique streetscapes. Each type of house carried its own connotations, fashion, and design. Nevertheless, they shared much and much discussion ensued regarding their differences.

Although the detached single family home is the icon of suburbia, most suburbs throughout the country harbor other dwelling types: the duplex, rowhouse, and garden apartment. Duplexes are the outcome of mixing the detached and rowhouse together. This mixing is a compromise written into the zoning law of 1923. Many areas in the annexed area were required to have at least one side yard. Today all suburban regions are a mixture of residential forms.

The oldest detached house type was the I-house, which dotted Northeast Baltimore as farmhouses for most of the nineteenth century. The I-house is a long, narrow two-story house. The I-house was sited on the street with either its gabled side (long side) or its gabled end facing the street. Gabled-end I-houses rarely had additions. However, the side-gabled I-house always had an addition to the main structure. Thus, the building made a square, "L," or "T" shape, depending on the design. The front façade was ornamented usually with a central gabled dormer with a "Gothic" (i.e. pointed) arch or semicircular window. Stylistically, the side-gabled I-houses were called "Carpenter's Gothic." In most cases the fronts had porches with the typical Victorian bracket.

This type of house proliferated throughout Northeast Baltimore during the latter half of the nineteenth century. It was built in the area as late as the first decade of the twentieth century. These buildings were constructed by local carpenters and farmers and mark the carry-over of the farm era. They were extremely versatile structures. First and foremost, they were quickly constructed. Since the main body was one room deep, only two load-bearing walls (walls that carried the weight of the second story and roof) had to be built. Also, additions were easily attached to the main house—just put an addition on the back, the side, or even the front. And in several decades maybe two or three more additions could be added.

By the early twentieth century, on many of the lots laid out, the building only fitted with the gabled end facing the street. Eutaw Heights neighborhood, at the corner of Belair Road and Parkside Drive, is an early subdivision built with gabled-end I-hous-

Southern Avenue in 1904. (Photo by James H. Lewis, courtesy of Jack Hennessy)

es. These houses lost favor when the bungalow and cottage were being offered by the developers of Overlea, Evergreen Lawn, and Montebello Park.

The bungalow and the cottage varied from each other by their visual verticality. The cottage was a wood frame house with two or two-and-a-half stories, whereas the bungalow was a one or one-and-a-half story structure that visually hugged the ground. The bungalow sported a low-pitched roof that protruded over the front porch. On the cottage the porch sported its own roof with Victorian or Colonial Revival porch details. In Baltimore during the 1910s, much debate centered on the cottage and the bungalow: they were compared and contrasted with each other. Tastemakers writing for local papers piped in with their own opinions of which house type was better, more artistic, or comfortable. They pontificated ceaselessly on which housing type was "true" to Baltimore. Throughout Northeast Baltimore, most streets harbor cottages and bungalows. On any given street, both—and sometimes their hybrids—center on front lawns. Although their origins are quite different, they go well together.

Cottages were direct descendants of A. J. Downing's era. They were vertical in nature

Turn-of-the-twentieth-century garden off Southern Avenue. (Photo by James H. Lewis, courtesy of Jack Hennessy)

and mimicked the massing and shape of Victorian and Colonial revival houses. On the other hand the bungalow was horizontal in nature, squatty in shape and massing, and reveled in all kinds of stylistic detailing. These house types as well as the meaning of the terms intermingled and began losing their distinction. In essence, they became names for suburban houses. Nevertheless, they started out as specific building types and gradually evolved to become harbors for grandiose associations. Here, national as well as local tastemakers became minutely involved with trying to defend the strict definitions between the cottage and the bungalow. They ultimately failed, but their efforts chronicled a chapter in suburban ideology history—a history wrought in Northeast Baltimore.

The bungalow migrated over thousands of miles and three hundred years, taking a windy road from India to Baltimore. During its travel, it picked up many nuances, associations, and physical characteristics. By the 1920s, the bungalow was so rich in nuance and connotation that it meant—more than anything else—a detached or semi-detached suburban home. The word "bungalow" is rich in meaning—not for its exactitude—but for its adventure from India to North America.

"I-Houses"—such as this one from the 3800 block of Parkside Drive—were a versatile design that carried over from the nineteenth-century house form. (Author's photos)

The word "bungalow" derived from the Bengali word "bangla," meaning "a low house with galleries or porches all around."[46] The word was introduced into English in the seventeenth century. Through the eighteenth century in India, the word bungalow became attached to the type of house that British imperialists would build for themselves. The house differed from the traditional British house. The bungalow's design took into consideration the climate of India: hot weather. A square-shaped, one-story-high structure with a low-pitched roof and deep overhanging eaves became identifying features of the bungalow. Verandahs or porches wrapped around the whole house, as each room was designed for maximum airflow. All rooms had at least three openings and at least one that opened onto the verandah. Its squatty land-hugging form was its most identifying feature.

In 1869 the bungalow first arrived in England as a vacation home. The word as well as the building type immediately became associated with vacation, a retreat from the hot, congested, and polluted industrial cities. You lived in a house and retreated to your seaside bungalow. Throughout the latter part of the nineteenth century many architectural books published different designs of the bungalow—most were one-story ground-hugging buildings. However, by 1891 "bungalow" as a term also included picturesque two-story structures. R. A. Briggs published a book entitled *Bungalow and Country Residences* in 1891. Here in the preface he pontificated upon the meaning of the bungalow:

A Bungalow in England has come to mean neither the sun-proof squat house of India, nor the rough log house of colder regions. It is not necessarily a one-story building, nor is it a country cottage. A bungalow essentially is a little 'nook' or 'retreat'. A Cottage is a little house in the country, but a Bungalow is a little country house—a homey, cosy little place, with verandah and balconies and the plan so arranged as to ensure complete comfort, with a feeling of rusticity and ease.[47]

Briggs tied associations such as retreat and coziness to the bungalow. In this sense the bungalow mirrored the underlying connotations of the picturesque. However, Briggs points to a slight, but extremely significant difference. Unlike the cottage, which was beautifying the country by adding to the country's landscape, the bungalow added the country to the suburban or semi-urban landscape by being a country house.

Typical I-House with gabled end facing the street. (Author's photo)

Thus, from England the term bungalow was shipped overseas to the shores of such places as Martha's Vineyard. Here, the bungalow began its relationship with America's cottages, which flourished in the stick and shingle style. The bungalow then began its westward trek and found common ground in the arts and crafts movement and in the Prairie Style (i.e., Frank Lloyd Wright) movement. It wasn't until it reached California that the bungalow became Americanized. During the first part of the twentieth century, California seized upon the bungalow as its main house type. The house here, more than on the East coast, lost a lot of its Victorian details and began its earnest search for low-hanging horizontal lines, and its one-story size. The popularity of the bungalow in California, and the popularity of California itself, created the bungalow craze, which proliferated throughout the country. The bungalow also carried the associations of exotic California (in Northeast Baltimore it also brought us the neighborhood Beverly Hills!).

Through mail order catalogues, the bungalow was shipped to all parts of the United States. Back in Baltimore, real estate sections of the newspapers as well as developers began defining "the bungalow." The *Baltimore News* real estate section of February 26, 1910, announced the arrival and proliferation of the bungalow:

Pre-World War I bungalow identifiable by ground-hugging shape and tiny shed dormer windows. (Author's photo)

Post-World War I bungalow in Arcadia. (Author's photo)

Typical cottage-style house from Montebello Terrace in Lauraville. (Author's photo)

> The bungalow habit, which has taken such firm hold on Baltimoreans is showing itself as a factor in suburban development more prominently this year than ever before. The number of these picturesque structures now under construction on the outskirts of this City is astonishing when it is considered that less than five years ago a bungalow was regarded as impossible for a permanent home here and was accounted as useful only for outing purposes in the summer. Now these low, one-story houses are getting to be as common hereabouts as the ordinary cottage.[48]

Another article of the same date described a bungalow/cottage combo built in the Baltimore suburbs. The house was one-and-a-half stories high, lending itself to a bungalow definition. It had a doubled-hipped roof with jergin head dormers peering on both roof hips. The porch roof was separate from the house roof while a couple of bay windows protrude from the front and side façades. These attributes label it a cottage.

By 1914 the *Baltimore News* tried (in vain) to separate the meanings of bungalow and cottage:

> The word bungalow says an authority on the subject is a curious example of how we Americans overwork a word that is euphonious and the meaning of which on account of its comparatively recent assimilation into the language has not become sufficiently defined.

Colonial Revival at 3210 Juneau Place. (Author's photo)

Four-square houses in the 2800 block of Hamilton Avenue. Identical designs form the signature of a single builder-developer. (Author's photo)

In this remark there is to quote again, "more truth than poetry." The results attained in the design of many of the so-called bungalows are a startling exemplification of this statement. They are, for the most part, little worthy of the name. For the many absurdities they exhibit, misunderstanding of the style on the part of the designer and inexpert dictation and interference on the part of the owner are mainly responsible....

In the first place it is a physical impossibility to make the orthodox "raised cottage" assume the lines and proportions so essential to the true bungalow, for its unnaturally stilted mass precludes all possibility of designing it with the low squatty effect that buildings of this description demand.

As for two story buildings, not even in the land where the bungalow grows are they so called. Double story houses with bungalow suggestion are properly called "chalets" as being in appearance more closely allied with the chalet of Switzerland and the ancient log chalet of Norway.[49]

The article goes on to describe how the bungalow in Baltimore got "bastardized" by the meddling of the owner in the design of his own house. Here, the owner requests such things as Queen Anne bay windows, asbestos diagonal pattern roof shingles, a second story with ten-foot ceiling heights. Through the owner's meddling in the architect's pure bungalow plan, the house becomes "another bungalow plan that its California sisters would have an extremely difficult time recognizing as one of their kin."[50]

Whatever the architects and builders were creating in Baltimore, the term bungalow latched onto Baltimore's suburbs. Baltimore's discussion regarding the "proper bungalow as well as its popularity" is telling of the changing attitudes throughout Baltimore and the nation. First, the exotic associations of the word to such places as India and California as well as associations with vacation resorts fit the early twentieth-century suburbs. Through the bungalow, the suburban ideal was captured, packaged, and mailed throughout the world. The mail order bungalow represented the American Dream of home ownership. It packaged California for everyone.

The last house type was the foursquare which was built between 1900 and 1930. This form is two-and-one-half stories high and sits on a raised basement. Usually the roof is of pyramidal shape with several dormer windows, mostly one to each façade. The front façade most always has a front porch. Ornamental elements can range from cedar shake shingles, stained glass to Colonial Revival door and window frames and Queen Anne bay windows. The size can vary from extra large to large. In many cases the foursquare was the larger option to the quaint bungalow.

Its origin is as eclectic and American as our society itself. Before 1890 their were no foursqaures throughout the country, but by 1900, thousands dotted the American suburban landscape. The building exemplifies the creation of the middle class. It became a counter-reaction to the picturesque irregularity. It also caught upon the symmetrical Colonial Revival bandwagon. Foursquares, in many aspects, hearken back to the form and layout of Georgian symmetry. However, this time the building was manufactured and disseminated through mail order catalogues and popular magazines. The orderliness of the house symbolically represented the new wave of science and its infiltration into home economics. In many ways it became the perfect combination of the bungalow and the cottage, and in Northeast Baltimore it fit perfectly next to both.

The Rise of the Lawn Care Industry

The American lawn industry began with the first lawn mower patent in 1869 and grew to be a multi-billion dollar industry with national and international companies serving homeowners from coast to coast.[51]

By the 1980s there was approximately thirty million acres of lawn—a strictly manmade encroachment into the natural landscape of America.[52] Two intermingling components created this multi-billion dollar industry: the ability and the desire for lawns. In the United States the proliferation and sudden growth of this industry changed the look of neighborhoods forever. Northeast Baltimore, like all suburban developments of the 1910s and 1920s, were not immune from the marketing influence of the lawn industry.

The lawn, like the suburban house, had its roots in England. During the eighteenth century the lawn was an integral part in the picturesque aesthetic found in country estates of English gentlemen. Not only did it provide outdoor recreational space, it also allowed landscape gardeners to create view sheds. The lawn became the border, the space upon to arrange flora ruins and woods. By the end of the eighteenth century London's suburbs were building around common lawn areas. Essentially, they were communal lawns. From here, the lawn crossed the ocean and became Americanized.

During the nineteenth century the lawn was directly transported from England. Servants with scythes or sheep and goats tended to the lawns. Lawns were also limited by climate. Few strains of grass could produce the aesthetic touches desired. However, grass seed of all kinds were being collected and disseminated through agricultural magazines and organizations. Experiments with grass growing abounded upon gentleman farms.

Before the 1870s most American country and suburban homes had dirt yards. By the mid-1880s, as tastemakers and architectural pattern books became common, lawns were touted as outdoor rooms in which the family could play upon the velvety green carpets. Advertisements led the popular culture to believe that tending to a lawn was easy. By 1883, several lawn mower dealers were marketing their new product. Several dealers created and distributed trading cards, while others promoted their mowers with images of finely dressed women mowing. This, however, did not influence a lot of people. Lawns were only feasible for the upper class.

Symbolically, lawns became extraordinarily important. First, as lawns blemished the landscapes of great country estates in England and America, the lawn was a symbol of man's dominion over his (or her) surroundings, security, and wealth. Lawns were perceived as outdoor rooms. It also became associated with security from nature itself. A low-cut lawn allowed the homeowner to spot and eradicate vermin, insidious weeds such as poison ivy, and thorn plants. As an outdoor room, it was man's realm—not nature's creation.

The lawn was also a mitigated response, a border to public and private spaces, to indoor and outdoor spaces, and to nature and to architecture. Here, with a low-cut space, the house could be seen from the driveway, and from the house, the vistas of nature, could be seen. Much like suburbia itself the lawn was a borderland in microcosm. It became an icon for the middle class.

Perfectly manicured lawns—the suburban ideal realized in Northeast Baltimore City. (Author's photo)

It wasn't until three organizations worked together that the lawn became available to suburban homemakers. The Garden Club of America, the United States Golf Association, and the United States Department of Agriculture began an all-out campaign to bring lawns to the American landscape. From the inception of the United States Department of Agriculture in 1862, the USDA judiciously catalogued lawn and agricultural grasses.[53] Their main purpose was to create agricultural grasses. It wasn't until the United States Golf Association approached the USDA that the government agency began a nationwide effort to create the perfect strain of ornamental lawn grass.

In 1912, Charles Vancouver Piper, a botanist at the USDA and an avid golfer, became very receptive to helping the USGA. In 1912 Piper began research on turf grass at the Arlington experimental farm. Here he created new strands of grass that could be grown in various climates. Through the judicious research of the USDA hundreds of strands and crossbreeds of grass seed were grown in order to find that hearty breed.

By 1928 the USDA had "480 test plots in Arlington devoted to trials of different putting green grasses, fairway mixtures, turf diseases and pests, fertilizers, cutting experiments, watering, and tests under playing conditions."[54] Furthermore, by 1927 test plots of turf and lawn grasses were grown at state agricultural stations throughout the country: Florida, New Jersey, Kansas, Minnesota, Wisconsin, and Nebraska.

This scientific information was disseminated to Garden Clubs throughout the United States and used in many magazines of the era, such as *Better Homes and Gardens*. With the scientific information conducted at government expense or on tax-exempt research stations of the USGA, the lawn became physically possible to be grown in every climate in the U.S.A. This in turn created a huge lawn care industry. The lawn care industry was comprised of three areas: growing grass, killing weeds, and the creation of chemicals and tools to control both. Much technological innovations were created for the care of the lawn. Everything from garden hoses, lawn mowers, and weed whackers to fertilizers, herbicides, and pesticides.

Northeast Baltimore was no exception. According to the zoning law, all detached, semidetached, and most rowhouses had to have lawns. In 1910 a subdevelopment in Hamilton was named Evergreen Lawn. Without the efforts of the USDA, USGA, and the Garden Club of America, Dr. George C. Wegefarth would not have named his development Evergreen Lawn. By the 1920s Clifton Park and Herring Run were developed as golf courses. Today, we view the front lawn as natural, but in reality it is as created as the house itself. The lawn in many ways became the component, the background green that visually holds the suburbs together.

Northeast Baltimore during the first

half of the twentieth century was a microcosm of the changing country. It became a unique conglomeration of neighborhoods built within a booming and transforming Baltimore. As Northeast Baltimore developed, Baltimore too changed into a city of skyscrapers, an immense industry base and a port rivaling any city. Annexation, more than any other legislative or bureaucratic undertaking, captured as well as illustrated the force of change upon Northeast Baltimore. Here, annexation exemplified the fight not only about what jurisdiction would develop the areas, but how and with what resources to develop. Once the city proved to have more resources—economic as well as bureaucratic—the boundaries were expanded. After 1918, the city stepped in and became the most significant partner in developing Northeast Baltimore. Roads, sewers, water, fire and police protection, streetlights, schools, hospitals, libraries, and parks underpinned the creation of every neighborhood. In addition, city regulation profoundly shaped the neighborhoods. Here, zoning and building codes, by law, had to be followed. Also, the city regulated telephone, electricity, radio as well as movie houses, saloons, and restaurants. Music, charities, swimming pools, golf courses, and recreation athletic leagues were organized by the city. By far, the City of Baltimore played the largest part in developing Northeast Baltimore.

Only from this bureaucratic foundation, private enterprise could begin its task. In democratic fashion, men of capital worked within the regulatory guidelines and built upon the municipal infrastructure. But it was the community that added the soul and essence to the area. Underlying the developers and the municipality's building of the suburban landscape was the taunting and sometimes daunting community. Here, the communities spoke their minds and were listened to by the city councils (there were two chambers in Baltimore until the early 1920s), the mayor's office and the department heads. During the 1920s, harmony existed between the community, the city, and the developers. Nevertheless, it was a harmony brought about by continuous fighting, nagging, politicking, and good-ole grassroots organizing.

Evolving tools of lawn care resulted in the finely manicured housefronts of suburban America. Above: The mechanical 1872 mower. (From the *Maryland Farmer*, courtesy of CHAP)
Left: The 1950s-era "Eclipse Rocket." (From *Gardens, Houses & People*, May 5, 1952)

From the *Maryland Farmer*, June 1872:
"The lawn must be often mown that the grass may thicken and improve. Nothing contributes more to the neatness of grounds than an evenly-shaven turf. To accomplish this desirable end, the hand lawn-mowers are indispensible to those who have ever used them."

Hamilton Mainstreet circa 1900. (Courtesy EPFL Maryland Room)

MAINSTREETS

DURING THE FIRST three decades of the twentieth century developers built subdivisions; residents created neighborhoods. Suburban neighborhoods were more than a group of homes laid out along streets. They were places where people did everyday activities in everyday ways. As a family member stepped onto the sidewalk in front of their house, inevitably they would wind up on the Harford or Belair Roads. These main streets were the backbone of the neighborhoods. Here, the commercial, business, religious, and social buildings were constructed. Residents mingled at the trolley stop, social club, church, barbershop, lunch counter in the drug store, department or grocery store. Here, the residents created communities.

As the streetcar ran along the Harford and Belair Roads, the old nineteenth-century farm villages were transformed into a hodgepodge of old and new buildings and businesses. The old farm villages thickened into viable mainstreets. They became dense as buildings stretched along the roads, creating a linear mixture of residences and businesses. Nineteenth-century frame houses added one-story additions, enclosed porches, and placed merchandise and signs in new store windows. Alongside these changes, old residences were razed, and new buildings were erected in new styles, materials, and sheer showy smoothness.

Church congregations built foundations of community while entrepreneurs added movie houses, halls, and bowling alleys. As Baltimore's industry and commerce provided jobs outside these city suburbs, the mainstreets—only through diversity—formed the backbone of community.

Like tentacles, side streets stretched from Harford and Belair Roads into the old farmsteads and connected the new subdivisions to the neighborhood mainstreets. Subdivisions became neighborhoods through creating a relationship with the mainstreet corridor. Along Harford Road the retail and community institutions clustered around the old farm villages of Homestead, Lauraville, Hamilton, and the twentieth-century creation of Northern Parkway. Along Belair Road, mainstreet centers were created near Georgetown, Gardenville, and the twentieth-century creation of Overlea.

Harford Road Mainstreets

Between 1898 and 1914, the number of buildings along Harford Road greatly increased. Around Grindon Lane the number of buildings doubled from thirty to sixty.[1] Between Echodale Avenue and Christopher Road the number of buildings increased from twenty-eight to sixty-four. North of Christopher Road the number of buildings jumped from approximately ten to twenty. Many of the new structures were made of brick or concrete block and were configured into an urban mass. Many buildings were two-story, slanted, and flat-roofed, and ornamented with a protruding Italianate, like cornice. Mainstreets first catered to walk-in customers. After World War I another wave of commercial development occurred, but this time catering to both walk-in and automobile customers.

A comparison of several gazetteers and city directories illustrated several general mainstreet trends. The number of businesses along Harford Road increased in direct correlation with the suburbanization of Northeast Baltimore. In 1894 only thirty-three businesses were listed on the Harford Road. By 1928 the businesses jumped to approximately 195.[2]

By 1917, types of listed occupations fell into three categories: building industry, professional occupations, and retail.[3] Building industry-related occupations were as follows: real estate and land companies, pump manufacturers, plumbers, lumber dealers, tinners, contractors, and stonemasons. 1917 retail stores selling goods to suburban residents included bakers, barbers, druggists, a pickler, a tobacco dealer, a laundry store, butchers, tailors, and notary publics. Other occupations increased, such as grocers, general store managers, restaurant managers, doctors, and shoemakers. Some occupations disappeared altogether: brick maker, canners, hotel worker, lawyer, huckster, and fence maker.

In 1930 the change along Harford Road was duly noted. The *Union News* on May 30, 1930, published a section exclusive to the development of Harford Road. The intensity of development captured not only the change and growth of businesses but also the increase in property values. Many lots along the Harford Road sold for a few hundred dollars in 1900, and by 1930 sold for twenty to thirty thousand dollars.[4] With this in mind, many of the buildings erected were considered taxpayer buildings. Here, speculative developers would buy the land as an investment. They would build one-

Opposite: Bromley's 1914 Atlas of Baltimore County shows a Gardenville's burgeoning mainstreet.
(Courtesy of CHAP Archives)

Harford Road 1911 improvements included a state-funded widening and hardtopping project seen here at the intersection with Homestead Street. (Courtesy EPFL Maryland Room)

story cheap structures that could be rented for enough money to pay the yearly taxes. Immense profit hoped for would come when selling. Sporadically it worked; many taxpayer buildings still exist today.

As Harford Road thickened with businesses many advertised in local newspapers. These ads, along with the gazetteers and city directories, shed insight into the commercial diversity of the area. All types of businesses catered to the Lauraville and Hamilton communities. The Sawyer Pharmacy, located at 4516 Harford Road, began in 1900 as the Weller Drug Company. Another entrepreneur, Mrs. Margaret Tregor, owned a dress shop:

> The Modiste shop at 5802 Harford Road was started three years ago (1927). Mrs. Margaret Tregor, the manager, at first was able to do all of the work herself, but the business has grown to such an extent that three persons are now required to handle it. In rush seasons more are needed.

> Mrs. Tregor, who has had 19 years experience in her line, has taken in addition, courses in dressmaking, designing, and women's tailoring. She is conducting the only exclusive ladies and children tailoring establishment on the Harford Road.
>
> Mrs. Tregor has lived in the Hamilton neighborhood for the last 15 years having moved there when it was a part of Baltimore County.
>
> She specializes in hemstitching, button covering and doll repairing, and her courteous treatment and good workmanship have built up a substantial business.[5]

The Arcadia Meat Market replaced Mann's Wagon Repair Shop at the corner of Weaver and Harford Road. Mr. Wilke began a "lawn mower hospital" in Lauraville, where he mostly sharpened the blades of the push mowers. His shop stood at 4523 Harford Road. Henry Sause opened an "Up to date Department Store:"

> In June of the year 1922 the Hamilton Department store opened its doors for business with Mr. Henry H. Sause, Proprietor, and for the past seven years has given the people of the Hamilton section a real department store's service. The store has always maintained a high class standard of merchandise which their customers have appreciated—evidence by the steady increase of patronage it has enjoyed from year to year.
>
> In 1929 an annex to the store was made by establishing a men's furnishing store at 5525 Harford Road connected to the store by a wide arch.[6]

The Hamilton Restaurant opened in 1927 which "catered to families and auto parties."[7] Frank Shirey's Auto Garage stood near current-day Shirey Avenue (4912-14

Surviving "taxpayers" on Harford Road. These one-story commercial buildings were constructed by real estate speculators in order to hold the land and to earn just enough money to pay the taxes on the property. Many, however, remain to this day. (Author's photo)

Harford Road). Since 1910, Mr. Wittner sold dry goods at 4615 Harford Road. Samuel Markley Supply Company first began in 1876 and thrived well into the 1930s. In 1917 Samuel bought the establishment from his father. In 1930 Samuel Markley had eighteen employees, six horses, and three trucks which sold farming equipment, which eventually catered to gardening.

Two laundries were located in Hamilton, one ran by the Maryland School for the Blind, and another by Lee Fang. Also a medical fraternity was located in Hamilton in 1914. It was comprised of Dr. Morris Green, Dr. Geary A. Long, Dr. George Vogler, Dr. Charles H. Heller, and a dentist, Dr. Benson Roberts. And four grocery stores were located on the mainstreet. In 1925 Parker, Thomas and Rice, architects of the Belvedere Hotel, built a new post office. In addition the architects designed the new bank building for twenty-four by seventy-six feet on the southeast corner of Hamilton Avenue.[8] Architect-designed buildings indicated the growing importance of the mainstreet to the Baltimore region.

Movie theaters were another neighborhood mainstay, creating spaces for social interaction. As early as 1916 movie theaters became an important institution in Northeast Baltimore. In 1916, at 3019 Hamilton Avenue, a half block from Harford Road, the "Community" opened in the former Hamilton Presbyterian Church. The proprietors were Captain W.A. Blake (Merchant Marine) and H.P. Mann (retired blacksmith). By 1919 it was part of the Durkee family dynasty who owned and operated many theaters in Baltimore. In 1927 the movie house closed. In 1929 or 1930 the old wooden church was replaced with a brick edifice fifty feet by one hundred fifty feet, including a mezzanine, where until 1933 it was used as a bowling alley and finally an indoor golf course. In 1933 the building was reconfigured as a movie house and renamed Avon. Owned and operated by the F. H. Durkee corporation, it operated as a 399-seat movie theater from 1933 to 1960, when it was finally razed.

The Arcade, which opened in 1928 by F. H. Durkee Enterprises, was one of Baltimore's three arcade buildings. The movie theater was located in the back of a long corridor, which was flanked by several stores: real estate offices, a drug store, barber shop, a shoe shine, and a building loan association. A true arcade, this structure became a precursor to the indoor malls of post World War II and has its roots in eighteenth-century Paris. The movie house seated 1,000 people and became the office of the Durkee family movie theater dynasty. Hamilton was the only suburban Northeast Baltimore mainstreet that had two movie houses.

In 1921 the Cameo opened in Lauraville at 4707 Harford Road. The Cameo was built in 1921 as the Parkside. In 1930 it was rebuilt as the Cameo for $30,000 with a seating capacity of 500. The theater was owned and operated by the newly formed

Hamilton Amusement Company. Catering to the German population, on Christmas Day 1953 it began showing German films. Shortly thereafter it became the New Cameo. Today it is a bar.

The Northway movie theater opened its doors in 1937, half a block north of Northern Parkway, and was built by John Zink and E. Eyring and Sons for Durkee Enterprises.[9] Its opening completed the establishment of a mainstreet commercial node at the corner of Northern Parkway and Harford. By 1928 there was a shoe store, auto shops, barber, confectioner, and a pharmacy. In addition, there was The Great A & P Tea Company grocery store, which was the precursor to the A & P super market.

Along with the growth of the area came neighborhood and community associations. Their main goal was to pressure the county and subsequently the city to provide the necessary infrastructure for the area. Sometime between 1898 and 1904, the Northeast Improvement Association was formed. In 1904, a reporter wrote about one of their annual picnics:

The streamlined Art Deco Northway Theatre, designed by John Zink and originally opened in 1937. (Author's photo)

> Yesterday afternoon and evening were gala occasions at Evergreen, Hamilton, as the Northeast Baltimore Improvement Association held its annual watermelon fete on the Estate of George Wegeforth. The celebration was to mark the phenomenal growth of the association from 25 to 535 members...
> At 6:00 supper was served to 90 guests in the Hotel Hamilton which has recently been erected.[10]

In 1906, The Northeast Community Association fought for the extension of the Baltimore County Electric and Water Company lines to service Hamilton. Many debates ensued in the Baltimore County chambers. Nonetheless, the lines were not extended and Hamiltonians still relied on well water until the 1920s. The Northeast Communi-

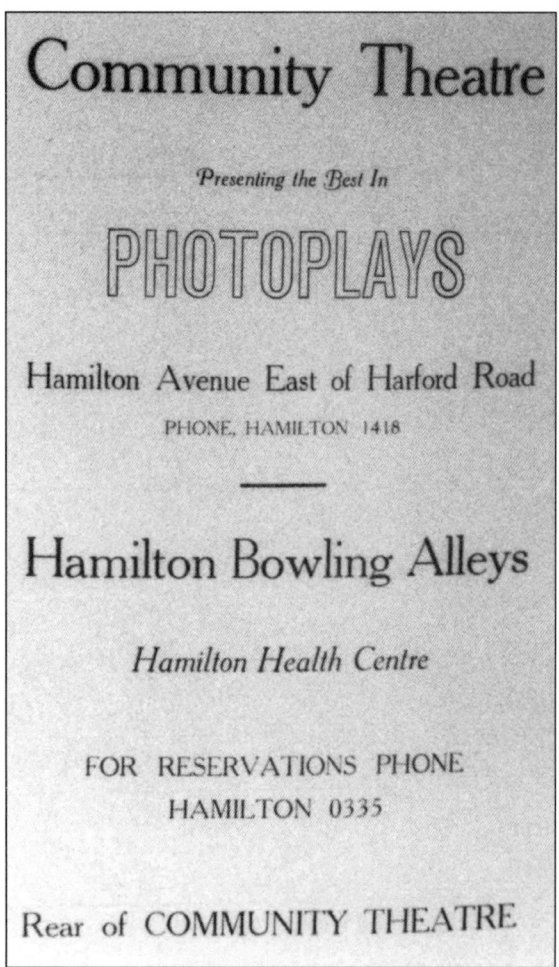

Neighborhood mainstreets became the center for social activity. (Courtesy EPFL Maryland Room)

ty Association was the first known organization advocating for improvements to the area.

As the area grew, Hamilton became big enough to create its own association in 1904. Here, the association ardently fought from 1904 until after 1930 for many of the improvements in Hamilton. By 1930 the association held an annual event, not in Hamilton, but in the Lord Baltimore Hotel. Between 1904 and 1930, William McCallister, then president, advocated and secured many improvements for the community such as the elimination of toll gates along the road, telephone service to Hamilton, gas lines, sewers, and electric lights. He advocated for state road money, fought for higher teacher salaries, secured better mail delivery, and much more.

The Hamilton Woman's club was another leading social organization.[11] Started in 1914, they met in the home of Mrs. Bradley K. Purdum and outlined their goals as civic, literary, social, and welfare activities. They worked with the Red Cross, and organized Liberty Socials during World War I. During World War II they again worked with the Red Cross, as well as the Civil Defense Department to spot enemy planes. They also encouraged people to raise vegetable gardens. They supported local activities for the improvement of Hamilton. They lobbied for a library, better sidewalks, a nursery school, and a recreation center.

A community would not be a community without churches. On and directly off Harford Road between 1900 and 1930 over a dozen church structures were built. Six churches in Hamilton first began meeting in Hamilton Hall: St. John's of Hamilton United Methodist Church, Hamilton Presbyterian, Grace Lutheran Church, St. Dominic Roman Catholic Church, the Methodist Protestant Church, and the Baptist Church. All these congregations migrated along with the residents.

St. John's began under the leadership of Reverend John B. Henry on May 17, 1903.[12]

Greek Revival columns mark the entrance to St. John's of Hamilton United Methodist Church. (Author's photo)

They first met in a rear room of Hamilton Hall. Reverend Henry was the preacher for Taylor's Circuit, a route which included Taylor's Chapel, Andrew's Chapel off of southern Avenue, Perry Hall, and Lorely. On April 24, 1904, St. John's of Hamilton United Methodist congregation was incorporated. On October 3, 1904, a cornerstone was laid for a church at the southeast corner of Harford and St. John's Avenue, where Coopers Camera Mart now stands. By February 5th, the congregation worshipped in their new church. The church, designed by builder-architect Hugh M. Magruder, was built in a country parish Gothic style. Its squatty-hipped roof accented the nave. A rose window capped a steeped gable entryway. The church, like many along Harford Road,

A Spanish Mission Revival gas station, currently used as a car dealership on Belair Road. (Author's photo)

was built of rough field stone from one of the local quarries. Nevertheless, by 1925 St. John's outgrew its church. The church bought property on the southeast corner of Gibbons Avenue and Harford Road. It erected its current edifice in the Greek Revival style in conjunction with the nation's Colonial Revival tastes.

Across the street St. Dominic's Roman Catholic Church was built for newly arrived residents who used to worship at St. John's and St. James the Less in East Baltimore.[13] Father J.B. Manley, who was a chaplain at the Dominican convent in Irvington, was appointed Chaplain. On July 1, 1906, Father Manley began the first Mass at Hamilton Hall. On May 5, 1907, the corner stone for the main building was laid. The plans were designed in a Gothic style and built of local stone.

Shortly thereafter, Father Manley established a parochial school in 1906. A modern fireproof building was finally constructed in 1919 to hold eight classrooms and a total of 725 students. Around 1930 a fourteen-room convent was constructed for the Sisters of Charity. Again in 1935 a junior high school building was erected. Finally, in 1958 the third floor was added to the school. Altogether, the architecture and campus is unified by the use of local quarry stone. Even the parish house, designed as a bungalow, but made entirely of stone, blended into the campus. From St. Dominic's two mission churches popped up on the Harford Road, St. Ursula at Carney and St. Francis of Assisi in Mayfield. Both mission parishes were active by 1930.

Calvary Lutheran Church also held worship in Hamilton Hall. In 1914 the congregation first held services in a small residence on Richard Avenue. Shortly thereafter, the church rented Hamilton Hall.[14] In 1917 the church purchased a lot at Roselawn Avenue. In 1919 the simple temple gable-end church was erected. In 1930 the church building was improved and enlarged. The church stayed until 1947, when they purchased a plot of land at Old Harford Road and Northern Parkway. And in 1951 the current church building was constructed.

First Presbyterian Church grew out of the Lauraville Presbyterian Church, which was organized in 1891. They first met at Hamilton Hall, and soon after in a structure located at 3019 Hamilton Avenue.[15] In 1911 they bought the lot at the southwest corner of Hamilton and Evergreen Avenues, which was dedicated in 1915. Later, the structure at 3019 Hamilton Avenue was turned into Hamilton's first movie house by retired Lauraville blacksmith, H.P. Mann.

The Church of the Messiah Episcopal Church originally was located in downtown Baltimore at the corner of Gay and Fayette Streets.[16] In 1921, they moved to their current location. Designed by Baltimore architects Mutto and White, the current church kept the furniture and a Tiffany window from the 1905 church. The new church was "designed to contain, besides the auditorium with platform on the main floor, a rector's study, assembly, choir rooms, Sunday school rooms, bowling alley, and a kitchen."

Throughout history, the church has always been the symbol of community. The church spire has always been a beacon of a neighborhood. In suburban development the same is true. A subdivision stays a subdivision until church structures physically and spiritually center a community. Communities are the extension of churches. The churches or religious centers are always the heart of the community. We do not go to Disney World to be married, to be baptized, to mourn the loss of a loved one, or to celebrate just "being alive." We do not go to Camden Yards to solve problems in our neighborhood, to find moral guidance, or to find strength to overcome personal problems. We go to our spiritual centers. It has always been, and it will always be.

Belair Road Mainstreet

Along Belair Road three crossroads villages grew into streetcar mainstreets: Georgetown, Gardenville, and Raspeburg. In addition, the Overlea neighborhood mainstreet grew out of the needs of the suburban community of Overlea. In 1894 above Herring Run, Belair Road had thirty-six businesses listed in the Gazetteer. By 1917 on Belair Road the number jumped to 117 listed occupations. By 1928, Polk's directory listed approximately 134 businesses north of Herring Run. Altogether, Belair Road harbored approximately 200 businesses by 1928.[17]

On the Belair Road north of Herring Run, the number of buildings jumped from approximately fifty-four in 1898 to 190 in 1914.[18] Interestingly, the Gazetteers of 1894, 1906, and 1912 suggest that the number of businesses along Belair increased, but there was no increase in the type of businesses. Nevertheless, the same occupations that decreased in number along Belair Road matched the same trend on Harford Road. The Maryland Gazetteers mapped out the changing crossroad villages, telling of the disappearance of agricultural business: fence makers, farmers, dairymen, and hucksters. In addition, blacksmiths, wagon builders, and wheelwrights slowly disappeared in the growing suburbia. And last, manufacturing such as brewing, cotton and flour mills, brickmaking, cloth factories, and shoemakers were all gone, making way for the picturesque suburbs. By 1917, Belair Road businesses were catering to the new communities.

In 1917 the Maryland Gazetteer described the Belair Road mainstreets of Gardenville, Raspeburg, and Overlea. At this time Georgetown was within Baltimore City, thus it was not listed in the Gazetteer. Much like Harford Road, the occupations were categorized into professions, building contractors, and retail. However, in 1917 the Belair communities of Gardenville and Raspeburg still held several truck farm professions. Although only one farmer was listed in 1917, eleven florists and four dairies were listed. In addition, there was one lumber company, and at least two quarries, many grocery stores, and saloons. No saloons were reported in the new mainstreet of Overlea. In Gardenville came Northeast's first automobile garage, opened by Joseph Lurman.

Later on, Belair Road invited automobile dealerships to locate on the corridor because of zoning and large parcels of land. By 1923, the Belair Road corridor was zoned completely for retail and wholesale businesses and light manufacturing. On the east side of Belair Road, from North Avenue to just north of Herring Run, was zoned for business and manufacturing.

In 1928, centered on Erdman Avenue, there were four grocery stores, two of which were chain stores. Drug stores, physicians, lawyers and banks were also estab-

An early Belair Road auto dealer, F. T. Gatch, supplied and serviced the automobiles of Northeast suburban residents, and the tractors of area farmers. Soon, many more automotive dealerships would compete along the Belair Road corridor. (Courtesy EPFL Maryland Room)

lished. Buildings were a mixture of rowhouse-type storefronts, and one-story Art Deco and Moderne commercial structures. Most interesting is the 3300 block of Belair Road. Here, the typical daylight rowhouse underlined the basic row. Nonetheless, the front porch was replaced by a one-story storefront. On top of the storefront was a balcony. This acted as a porchfront for the second floor apartment above the store. In this sense, the urban form of store with living space above has become suburbanized (but not very well). Subsequent additions have closed in the second-story porch front. These enclosures occurred concurrent with the widening and increased traffic of Belair Road. And further additions and renovations have combined some units or expanded restaurant space to the second floor while others have replaced porch columns with Ionic concrete columns—a common renovation on porch front rowhouses.

On Erdman Avenue, the last White Tower building used to stand. Along with much of the one-story Art Deco buildings, the White Tower opened in 1945. The chain came out of Milwaukee in 1926 as a direct imitation of its competitor, White Castle. By the mid-1950s there were 250 stores throughout the United States.[19] It was opened twenty-four hours, seven days a week and finally closed in the mid-1990s.

The Overlea movie house, located at 6805 Belair Road, opened in late 1927 and lasted until shortly after 1952. It seated five hundred persons.[20] The Earle, at 4847 Belair Road, was built by John Eyring. It opened in 1937 and seats 700 persons. Down in the mainstreet of Belair/Edison, the Vilma was also designed by John Erying and opened in 1928.[21] The Belmar (6313 Belair Road) grew up with the neighborhood and opened in 1920. It was only opened two days a week and probably closed down shortly after the larger theaters were built. The Paramount at 6650 Belair Road was built in 1946 and designed by architect Hal Miller, who designed many of the 1950s apartment houses around town.[22] In 1974 it was still operating, but closed down several years later.

Churches also lined Belair Road. Many of the churches were formed in the nineteenth century as village churches, but grew to accommodate the new communities. The Jerusalem Evangelical Lutheran Church, in the 1910s or 1920s, redesigned its front in a Gothic collegiate style. This remodeling transformed the church from a country parish to a city establishment. Gatch Memorial Methodist Church and St. Andrew's Memorial Methodist Church were outgrowths of the nineteenth century. Both churches added and reconfigured its shape in the 1920s. These churches were centered around the old village of Gardenville. St. Anthony of Padua Roman Catholic Church, established in 1885, grew significantly. In 1886, the church established a school. In 1889 a two-room school building was constructed, and in 1899 three more rooms were added. In 1924 prominent local architect Lucius White designed a school building with eight classrooms, an auditorium, and a school office.[23]

Just south of Gardenville, in newly entitled Belair Edison, Little May Flower Roman Catholic Church was built on the Erdman estate. Bethlehem Evangelical Lutheran Church, located in Belair Edison, was established in 1928. North of Gardenville, in 1908 Frederick Powel laid the cornerstone for the Increasing Light of the Epiphany Lutheran Church. The church expanded in 1923 with a design by Clyde and Nelson Friz. In Overlea, local architect Francis Tormey designed St. Michael's Church sometime around 1918.[24]

As the subdivisions were partially defined by their relationship to their mainstreets, the mainstreets were also defined by the subdivisions growing up around them. These subdivisions have become the neighborhoods of Baltimore.

1939 aerial photograph of Walther Avenue. (Photo by Fred Kniesshe, courtesy of the *Sun*)

DIVERSITY *in* CITY SUBURBIA: SUBDIVISIONS MATURE *into* NEIGHBORHOODS

BY THE BEGINNING of World War II, the hundred or so subdivisions coalesced into a menagerie of complementary neighborhoods. Though they shared shade under the suburban umbrella, Northeast's neighborhoods differed greatly. They varied in architecture styles, building types, streetscapes as well as social class, ethnicity, religious affiliation, and race. Much of their characteristics spawned from history, location, period of construction, and the developer's personality. However, each neighborhood's unique characteristics ultimately sprung from Baltimore. Northeast's neighborhoods—though suburban in many aspects—were Baltimore City neighborhoods. Only urban areas embody such diversity. Northeast neighborhoods are the city's suburbs.

Nevertheless, the creation of such diverse neighborhoods was predicated on interdependency between neighborhoods, mainstreets and Baltimore City. As the subdivisions matured into neighborhoods, each reflected and influenced the other. Eventually, many subdivisions lost their original developer-given names and merged with one another. The changing landscape slowly shifted boundaries of neighborhoods. Together, the neighborhoods typified the diversity of Baltimore, albeit segregated neighborhood by neighborhood.

Rowhouse Suburbs: Urban Forms in Suburban Clothing

By the turn of the twentieth century, Baltimore's ubiquitous icon was the rowhouse. Simply clad or bulging with Victorian doodads, Baltimore's rowhouse multiplied further and further into the hinterlands. The rowhouse was built for everyone, rich and poor, and sized accordingly. Small alley houses were built for first-generation immigrants as well as first-time homebuyers. Smaller two- and three-story rows flanked the streets of East and West Baltimore. In contrast, mansion rows were built in Mount Ver-

*Just the wee cot—the crickets' chirr—
Love and the smiling face of her.*
—JAMES WHITCOMB RILEY

E. J. Gallagher Realty Co.

MUNSEY BUILDING

Homewood 9596

A direct mail advertisement uses Romantic poetry to create an air of sophistication in this tiny Ravenwood rowhome. (Courtesy UB Archives Gallagher Collection)

non, Bolton Hill, and Reservoir Hill. Baltimore's signature was not just the rowhouse, but rows upon rows upon rows. The rowhouse became synonymous with urban living. Thus, a rowhouse suburb seems to be an oxymoron. Nonetheless, by the time the rowhouse ventured in force into Northeast Baltimore, it had no choice but to adapt.

Eighteenth-century Baltimore built one-story-plus attic rowhouses for the working class of Baltimore, Jonestown, and Fells Point. Between 1800 and the 1840s, carpenters built two-and-a-half story two-bay, gabled-roof rowhouses along the edge of the Inner Harbor. With a flat façade, gabled roof, and a pedimented dormer, these resembled the bigger Federal Period homes of the area. A major adaptation to these small rowhouses was the attic eyebrow windows. By adding two six-lighted windows, the pedimented dormer disappeared, the roof pitch decreased, and, consequently, much needed space was added as a third floor. After the Civil War, three-story rowhouses were being built for the middle and upper classes. By the 1860s this configuration was adapted to working class houses. The roof flattened into a slanted flat roof and the cornice became the ornamented centerpiece.

During the last three decades of the nineteenth century, rowhousing experienced an influx of many new materials and ornamental features such as bay windows, terra cotta blocks, decorative

Original advertising pamphlets for Montpelier homes showing front, rear, and interior details.
(Courtesy UB Archives Gallagher Collection)

Historic photo of houses facing Clifton Park in Belair-Edison. (Photo by James H. Lewis, courtesy of Jack Hennessy)

brickwork, yellow brown, and iron-spotted bricks. The massing of these eclectic rows resembled the basic massing of the earlier rows, but decorated themselves differently. During the 1910s, the rowhouse massing grew wider and shorter. Through several years the massing transformed into what is known as the "daylight house." Twelve- or fourteen-feet wide houses grew to twenty- or twenty-two-feet wide. This transformation occurred to shorten and widen the structure in order to eliminate dark center rooms. They went from three rooms deep to two rooms deep and two rooms wide. The transformation into daylight housing directly corresponded to the growth of rowhouse neighborhoods in borderland truck farm and suburban areas.

In addition to changing its shape, the rowhouse added suburban characteristics in various ways. The rowhouse neighborhoods of Northeast Baltimore illustrate the change of the rowhouse, and conversely how the rowhouse changed Northeast Baltimore.

South Clifton Park

South Clifton Park, located between North Avenue and Clifton Park and between Washington Street and Belair Road, was built between 1896 and 1906 in the old village of San Domingo. The construction of rowhouses vanquished the village of San Domingo by extending Baltimore's urban center beyond North Avenue. The development of duplexes and two types of rowhouses illustrated this change from a suburban to urban neighborhood.

Before the urban grid jumped over North Avenue, the area was a mixture of marble yards, breweries, and suburban residences lining North Avenue. The first phase of urbanization was the development of duplexes on Washington Street. Built between 1892 and 1896, the duplexes were a mitigated architectural response between rowhouse and detached house. This architectural form was extremely appropriate as a transition streetscape from rural Clifton Park to the urban grid south of North Avenue. Washington Street at the time—not Broadway—connected the southern portion of Clifton Park to East Baltimore. It was the gateway to Clifton Park. Economically, the duplexes were again a compromise between urban efficiency and suburban desire. Developers could double the density of detached suburban housing, while building a suburban streetscape.

Next, narrow two-story Italianate style houses with the ubiquitous marble steps were built on Pearlman and Patterson Streets during the first decade of the twentieth century. These houses were built for the working class and in all aspects were extensions of the neighborhoods south of North Avenue. With the presence of Pearlman and Patterson Streets, the older suburban-like setting vanished. However, the next type of rowhouse built just west of Patterson Street during the second decade of the twentieth century made a conscious effort to look suburban. These homes dropped their marble steps and replaced them with the porchfront. Porchfront rowhouses laid out on the urban grid in the same density as their Perlman Street cousins did little to suburbanize the rowhouse neighborhood. Nevertheless, the porchfront was a major step towards the suburban rowhouse neighborhood.

Coldstream-Homestead-Montebello

This neighborhood gained its name from the great American tradition of naming subdivisions after the estates demolished by the developer. Although suburbanization began in 1852, the neighborhood was not completely developed until the 1920s. Coldstream-Homestead-Montebello derived its character from the incredible mix of residential building types and styles. The neighborhood, primarily a rowhouse suburb, retained much of Homestead's nineteenth-century housing. The mixture of the historic nineteenth-century Victorian cottages with over a dozen rowhouse designs, created an odd, though common, early twentieth-century suburban character.

Unlike the purely planned suburbs such as Roland Park and Sudbrook Park, most suburban areas were a constantly changing environment made up of the old, new, and a sense of becoming. Dozens of players made hundreds of little decisions, which changed the neighborhood from a rural to a suburban to an urban landscape. By 1923, the comprehensive zoning ordinance crowned the area a rowhouse community. The first large wave of rowhouse development occurred in 1913:

> The development along the Harford Road is twofold—City and Suburban. There are along its pathway within the city's limits some of the choicest tracts for development in Baltimore today...
>
> The Rochester-Kirkness Realty Company is now rapidly progressing in the development of this property. Its plans are different radically from Mr. Novak's proposed scheme, and conform more to the distinctly city style of house. The first installment of dwellings to be put up by the company are along the Harford Road. Perhaps the finest thoroughfare in the development will be Alameda Avenue, a broad and smooth road, which comprises a portion of the Park-to-Park Boulevard plan.[1]

The first of the rowhouses were built at the 2700 and 2800 blocks of Harford Road. According to plans by Architect C.W. McKewin, the rowhouses contained seven rooms and a bath. The houses were equipped with the latest fixtures for gas and electricity. T. H. Disney built thirteen other houses in the 2000 block of Rob Street. E. J. Gallagher also built many of the homes, including many centered around Homestead Street, near Darley Avenue.

These houses were not considered daylight housing. They had the same massing as older Baltimore rowhouses. In between rowhouse units long exterior halls or alleys were punched inward from the rear façade. Known as "areaways" they allowed for the middle of the rowhouse to receive light. Nevertheless, these rowhouses did suburbanize themselves with porchfronts, and rather large front lawns. Also, the houses stylized their front façades with bay windows, crenellation, and turrets. Many of the porches were built on a foundation of fieldstone, instead of "urbany" brick.

In 1914 The Alameda was laid out. Shortly thereafter, large-scale rowhouse developer E. J. Gallagher built porchfront housing with front yards.[2] These houses were designed without "areaways" and with several suburban design elements. Finally, right after World War I, along 32nd Street and in pockets of undeveloped land in the neighborhood, full-fledge daylight houses were constructed. The daylight house fashioned itself with parapet edges that visually separated each unit, a front lawn, field stone, a porchfront, and a green-tiled faux double-hipped roof. These elements together visually detached the suburban rowhouse from its urban ancestor.

Coldstream-Homestead-Montebello, though a mixture of different style rowhouses and nineteenth-century Victorian structures, created a unique neighborhood that still retains a suburban flare. The next rowhouse suburb is a medley of suburban rowhouse styles.

Belair-Edison

Belair-Edison streetscapes are rarely tarnished with detached housing.[3] Except in a few places, the rowhouse muscled all detached housing from the streets. Remarkably, dozens of developers independently built one of Baltimore's most cohesive rowhouse suburbs. More astonishing, the period of development ranged from 1916 to the 1950s. Although laid out on the urban grid, and similar in density and massing to inner-city rowhouse communities, Belair-Edison is different. Belair Edison is Northeast's quintessential rowhouse suburb.

Builders of Belair-Edison worked in a rich tradition of ornamenting rowhouses. Most of the architects that peddled the rowhouse artistry were professionally trained; the builders of Belair-Edison were not. Thus Belair-Edison's designers freely and creatively mixed and matched architectural features in ways that were not constricted by a formal training in architecture. The upscale suburban neighborhoods like Roland Park gave Belair-Edison's builders an architectural vocabulary in which to work. Two architectural styles, as Walter Leon of the Commission for Historical and Architectural Preservation pointed out in CHAP's 1994 historic resources survey of Belair-Edison, dominated Belair-Edison's rowhouses: the Italianate Style and the Colonial Revival. In addition, other stylistic features were used from the Craftsmen style to Queen Anne style. The architectural details of Belair-Edison rowhouses were stripped down versions of the "high-style" (and high cost) architecture. They enlivened the streetscapes of Belair-Edison.

Before ornamenting Belair-Edison, the Italianate style fashioned much of nineteenth-century Baltimore. More than the bulging asymmetrical Victorian styles, it settled nicely next to the older classical-styled rowhouses. In the Italianate style, the cornice grew in size and obtained scroll-sawn brackets, modillions, and ventilator panels

Different architectural rowhouse styles as seen in Belair-Edison.
(Photos by Walter Leon, courtesy of CHAP Archives)

while the roof changed from a gable to a slanted flat roof. Ornamental features capped windows. The second and third stories were articulated on the front façade by a belt course. The basement was an articulated marble foundation. More than any other architectural feature, the cornice on the Baltimore rowhouse defined the Italianate style. In addition to a stylistic feature, the cornice also had a utilitarian use. Baltimore City fire codes demanded a firewall that was higher than the roofline. Therefore, the builders sloped the roof towards the back while raising the front façade higher than the roof. Vernacular builders copped the Italianate style by copying the cornice. The cornice also came to be the builder's unique mark on the rowhouse. It was the developer's way of initializing their buildings. On any given streetscape in any rowhouse neighborhood, counting the different cornice designs can identify the number of developers. The same is true in Belair-Edison.

Belair-Edison's early rowhouses inherited the Italianate style in two general ways: a blocky projecting cornice, or a green-tiled faux double-hipped roof that copped the suburban foursquare look. This time, though, the style was blended into a suburban streetscape of porchfronts, fieldstone foundations, and lawns.

The second style prevalent was the Colonial Revival style. Here, the developers replaced the Italianate cornice with a gabled roof. Door surrounds and windows were fashioned with classical details. In addition, several rows were designed as an harmonious whole with cross gables at each end. This style was built in the 1930s after the popular reconstruction of Colonial Williamsburg. The Colonial Revival houses in Homeland also influenced the developers of Belair-Edison.

Although Belair-Edison's developers weren't building for Baltimore's elite, they influenced Baltimore's architectural drapery. The three largest Belair-Edison developers cumulatively built over fifty thousand homes in and around Baltimore. The architects in Homeland may have had influence regarding house design, but E. J. Gallagher, Frank Novak, and Ephraim Macht built more of Baltimore than any other developers. Only James Rouse can be said to have had more influence on the shape and design of our region.

E.J. Gallagher was the first large-scale developer in Belair-Edison. Between 1919 and 1926, Gallagher developed thirty-three rows of housing north of Sinclair Lane and east of Belair Road. Known early on as the four-by-four neighborhood, it was the first rowhouse development in the area. Here the housing was the typical porchfront front lawn housing. These houses, however, were not of daylight width. Nevertheless, they had all the trimmings of a suburban rowhouse.

Gallagher pulled the row back from the street and planted a front yard. This allowed for a large green swathe throughout the streetscape. Furthermore, the residents owned the front yards. They had control over the plantings. This differed greatly from the inner-city rowhouses in which a green swathe separated the sidewalk from the street and was owned by the City. Needless to say the green swathe was extremely wider in Belair-Edison than the other developments in the inner city. Secondly, Gallagher replaced the marble steps with a front porch made out of field stone. The field stone symbolized the country whereas the marble symbolized the city. Gallagher visually emphasized each rowhouse with parapet edges, the chimney-like brick details that protrude beyond the cornice. They acted to differentiate each house, while again, in the city the Italianate houses did not separate themselves with an architectural detail.

In terms of space the front porch acted as an outside room. The suburban ideal emphasized privacy while in the city all exterior space was communal. Therefore, the front porch and front lawn acted as a buffer zone from public and private space. Stoop sitters by the very nature of being on the sidewalk must act within the public theater. Porchfront sitters can choose to be an observer or a participant. In addition, the small front lawn also pulled the porchfront further from the street scene. Finally many porchfronts today have been turned into sunrooms.

Gallagher also provided several interior innovations as well as selling techniques. Gallagher built not a kitchen but a kitchenette in the houses in the four-by-four area. The kitchenette was organized as a cooking zone where "everything" was in the reach of the cook. Gallagher described the kitchen as being "beautifully papered... amply large and the arrangement of the range, sink and cabinet made to save many steps for the housewife." Gallagher thought much like early twentieth-century progressive thinkers that viewed the house as a sophisticated machine. Gallagher introduced the breakfast nook into the rowhouse, promoting to potential buyers that "the breakfast room adjoining the living room and dining room is one of the newest developments in the construction of homes of moderate cost."[4] Most significantly, Gallagher expanded the home downward into the basement by pouring a concrete slab. Again, this innovation was full of foresight, as we see the development of the club basement in later years. Along with Gallagher, who championed the affordable rowhouse and couched it in a suburban architectural vocabulary, two other major developers began building in Belair-Edison—Frank Novak and Ephraim Macht.

Frank Novak brought to Belair-Edison the full-fledged daylight house. He developed most of the houses directly north and south of Herring Run. Novak's housing was a stripped down version of the Italianate style: beige-colored brick, wide rowhouses, and sheet metal Italianate cornices. He built kitchenettes and front porches, pulled the row back from the street, and also introduced the garage to the neighborhood. Novak used thin second-story bay windows, and a combination of Italianate styles and Tudor details.

On Shannon Drive, he replaced the porchfronts with an enclosed sun room, and fashioned the front entrance with an Italianate hood—all looking out towards the park. Another innovation Novak brought to the neighborhood was the small mansard-like roof. Many have green tiles that mimic the Italian Renaissance style seen on many detached houses in Northeast Baltimore. Also, they mimic the very popular foursquare.

Ephraim Macht, owner of the Welsh Construction Company, introduced the Colonial Revival style into the neighborhood. These houses mimicked the Georgian revival houses found in Roland Park. The ends of these rows are capped with cross gable dormers, making the whole row one architectural design. These were built just before and after World War II and differ from the earlier houses.

By World War II the porchfront diminished into a concrete slab enclosed by a thin metal rail. The demise of the porchfront rowhouse in Baltimore followed a national trend set into motion by the growing dependence upon the automobile. When Gallagher built his "four by four neighborhood," the workers relied on streetcars to carry them to and from work, shopping, and play. By the time Macht was building in the area, the automobile was the main means of transportation. This changed the resident's relationship with the street. The street was no longer dominated by pedestrians, young and old playing street games. The street was for the car, which doesn't mix easily with stickball. Secondly, the radio and finally the television competed with the front porch. Thus, Belair-Edison residents found the street "theater of characters" usurped by cars, radio, and television. People parking became less interesting to watch than television. In short, people stopped sitting on front porches, and Macht stopped building them. They became an entranceway into the house. Meanwhile, other changes occurred to accommodate the car.

The alleys changed. When Gallagher built his rowhouses, he didn't make accommodations for the automobile. When the residents finally bought a car, they also bought a prefabricated garage sold by Sears, Wards, or the local hardware store. Many of these structures still exist. They are made of sheet metal with the low sloping gable roof. In addition, some homeowners bought concrete block and built their own garages. In a matter of five years developers caught on to the necessity of the car and began building detached garages out of brick. In fact, in many alleys, one side is a mishmash of garages built by residents, and the other side is uniform—built by developers.

Belair-Edison, one of the City's largest rowhouse communities, encompasses not only rows of houses but several churches, remnants of Georgetown, a library, a shopping center, many industrial buildings, several cemeteries, and Clifton and Herring Run Park. Although the neighborhood contains buildings built between the 1830s to the 1970s, it is a viable cohesive Baltimore City neighborhood.

The Cottage and the Bungalow Prevail: Pre-World War I Neighborhoods

Mayfield

Mayfield is Northeast's only pre-World War I cottage bungalow neighborhood built within the 1888 city limits. At the turn of the twentieth century several wealthy families owned most of the land couched between Herring Run, Clifton Park, and Lake Montebello. The land was dotted with truck gardens and hot houses (or "greenhouses"). Nonetheless, with the electrification of the streetcar, and the establishment of Herring Run and Clifton Park, Mayfield became ripe for suburban development. Today, the area is a mixture of six periods of residential architecture, three residential building types, and two periods of landscape architecture. In addition, five churches were built within the neighborhood. As a whole, Mayfield is one of Baltimore's most diverse, yet intact and cohesive neighborhood.

Nineteenth-century farmhouses first nestled in between the large summer estates and Lake Montebello. However, with the 1888 annexation came slow development of parcels lining Harford Road. By 1896, west of Harford Road, fifteen detached houses and two duplexes were constructed.[5] The old Erdman farmstead was built before 1877 with a beautiful Victorian bracketed porch. Built in the I-house form it was stylized with the typical Rural Gothic center gable. The porch was removed before 1926 and replaced with a simple Colonial Revival entranceway. Most likely this remodeling occurred around 1911 when Harford Road was widened. The other nineteenth-century houses varied from small worker houses, duplexes, and large suburban residences that sat next to working ten-acre truck gardens. All the suburban houses were built on the west side of Harford Road. The next development was a comprehensive attempt to build an elite neighborhood.

Around 1905, a quiet but adventuresome judge saw the advantage of a subur-

One of the original homes in Mayfield.
(Author's photo)

Diversity in City Suburbia 197

The homes at 2108–2116 Kentucky Avenue are large Victorian cottages built prior to 1914. (Author's photo)

ban neighborhood in the area. In 1908 Judge John J. Dobler bought a tract of land from Mary Garrett, laid out Mayfield Avenue, and built a house. Here, Erdman and Mayfield Avenues were showcases of large upper-class suburban mansions. 2200 Erdman Avenue exemplifies the story of many of the suburban mansions on Erdman and Mayfield Avenue. On March 14, 1913, John Dobler sold the tract of land to John Bauernschmidt of the beer baron family. In the deed, like all others, restrictions of land use were unequivocally spelled out:

> The sale of the land is subject to the following conditions "no residence or dwelling house or other structures shall be erected or kept on said land wholly or partly within 25 feet of Erdman Avenue. There shall not at any time within twenty years from the date hereof be more than one residence or dwelling house erected on said land and that no house to be erected on said land shell ever be used as a factory or as a beer saloon nor for the sale of spirituous or malt liquors of any kind whatsoever. No house to be built on said land shall cost less than $5,000."[6]

These restrictions did two things for both the buyer and seller. First, the seller was insured that he would sell his lots to the upper middle class (thus receiving more profit) and secondly, the buyers were insured that their neighbors would be from the upper middle class. It worked for this single block. Deed covenants were a common practice in many of the late nineteenth- and early twentieth-century suburbs. They were the predecessors of zoning.

Today, the houses on Erdman and Mayfield Streets from Harford Road to Norman Avenue are Northeast Baltimore's largest collection of high style suburban architecture.

The Bauernschmidt Mansion, built by John Bauernschmidt around 1913, is obviously an architect-designed home that encompasses various architectural styles. (Author's photo)

For example, the Bauernschmidt house stands as one of Baltimore's most uniquely designed structures. The design marks the transition in architecture between the Victorian era and the mass-produced houses of the 1920s. The house, which is predominantly a foursquare in shape, is detailed with a variety of architectural ornamentation. The chimneys and gables resemble English architecture at the time of Maryland and Virginia colonization. The brick arcaded porch breaks up the foursquare massing and adds a horizontal dimension to the structure. The brick balustrade on top of the porch arcade borrows proportions from classical architecture, but the building materials are from American Arts and Crafts movement. Only during a transitional period could a house be designed with such diverse detailing.

On the west side of Harford Road before World War I Atlantic (Kentucky) and Lake avenues were developed with large Victorian cottages and duplexes. Also lining Harford Road were typical urban rowhouses and small urban style duplexes. The change in building type and design also illustrated the boundaries of land ownership. Many decisions culminated in creating a mixed-class suburban neighborhood. Mayfield is the product of hundreds of development decisions and not a comprehensive plan.

After World War I the largest building boom occurred. Streets were developed with the typical 1920s bungalows, duplexes, and cottages, most of which followed

This home in the 2200 block of Mayfield Avenue is a grand example of High-Style architecture found on Judge Dobler's original subdivision. (Author's photo)

zoning regulations. The financing for these houses usually was secured from small-time building and loan associations. Judge Dobler's lots were mostly financed by the German Savings and Loan Association. The other properties were financed by a myriad of other building and loan associations. By the 1920s many of the house lots were erected by several different builders, while the land was controlled and dished out by a few land speculators. This mix-match of financing and the weaving of builders created an eclectic mix of house styles. Much like the rowhouse builders who "signed" their row by the cornice design, developers chose their signature suburban design.

Mayfield is Northeast Baltimore's only detached suburban development built on the urban grid. Bisecting alleys are the city's largest stamp on the neighborhood. All other Northeast neighborhoods—although several had alleys—were not built on a grid pattern. Mayfield's street pattern orderliness was the result of the city's Municipal Annex Street Plan started as early as 1888. North of Herring Run along the Harford Road, developers deliberately skewed the grid or abandoned it altogether. Mayfield is the gateway from the urban rowhouse landscape into the twentieth-century city suburb. Moreover, it marks the transition from "city" design to suburban design. From Erdman Avenue, looking south one sees the attentive rowhouse. Looking north, one sees the ubiquitous gabled roof dispersed between trees.

Large subdivisions were laid out during the first two decades of the twentieth century. By the beginning of the 1918 annexation there were over thirty-four subdivisions. The street layout was oriented towards Harford and Belair Roads. The streets were mostly macadamized and the houses were hooked up to wells and septic tanks. The first houses were usually built on double lots with large three-story cottages or foursquares. Architecture styles differed greatly as many of the houses were architect designed. Today many of these neighborhoods are a mixture of large houses on double lots and small cottages and bungalows of the 1920s. Many neighborhoods have paved and unpaved alleys as well as detached garages. Several of the older homes have two-story stable garages. Also interestingly, the older pre-World War I subdivisions occupy the tops of hills offering expansive views. Hence, the many names donned with "terrace" and "heights."

Lauraville

By 1915 Lauraville consisted of several subdivisions. On the west side of Harford Road Lauraville consisted of Montebello Park, Lauraville Park, Ailsa Terraces, and Ailsa Heights. On the east side of Harford Road, Lauraville consisted of Echodale Terrace, Rosekemp, and Richard Estates. As early as 1898 lots were being laid out. However, as subdivisions sprung up along Walther Avenue in the 1920s, the west side of Harford Road lost its affiliation with Lauraville. These Walther Avenue-inspired subdivisions became new entities, and Lauraville neighborhood boundaries shrunk to only encompass the west side of Harford Road.

Lauraville's first subdivision occurred by 1898, one block west of Harford Road on Grindon Avenue. Here only eleven single-family homes and five duplexes were constructed. Interestingly, these were the only duplexes developed before World War I. In addition, Echodale Terrace was laid out on the estate of the Van Reuth family just east of Harford Road. By 1914 several houses lined Echodale, Batavia, and Rueckert Roads.[7]

Directly north of Montebello Park was Ailsa Terraces. Ailsa Terrace was laid out by realtors Webb and White on the Nicholson's summer estate. By 1910, the street was in full swing. These houses were built with close supervision from the residents themselves. A *News American* article of March 26, 1910, specifically mentioned the owners and identified them as the builders: August Famme, Herbert C. Aiken, Charles H. Carroll, Joseph T. Martin, R.S. Wrightson, F. K. Rogers, Harry Mason, and Webb & White. These houses were commodious and cost an exorbitant $4,000, well above the average price of $1,200. Developers Webb & White not only laid out the lots of Ailsa Terrace, but also Westphal Lawn in Hamilton, Hilltop in Mt. Washington, Forest Park in Northwest Baltimore, and another development in Florida.

The development that occupies most of current-day Lauraville was Montebello Park.

Guided by deep pockets and the business savvy of Ephraim Macht, who had been building rowhouses since 1891, Montebello Park quickly became a hit. Montebello Park first opened its doors to development in 1913:

Original 1913 ad. (Courtesy of CHAP Archives)

> The newest and possibly the lustiest of the suburban developments in this section is Montebello Park, owned and operated by interests identified with Ephraim Macht. Montebello Park has just about completed its first Anniversary. It was purchased early last spring and was open for the sale of lots in April.
>
> One point that makes a great deal for the impressiveness and prosperity of any development is the quick improvement by purchasers of the lots they have bought. A suburb may be well sold, and yet if there are no outward and visible signs of sales in the presence of houses completed and building the effect is apt to be a little forlorn. Montebello Park escaped this appearance of desolation. Aside from its well-laid and kept roads and sidewalks, numerous cottages have made their appearance within the year. An official census taken the other day gave the number as 30.[8]

Overland and Montebello Terrace Roads were developed first. Here, all the houses were built on double lots. Although Macht was selling lots for smaller houses, these roads were developed with larger houses for the upper middle class. This is typical of

2809 Montebello Terrace. This house draws from characteristics of the bungalow, cottage, and four square. (Author's photo)

most development in Northeast Baltimore. The Northeast Baltimore suburbs were still out of financial reach of the middle class. In the 1920s, with the help of Baltimore City, Lauraville saw the solid middle class lay claim to lots and build a menagerie of bungalows and small cottages. Here Lauraville Park, built two blocks away from Harford Road, began to be developed, this time with slightly smaller houses.

At the turn of the twentieth century Lauraville was an agricultural community with no specific boundaries. It was the community that centered on the Harford Road from Herring Run to Hamilton. After World War II and with many subdevelopments laying claim to old farmsteads, the community of Lauraville shrunk into a neighborhood. Today the neighborhood encompasses the subdivisions of Montebello Park, Lauraville Park, and Ailsa Terraces. In 1940, the area encompassed 724 houses.[9] Today the number is slightly higher.

Hamilton

Hamilton developed much like Lauraville, but bandied together at Hamilton and Harford Roads. It was developed on a much larger scale containing approximately ten subdivisions. The scale of development during 1900 to 1919 surpassed Lauraville. The subdivisions moved further away from Harford Road making significant entryways along Hamilton Avenue. The developers of Hamilton specifically marketed to the growing white-collar workers:

> The aim has been to realize a development of moderate price, without unnecessary embellishments but with all the essentials for comfortable living, which will be within the reach of very modest incomes.

All ten subdivisions aimed their advertisements at the growing middle class.

Evergreen Lawn was the first subdivision in the area. In 1905, Dr. Wegefarth, a local landowner, began selling lots located off Evergreen Road, one block north of Hamilton Avenue and one block west of Harford Road. Eight years later, the *American News* stated the following:

Diversity in City Suburbia 203

Historic photo of Hamilton houses. (Courtesy of CHAP Archives)

> At Hamilton there is the extensive improvement of the Evergreen Lawn Company, which under the capable management of Dr. George C. Wege-farth, has evolved a suburb that is second to none in its own particular class.[10]

The average cost was between $2,750 to $4,000. Houses that cost $2,750 were built in six weeks after purchase. Several financing options were available, including purchase cost of $1,750 with an annual ground rent of sixty dollars. Typical houses had five rooms on the first floor: a reception hall, parlor, dining room, kitchen, and pantry. The kitchen contained an enamel sink, a "range," and modern plumbing. The second floor contained three bedrooms and one bath. The attic space had room for two extra bedrooms. The homes were rigged with "handsome combination fixtures" for gas burners or electric light.[11] Shortly thereafter, other subdivisions quickly took off, especially after the announcement of the Harford Road state-funded improvements.

In addition to local developer Dr. Wegefarth, other local residents of the pre-suburban era entered into the development game. John H. Tames became president of the Grindon Building Association. In the beginning, they met every week in Dressel's Store. Also, the Hamilton Building Association was established with Joseph Dunn as presi-

Eclectic mix of architectural details at 2700 block of Evergreen Avenue. Note the gambrelled roof, bay window, and enclosed porch. (Author's photo)

dent. Local builders were Gustav Runge, John F. Neidhardt, Lewis Mulsky, James Vanburen, William Proctor and Son, and Grant German.[12]

By World War I, Echodale Terrace, Altoona Park, Royston, and Westphal Lawn all abutted the east side of Harford Road. Further east and in between Harford and Belair Roads were Hamilton Park in two sections and the Ciconia development. On the west side was Evergreen Lawn, Hamilton Addition, and Idlewild. Together, prior to World War I local builders built over five hundred houses. Between the wars, the number at least quintupled. The *New Era Towson* in 1914 pegged the population of Hamilton at 4,000 (most likely an exaggeration). Nonetheless, by 1914 it surpassed all other northeast communities in size.

After World War II, with the onslaught of suburban expansion out into the counties and the slow devolution of the Hamilton mainstreet, neighborhood associations popped up within the old limits of Hamilton. Today, the Hamilton mainstreet is the convergence of the surrounding neighborhood associations: Glenham Belford, Waltherson, Lauraville, and Harford-Echodale-Perring Parkway. In fact, the Hamilton Business District centers on the four corners of these neighborhood associations. Hamilton

Original house in the "chicken coop suburb" of Woodhome. (Author's photo)

as an official neighborhood name disappeared off the city planners 1990 map. Today, it is an official urban renewal commercial revitalization district. Nevertheless, Hamilton is the historic name—a name used most often for folks living off the Harford Road and between Echodale and Northern Parkway.

Woodhome Heights

Another pre-annexation development on the Harford Road was Woodhome Heights. However, Woodhome Heights added an extra angle to suburban development. Picking up on the particular rural attributes of suburban development, Woodhome Heights advertised itself as prime lots and location for chicken raising and gardening. Prior to World War II several subdivisions advertised themselves as "chicken farms." California Grove, just a half-mile up Harford Road, was marketed as lots for chicken farms. The desire to build little farms for city-centered suburbanites was part of the back-to-the-land-movement. Here, as the country transformed into a more industrial society, rural living was touted as morally superior to urban living. Thus, this movement emphasized rural attributes as refreshing the soul. Needless to say, the labor and work of even one acre proved not to refresh anybody's soul, but to exhaust the city worker.

Developed by Theodore Messerschmidt and Kohlstead, Woodhome was located north of the proposed Northern Parkway just below Parkville.[13] It began in 1910 with approximately forty-nine one-acre lots. The first couple of years saw little development. By World War I there were approximately eleven homes on the site. Among the first six residents to erect a home, five built cottages while one built a bungalow. By 1913 the *Sun* real estate section highlighted Woodhome Heights:

> We offer you acre lots surrounded by homes worth from $2500 to $5000 within walking distance of 5-cent fare. Each Acre has a frontage of 100 feet on macadamized Forest Avenue, and a depth of over 400 feet. Fine size for bungalow or cottage, giving plenty of ground for chickens and gardening.[14]

Most of the development occurred after urban amenities were insured through annexation. By the end of the 1920s Woodhome Heights was one subdivision amongst many that straddled Harford Road. In addition, Woodhome Heights on the East began to visually merge with the expansion and development of Overlea. After World War II, in the 1950s, Woodring Road was laid out and brick duplexes were built in mass. This subdivision usurped the older neighborhood name. Today, the North Harford Road and Woodring associations identify this area.

Overlea

On the Belair Road corridor, subdevelopment began not near the city, but at the northern end of 1918 city limits. Overlea was a well thought-out development that straddled the 1918 city/county lines. First conceived around 1910 the subdivision was laid out between Raspeburg and Fullerton villages. A 1911 *Sun* article featured the young suburb:

> Situated on the high ground just east of the Belair Road at the terminus of the car line and overlooking miles of beautiful countryside, is Overlea Park. As one enters Overlea Park by its main thoroughfare, Willow Avenue, he is struck by the beauty and extent of the view afforded. He sees across and beyond the suburb proper and beholds luxuriant cornfields and meadows and woodlands, and circling all, in the distance, a range of hills which lend an almost mountainous touch to the landscape.
>
> The Overlea Park tract comprises some 14 acres, which are divided into building lots of various sizes. On Willow Avenue the lots have a frontage of 25 feet by a depth of 150 feet. On Madeline Avenue the depth is much greater. Most purchasers, however, are not content with buying one lot, they buy several.
>
> Willow Avenue is the most prominent thoroughfare, forty-eight feet wide it stretches, inclusive of sidewalks. The roadbed proper is of fine macadam; the sidewalks are of concrete, and so are the gutters. Other prominent avenues are Linden, which intersects, and Madeline, which parallels.[15]

The article goes on to state that electricity is available, but it is a "pilgrimage" to obtain. Nevertheless, sewage is readily available. The first purchasers, as mentioned were

Above: Historic photo of the Overlea area (1912 or 1913). (Courtesy of CHAP Archives)
Below: 3900 block of Northern Parkway, Overlea. (Author's photo)

small-time builders. Sumner and Gerlach bought six lots on Willow Avenue, Alfred Cross bought two lots on Madeline Avenue, C. Strobel acquired four lots on Willow Avenue, and William Salchuner bought three lots on Madeline Avenue. At the beginning, Overlea was laid out by a citywide developer, but built on speculation by local small-time builders and several residents building their dream.

Very quickly Overlea expanded into a suburban community. By 1918 when the community was divided between city and county municipalities, the area comprised approximately fifteen subdivisions, and engulfed Fullerton and Raspeburg into their new bedroom community. Not as developed as Hamilton by World War I, the area surpassed Harford Road in density and development activity shortly thereafter. These large developments were engineered by large-scale developers, Kennard and Company and Henry Kolb being the most prolific:

> The Overlea group comprises an important section of the Belair road developments and is composed of Overlea proper, South Overlea and Overlea Park. Kennard and Co. were the developers of the original Overlea, and South Overlea. Overlea Park is the development of Henry Kolb...
>
> About 700 building sites have been sold at the Original Overlea, and more than 200 houses have been build. Its younger adjunct, south Overlea, which has been laid out in 710 building sites...[16]

Overlea became the largest community to straddle the city/county boundaries. Even today, the neighborhood association draws from both city and county residents.

These pre-annexation developments started the momentum of sprawling Northeast bedroom communities. Nevertheless, their most defining quality was the open land that was diminishing year by year. This fleeting quality of suburbia captured not only beautiful vistas but also suburbia's "sense of becoming." On Northeast's fields laid the future reality of a developer's dream, subsequently marketed and sold to homeowners. Suburban developers were not building a "city upon a hill," but houses placed in a diminishing bucolic landscape.

Suburbs Built Under the City's Annexation Policy

Between the wars, Northeast's suburbanization accelerated as developers broadened their market to a wider audience. The first activity after World War I was the continual building in older subdivisions. Second, development activity occurred on those subdivisions laid out before World War I, but not developed. And third was large tract developments. The biggest change was the diminishing size of house and lot. Here marks the great expansion of middle-class Baltimore. Partnering with developers was the city with its constructions of schools, firehouses, and playgrounds. As a result, open land disappeared. Suburbia was losing its precious evanescent quality.

As developers engulfed large tracts of land, they also inherited sporadic splotches of earlier development. Mostly on the edges and near the Harford and Belair Roads, big and small suburban homes were built. As the new subdivision grew into a neighborhood, these edge areas became affiliated with the modern subdivision. They became part and parcel of the neighborhood association.

Arcadia

> The name Arcadia comes to us out of Greek history. Arcadia was a mountainous and picturesque district of Greece Inhabited by a simple pastoral people, distinguished for contentment And rural happiness. Hence, figuratively, any region or scene of simple pleasure, rustic innocence and untroubled quiet. How appropriate as the name for our beautiful locality, and the name of our association which has made the improvements possible (written in 1938 Arcadia History).
>
> —*Sun*, October 28, 1913[17]

Arcadia comprises three distinct development periods: the Heckel family and Eutaw Heights, post-World War I development of Arcadia, and post-World War II Eastwood Drive and infill development. Though these periods differ significantly in house type and design, they make up a cohesive neighborhood. The first era of development was between 1898 and 1914 and center around the Heckel family on Heckel Avenue. Between the late 1880s and mid-1890s Gottleib Heckel, a cobbler on Gay Street moved his family into a log cabin located near today's Parkside Drive and Prior Avenue. Shortly thereafter, they bought nineteen and one-half acres of the eastern portion of Eutaw Farm tract. Gottleib Heckel started building Eutaw Avenue (which became Parkside) from Belair Road to the farm around 1895. In 1902 he laid out and built Heckel Avenue as his driveway. His son, Charles Heckel, described growing up in Arcadia:

> ...and let me tell you it was a fine place. We lived a good life there, a life of bounty. There were tons of vegetables and fruits, plenty of meat and eggs and milk. Herring Run was loaded with Fish. There were berries of every kind too. And better than that, there were chestnuts. They would fall off the trees at night and in the morning before breakfast my brothers and I would gather them by the basket.[18]

Charles at the age of sixteen entered into the carpentry and masonry business. By the 1890s, the Heckel family opened a sand and stone quarry that catered to the local builders.

Three-dimensional billboard welcomed visitors to the new development of Arcadia. (Photo by James Lewis, courtesy of Jack Hennessy)

By 1898, the Hall's estate and gristmill were abandoned. In 1902 the Heckels sold two lots to Dr. Giering and built for him the field stone house on the north side of Parkside. The driveway to the Giering's stone house became Harris Street. Between 1898 and 1914 forty-nine single and duplex houses were built. By 1914 much of "Eutaw Heights" was constructed.

Arcadia was officially created on March 28, 1914:

> Another new development in the northeastern section will be the result of a recent purchase by R. Stanley Carswell, who has bought a tract of 41 acres binding on the north side of the property acquired by the city for a park between the Harford and Belair Roads, Including all of the Herring Run Valley.
>   The tract is located so as to overlook all of this park, Lake Montebello and a large portion of the city and surrounding country. It is covered with a fine growth of original timber. Which will be thinned out to give the best effect and the streets will be laid as to enhance the natural beauty of the location.
>   The work of clearing, grading and improving the streets, laying of drain and sewer pipes and cement sidewalks will be pushed this summer, and the tract should be ready for development in the early fall and will be improved by high class cottages, for which purpose the location on a direct car line with a running time of 25 minutes to the City Hall and a five cent fare adapts it.[19]

The Arcadia Improvement Association formed in 1923 in order to address the many issues that plagued the growing suburbs. By 1923 the area looked different than the bucolic scene painted by Heckel's words. In 1938 Arcadia was described as follows:

> What I found In Arcadia, 'the land of ideal conditions' in March 1921, was open ditches cut through the woods for roads; no pavements or side walks; no mail boxes; water piped over ground; oil stoves for cooking—no gas; mosquito breeding swamps in lowlands; open sewers running through development carrying drainage from cesspools and all manner of diseases.[20]

The importance of the improvement association to deal with basic infrastructure problems was essential. With the collective voice, according to the 1938 history, the Arcadia Improvement Association advocated for the following physical improvements: tree plantings along sidewalks; sewer hook ups for individual houses; removal of trolley poles; donated Harford Terrace slope to park board; beautified Herring Run Park; the opening of Walther Avenue; and the installation of safety traffic lights, streetlights, and sidewalks across vacant lots. In addition to physical infrastructure, Arcadia jumped into the zoning battle in regards to rowhouses planned for Eastwood Drive. Here, the developer attempted to rezone Eastwood Drive for rowhouses. After several court battles and countless zoning hearings, the neighborhood improvement association helped to uphold the zoning of Eastwood Drive, which required at least one side yard. In addi-

The construction of Iona Terrace located in Arcadia, circa 1920. (Photo by James H. Lewis, courtesy of Jack Hennessy)

tion, the neighborhood fought against dance halls and saloons. However, they did not mind corner stores and they held their first anniversary in the banquet/store room at 3201 Berkshire Road.

Finally, after 1940 the housing in and around Eastwood Drive was developed. Here the homes were developed in a stripped down version of the Colonial Revival. They were built as red brick duplexes to overlook Herring Run Park. Arcadia's housing was the epitome of 1920s suburban housing. Each street is full of dozens of designs, shapes, and styles of middle-class housing.

At first the Neighborhood Improvement Association drew from Carswell subdivision only. Nevertheless, throughout the years and as the issues confronting the Association changed, the Improvement Association expanded its boundaries. Just recently the association considered adding Woodstock Avenue to the Association.

Beverly Hills

Beverly Hills was created a couple of years before 1926.[21] In 1926 the Beverly Hills Neighborhood Association was formed. Beverly Hills and Arcadia are spitting images of each other except for slight variations. East of Walther Avenue, Beverly Hills resembles Arcadia. Today no visual boundaries separate the neighborhoods. On the east side of Walther Avenue, several housing options are available. Along Harford Road are rowhouses ranging from the 1910s to the 1920s. A range of Tudor-style duplexes sheathed in stucco line several streets. Along Arabia Road are three large pre-World War I houses. Also, Beverly Hills off Harcourt Road has three Mission Revival houses. In name Beverly Hills captured the California rave.

Architecturally Arcadia and Beverly Hills illustrate the evolution of the garage. First, the garage was non-existant. The houses built during the first decade of the twentieth century relied strictly on streetcars and horse-and-carriage. By the early 1920s the garage came into being. It was a detached structure placed in the back of the house at the rear of the lot. It was positioned like a stable. However, by the late 1920s the garage became an integral part of the house. This time though, the garage was in the back usually next to the laundry room. However, no door connected the two rooms. The garage was completely finished in fireproof materials. The walls were concrete block or brick. The ceiling was a cement finished plaster, and the floor was poured concrete. People feared that the automobile was a fire hazard. Just after World War II, the garage moved to the front of the house. In Arcadia and Beverly Hills, there are several examples of pre-World War II housing types with attached front façade garages. After World War II things changed.

4403 Harcourt Road located in Beverly Hills. This is one of only a handful of Spanish Mission Revival houses in Northeast Baltimore. (Author's photo)

Waltherson

In 1927 the City began buying tracts of land for the creation of Walther Avenue. By 1938 Waltherson was zoned for fifty-four duplexes. Waltherson was a linear development spawned by Northeast's first auto boulevard. In one year forty-six houses were built and sold. Thus, Waltherson became Northeast Baltimore's first automobile development. This also allowed the necessity for garages to be built. In a newspaper article of the *Baltimore American* on July 10, 1938, the following was stated:

> Just a year ago, July 11, saw the opening of Waltherson, new residential development on Walther Boulevard at Gibbons Avenue, by Robertson Realty Inc.
>
> Already streets and sewers had been laid, all the ground graded. Space was available for 106 houses in pairs.
>
> Building has continued without pause. Forty-six houses have been completed or nearing completion. All of the finished houses and three of those not yet under roof have been sold.
>
> It has been a really remarkable record. Reasons are found in the unusual features of the site and the buildings themselves.
>
> All of the houses have completely private entrances. All are of brick and

One of the earliest houses in Morgan Park—most likely architect designed. (Author's photo)

This small bungalow located in Morgan Park was a contemporary of the large Colonial Revival illustrated above. (Author's photo)

stone. Each has two baths and an extra toilet. Each has a built-in garage and basement playroom. Designs avoid monotony.

There is automatic oil heat with summer hookup for hot water; there are weather-strips and insulation. Laundry is fully equipped.

Elevation is high, affording a good breeze and Walther Boulevard at the entrance give immediate access to lines of traffic.

Two working fireplaces, a large living room, an extraordinarily well equipped kitchen. French doors to the rear porch—there's a front porch, too—are among the features.

Paul Robertson, general manager, issued a general invitation to builders as well as the public to join the company in celebrating its first anniversary by an inspection of the work.[22]

These houses mark a new era in house fashion. First, the houses have built in garages, though they haven't made it to the front of the house yet. Secondly, the basement playroom is a precursor to the 1950s club basement. The parents who created the club basements were kids who played in the basement. Also, there is reference to modern appliances and two full baths and an extra toilet (which today we call a half bath). The houses are of the English Tudor style. There is also a rear porch—again, a precursor to the backyard sun deck and barbecues of the 1960s.

Morgan Park

Throughout the Baltimore region, there were at least six African-American suburbs built prior to World War II. Out of all of them Morgan Park was the fanciest. Many houses were architect designed and built by the shakers and movers of Baltimore's African-American elite. Morgan Park was a small thirteen-acre development attached to Morgan College. But the story goes deeper into Baltimore's history revealing the intricately convoluted snares the city set at the heed of xenophobia and racism.

Sometime before 1917, the Board of Directors of Morgan College bought the old Ivy mill tract, approximately seventy acres, in order to relocate Morgan College from West Baltimore. In 1867 Morgan College was founded as a Centenary Bible Institute by the Methodist Conferences of Baltimore, Washington, Wilmington, and Delaware.[23] In 1890 Dr. Lyttleton F. Morgan donated a significant sum of money, which enabled the school to expand to offer collegiate courses. Shortly after March of 1918 buildings for Morgan College were being constructed. In 1935, by court order, the State of Maryland had to provide equal college education for blacks. Shortly thereafter, the Methodists sold the college to the State of Maryland. Today, the school is well renown throughout the country and is continually expanding its campus as well as the diversity of students.

One of Northeast Baltimore's few modern houses can be found in Morgan Park. (Author's photo)

In the mid-1990s the college bought the old Sydenam Hospital complex and is now expanding south of Argonne Drive.

In 1917, many of the suburban residents living in Northeast Baltimore reacted negatively to the proposed move. Racism prevailed and guided many Northeast residents' opinions. Thus, the newly formed suburban developments of Northeast Baltimore fervently fought the location of the college and residential community. In full, the *Afro-American* printed on May 5, 1917, the following article:

> Another manifestation of hostility on the part of the white people to prevent, if possible, any expansion on the part of colored people, is manifested in the protest that residents of Lauraville are making against the location of Morgan College on the Old Ivy Mills property on the Hillen Road. A number of the residents gathered together Tuesday night and professed to see dire results should the college and a high class residential district for colored people be located on the property. A number of the kickers declared their intention of visiting the college and lodging a protest against its location in the suburbs. Several automobiles drew up in front of the College at Edmondson and Fulton Avenues, Wednesday, and the occupants went in to see Dr. J.O. Spencer, president of the college. President Spencer invited the delegation into the chapel and soon he and Dean Pickens were hearing the various tales of woe.

Fredereic Evans, president of the Lauraville Improvement Association headed the delegation. He and Henry P. Mann, Albert Strobel, Bradley K. Purdman, Charles E. Dobler, Elmer Weisheit and Frederick Kohler argued that the location of the college at Lauraville meant depreciation of the property values of the whites. Someone suggested that the building of the Union Protestant Infirmary on Division Street be secured for the future Home. The regular buncombe about the presence of colored residents depreciating property values was gone into as is usual on such occasions when influential white citizens protest against invitations of their property by Negroes. President Spencer told the delegation that the trustees of the college would have secured a still better location had it not been for the breaking out of the European War. He said inquiries had been made in other cities only to find out that property near colored colleges always increased in value.[24]

The neighborhood residents did not stop at just hemming and haggling. They turned to the courts and eventually to the state legislature. However, during 1917 the Supreme Court struck down the several laws segregating African-Americans through zoning laws. Once the surrounding neighborhoods lost in court, they tried state legislation:

Morgan College has bought 70 acres there and whites are opposed to its being located on the tract. Their opposition was first manifested last spring when a bill failed in the extra session of the legislature preventing its acquiring the site. Two bills have been introduced in the present session of the legislature. One prevents its locating on site within five miles of Baltimore and another would forfeit its charter should it sell residential sites from the tract to colored people.

Dr. Ernest Lyon and Delegate William Pickens appeared before the Judiciary Committee of the legislature Thursday of last week, protesting against the bills. More than 150 whites were on hand Tuesday to urge the passage of the bills. Dr. John O. Spencer president of the institution was on hand to urge the claims of the college.[25]

Wasted were thousands of dollars and hours. However, the local chapter of the NAACP raised a large amount of money to fight for the right to move to Northeast Baltimore.

Although the creation of Morgan Park was a triumph in civil rights, the neighborhood grew slowly. Two houses were built by 1919 and twenty-seven by 1940. These houses were of Baltimore's African-American elite. In addition, many were architect-designed. Some of the builders and architects were as follows: A. J. Klunk, builder; Johnson and Lokeman, builders; C. J. White, architect; M. M. Sykora, builder; Lawrence Menefee, architect; Howard Mason, architect; Carl J. Haug, builder and architect; Sylvester W. Ginn, builder and architect; W. J. S. Standyard; Joseph G. Martin, architect; John W. Ross, builder; James Martin, architect; and J. B. Spittel, architect.[26]

In addition, many of Baltimore's famous African-Americans lived in the area: W. E. B. Dubois, Eubie Blake, Cab Calloway, the Murphy family—and the list goes on and on. From the outset, the community was closely held together with strict deed covenants. Like Dobler's covenants in Mayfield, some of the restrictions created setbacks, insured side yards, and prohibited the construction of factories, saloons, or hospital asylums within the neighborhood. In addition, they prohibited fences, raising of swine and cattle, and any nuisance, which could be noxious or dangerous to human health. Most restrictive was the covenant that set up a committee to approve or disapprove potential buyers, house design, and type of building:

> All designs and plans of dwelling and all other permitted buildings including exterior color scheme and values and costs of dwellings or buildings to be erected and the character and nationality and color of prospective purchasers of lots or such questions of developments of this tract may arise. From time to time are to be approved by a committee consisting of John Spencer on the part of the grantor and in case of death or removal of either a successor to be nominated by the grantor on its part and the grantee on its part.[27]

Slowly, the neighborhood filled its lots with a wonderful diversity of bungalows, cottages, and modern ranchers built with international style influences. Today, Morgan Park is a quiet neighborhood of homeowners. Little to no houses are rented.

Subdivisions that Have Outgrown Their Name
Powellnaron

Powellnaron illustrates the relationship of suburban development with church development.[28] In 1908 a group of newly arrived suburbanites met in Powell's haybarn for the first service of the Epiphany Lutheran Church of Powellnaron. Here, the men in the newly formed congregation moved the hay to one side of the barn, built makeshift pews, and set up a reed organ, which was a gift from the Epiphany Lutheran Church in Baltimore. There were fifty-two chartered members and thirty-one showed for the first service. The church drew from Raspeburg, but at the time the area was considered as four small settlements (which were really new subdivisions): Raspeburg Heights, Belgravia, Raspeville, and Powellnaron.

Powellnaron was the newest real estate venture of Mr. and Mrs. Powell, who owned several large tracts of land. Powellnaron was built on the old Deitz estate. It was in the beginning a thirty-acre development which by 1914 added greatly to the area. Mr. Powell stated to the new residents that if they got fifty members, they too would join the church. And they did.

Shortly thereafter, Frederick Powell donated the land for the first church building. By November 22, 1908 the cornerstone was laid for a one-room church structure to be built by Otto Schrotke for $3,800. The first service was held in February 21, 1909. In 1912, Mr. Leurson who lived in the city bought two lots for his retirement home. Unable to convince his wife to move to the country, he sold his lots to the church, which promptly expanded.

On April 10, 1919, Mr. Powell made plans to lend the church $15,000 at 4% until his death. The church accepted and began another building campaign. In 1923 the church had plans drawn up by Clyde and Nelson Friz. Ground was broken on March 4, 1923. After Mr. Powell died in 1927, Mrs. Powell donated $20,000 to the church. In subsequent years, the building grew according to plans drawn up by Philadelphia architect Norman T. Mansell, and by 1958, the church had plans for another addition.

Epiphany Lutheran Church—corner of Raspe and Marluth avenues. The church that Frederick Powell built. (Author's photo)

Interestingly, Delaware Avenue, which ran almost directly south from Belair Road, was getting confused with another Delaware Avenue in Baltimore City. At this time, the City wanted to rename it St. Anthony. In response, Epiphany Lutheran Church suggested renaming the Street "Marluth" Avenue. Although the city had no idea of the meaning, they went along with the suggestion. It was only later that the meaning was revealed to be Mar(tin) Luth(er).

The expansion of the church was in direct response to the development of the area:

> Expansion—more space—was the second big problem. Since the church was built in 1924, several more of the great land tracts about the edge of the community had been developed. Among them was the old Neubauer property, which adjoined the Belmar settlement back of Kolb Avenue; the Weilbrenner farm, east of Springwood; the Plumer place, which ran back of Cedonia below Powell to Hazelwood.

The new settlements built upon these lands were known as Elmwood, Westwood and Plumer Heights. On the other side of Belair Road the Thomas B. Gatch land, which ran between White and Parkmont, had been sold and developed, and farther up the hill the Greenfield and Moyer lands. Moyer's woods had been cut down; the Glenmount School had gone up in their place. All this was within walking distance of the Sunday Schools.[29]

Always, with community development, the church in its various denominations was an integral part, either being formed after a subdevelopment was created, or concurrent with the developments. The church always reached out and was more than a place of worship—it was also a social building. Here, Boy Scouts met and home economic classes were held. Campfire Girls played "dodge ball" in the social rooms. Plays were put on, operettas sung, and socials were held out on the lawns lighted by Japanese lanterns. Devotion to worship was always at the center of activity. Most unique about Powellnaron was the close affiliation of the developer with the church. Though Frederick Powell did not set out to build a Lutheran community, he wound up creating one. As the church thrived, the surrounding suburban neighborhoods grew and the Grace Lutheran Church became one of many centers in the burgeoning Belair Road bedroom communities. For Powell, the church's existence was almost as important as the neighborhood itself.

Belmar and Belgravia

Henry Kolb, another citywide developer, laid out Belmar in 1913. The subdivision was part of the Deitz and Mann tracts and was thick with mature woods. Kolb, a thrifty developer, set up a sawmill to make the lumber from the trees on the old farmsteads. The roads were macadamized and sidewalks were concrete. Kolb poured 120,000 feet of walks, which lined fifty-foot avenues. In addition, modern improvements were installed (electricity, water and sewerage). By March 27th, 1913, 210 lots were sold to eighty purchasers and thirty-four cottages were built.[30]

Also, Kennard and Company built another house subdivision called Belgravia. In 1910 Belgravia was being advertised with a picturesque view of a sample cottage which is now known as the Belgravia Castle. Much like Belgravia Castle, other houses were built of concrete block. Set on top of a hill the neighborhood first overlooked Gatch's quarry. Today, the neighborhood overlooks the Bi-Rite Supermarket.

Anthonyville

Unlike Powell, who developed the neighborhood and then built the church, in Anthonyville the church was built and the neighborhood developed around it. Although

Diversity in City Suburbia 221

Advertisement from the *Baltimore News*, 1914, for the "Belgravia Castle."
(Courtesy of CHAP)

developed on a scale much smaller than Lutherville or Mt. Washington, Anthonyville was an attempt to build a neighborhood around the church. St. Anthony's Church was established in the mid-1880s and quickly set up a Catholic school for the surrounding Gardenville children. During the subsequent decades the church expanded along with the school. But by 1903, the school and church saw the impending change and acted proactively, hoping to build a Catholic community.

However, by 1915 the subdevelopment lost its name and became part of the Woodrow Development. The original Anthonyville development consisted of one street laid out and developed with only fifteen houses.[31] However, the school contin-

The Anthonyville subdevelopment was laid out, with St. Anthony's Church as the center. (Drawing from St. Anthony's Golden Jubilee Souvenir Album circa 1934)

ued to grow and prosper, but the original Anthonyville development scheme—like Gardenville—was lost in the shuffle.

Within the vicinity of Gardenville over half a dozen subdivisions popped up: Woodlea, Wilson Heights, Woodrow, Fairlee, Rockdale, Hazelwood Heights, and Valley View Park. Surrounding the old Gardenville center, two landscape plans were proposed. The development of Woodlea is centered upon a green common one block west of Belair Road. This open space was a common green, a communal front lawn for the surrounding houses. It may have been consciously or unconsciously modeled after the New England town common. Nonetheless, this was an intentional ploy by Henry Kolb to vary his product from the numerous other developments in the area.

Across the street, another landscape element was planned. In the midst of lots laid out behind the Jerusalem Evangelical Lutheran Church was a proposed small, elongated square. It was approximately one block long and was perpendicular to Belair Road. Named Furley Square, the design was overwhelmed when the street was widened. Gardenville remained compact until the garden and dairy lands east of Belair Road were developed after World War II. Much of the development was the newest suburban building type—the garden apartment and ranch houses.

Public Housing: for the Poor, Defense, and War Workers

Northeast Baltimore has a long and ruckus history with public housing. Today the words connote fear. In the early 1940s the words connoted fear. Nevertheless, public housing has an incredible history of helping literally hundreds of millions of people rise from poverty into mainstream America. Everyone knows several families that have benefited directly from the government housing. It could have been your parent, grandparent or great grandparent, or your best friend's grandparents.

Armistead Gardens was one of the oldest housing projects in the city. It first began as a slum clearance project, became defense housing, and metamorphosed into war housing. Eventually it was sold to tenants in the 1950s.

In 1937, the U.S. Housing Act was passed through Congress. That same year the Maryland State Legislature passed a bill enabling local jurisdictions to create housing authorities. In December of 1937 Baltimore City created the Baltimore Housing Authority. The U.S. Housing Act allowed the Federal Housing Agency to allocate federal dollars to local housing agencies for slum clearance and the building of public housing. By 1943, the Baltimore Housing Authority spent twenty-four million dollars building eight slum clearance projects and six war housing projects. By 1940 housing for war workers took precedent over slum clearance. The 1940 Lanham Act drastically altered the 1937 Housing Act by imposing federal control onto local authorities in areas affected by defense industries. In effect, war housing was built with federal dollars for migrant civilian war workers.[32]

The 1940 Lanham Act was a reaction to huge demographic shifts of rural workers relocating near major U.S. industrial areas where jobs were plentiful. By 1943, the Baltimore Housing Authority estimated that 40,000 immigrants poured into the Baltimore Area searching for war-related work. In Baltimore, like all U.S. cities, this huge influx of migrants spawned private development for white housing. Nevertheless, it wasn't enough.

Two organizations, the Baltimore Housing Authority and the Commission on City Plan were endowed by the Baltimore City Government and federal officials to approve war housing site location. The Housing Authority dealt with the short-term management of war housing, and the development and site location of permanent slum clearance projects. The City Plan Commission dealt with issues concerning the long-range planning of the physical development of Baltimore. Nevertheless, according to the 1940 Lanham Act, the federal government had ultimate authority to place temporary war housing where needed, but federal practice requested approval of site location from local authorities.

Detail from the 1914 Bromley Map of Baltimore County shows the Woodlea Green Common— a developer's perk to stimulate house sales in a competitive market. (Courtesy of CHAP Archives)

Thus on June 1, 1939, Armistead Gardens was introduced as an area D housing project to the Baltimore City government. By June 10th a flier was widely passed around the neighborhoods that surrounded the site. The flier in full stated the following:

700 Slum Families from Baltimore's Slums to Move into Our Community.

The Board of Estimates has been asked to approve a site of 86 acres on the Philadelphia Road, for the construction of seven hundred—perhaps two or three times that many—tax exempt housing units for slum families.

It is a notorious fact that vile social diseases, tuberculosis, juvenile delinquency and mental ailments prevail to an alarming extent in slum areas.

Our school children and people should not and must not be subjected to the dangers of a slum housing project in our community.

These slum families will of necessity use the same public transportation facilities—street cars and buses—as other residents of the northeastern section—and the same public schools.

Don't be Deceived. If this housing is not for slum dwellers for whom is it intended—and why should the taxpayers pay millions of dollars to provide tax exempt housing for any group except the underprivileged slum tenants?

We must Protest this proposal with all of the force at our command.[33]

In order for the Baltimore Housing Authority to sign a contract with the United States Housing Authority, the contract had to be approved by the Board of Estimates. The meeting proved to be a raucous event as 300 residents packed the second floor of City Hall. Not only was Armistead Gardens submitted for approval but six other areas were also. Here many of the opponents came to protest any "slum clearance projects" anywhere. Rhetoric was effulgent with passion: "We're here to protest primarily against this undertaking as a slum-clearance project." The president of the Hamilton Improvement Association declared the group to be "absolutely opposed to any slum-clearance project in the northeastern section." C. A. Kauffman, chairman of the slum clearance committee of the Hamilton Improvement Association, speaking for the groups of North and East Baltimore, viewed their action as "taking time by the forelock" to curb low rental housing projects. He further stated, "We are fighting a battle for the taxpayers of Baltimore, we object to putting slum dwellers in or adjacent to our midst, and protest the tax load saddled on home owners and buyers struggling to get along."

The rhetoric described in the newspapers went on and on. Nevertheless, sixty years later, the rhetoric is very revealing. Here, the lower class is identified as "slum dwellers." These slum dwellers were considered American citizens. Furthermore, they were touted as carrying disease, mental illnesses, and overwrought with juvenile delinquents. Though the rhetoric has changed slightly, the same issue plagues us today.

The Board of Estimates finally approved Armistead Gardens, but the residents were not finished fighting. On September 27, 1939, Abraham Kreshtool hired two lawyers who filed an injunction against the project. The lawyers asserted that "they brought no action against and had no objection to the various other projects in the $21,343,206 worth of slum clearance projects in Baltimore, since those other projects were situated in Downtown sections and called for demolition of outmoded buildings. However, they challenged the right of the Housing Authority to go out into the suburbs and build on vacant land in practical competition with private building developers."[34] Here's the rub —if the suburbs are by definition a commingling of rural attributes and urban amenities, they should only be the best of rural and urban. When the development patterns of the urban form bring to the suburbs the very problems suburbanites want to leave behind (real and perceived) then the suburbs are in jeopardy of losing their identity.

However, on October 18, 1939, the judge refused to enjoin the Housing Authority. He flatly stated that the housing project was within the authority of the Baltimore Housing Authority. On November 5, bids were put out on the street for contractors of Baltimore's first suburban public housing development. Finally, on December 6, 1939, John McShane Inc. was selected to erect the 700 units at Armistead Gardens. A year later, on December 8, 1940, the project was nearing completion.

Nevertheless, the building did not stop with the original plans. As the defense built up increased pressure in Baltimore, the National Housing Association began phase two and phase three in 1941. Here, the housing project specifically catered towards the workers for the Glen L. Martin Aircraft Company. This added another 694 units to the area.[35] As the war began, the housing was strictly limited to war workers. In September 1941, five social security workers were forced out of Armistead Gardens because they were not considered defense workers. This statement shows the immense control the federal government had on war housing. Many of the housing projects in

Sprawling "ranch rowhouses" attached to a Colonial Revival home in Armistead Gardens. (Author's photo)

Baltimore, born of the desire to house the underclass, were quickly swooped up for defense housing. In Baltimore several of the defense housing projects were located in the suburbs and based upon suburban ideals. Several were Cherry Hill, Aero Acres, Armistead Gardens, and Turner's Station.

Architecturally, Armistead Gardens was based upon the prominent thinking of the time. Streets were laid out in curvilinear patterns, and set in a garden-like setting. The housing itself was best described as Colonial gabled rowhouses. Here, the architecture, though based upon the same density as Baltimore rowhouses, was designed to mimic the individual rowhouses. The two end units on the first addition were only one-story high. Again, even in the public housing projects, the suburban ideal ran deep. After the War, the housing was sold off for private homes. Today, the area looks like many of the townhouse developments found throughout many of Baltimore's older suburbs.

Another story of public housing found great controversy within Northeast Baltimore. In 1943, the Federal Public Housing Administration announced that they were to put their efforts into creating 2,000 publicly financed Negro war housing units.[36] This effort spawned five public housing projects, of which three turned out to be permanent developments: Banneker Homes located in Fairfield; Turner's Station located in Dundalk; Soller's Point located near Turner's Station; Holabird Avenue; and Cherry Hill.

The rush was on to provide housing for Baltimore African-Americans. In April of 1943, when discussing the project that eventually became Cherry Hill, the Baltimore Housing Authority went to the federal agencies and asked if they could build permanent homes. With much discussion they agreed, but the question of where still loomed in the minds of the public officials. They first thought of building a project near Canton on Eastern Avenue. That site was eventually decided against. The second choice was directly north of Armistead Gardens, north of the Herring Run.

This too ran against opposition. This time, the fight went all the way to Congress. Eventually the decision fell into the lap of newly elected mayor McKeldin. As a card-carrying NAACP member he was receiving much pressure from the both sides. During his absence, a city council ordinance was signed into law by the acting mayor to forbid the Negro housing project on the site. Nevertheless, the federal public housing administration had the ultimate control, since this was during Wartime. They finally approved the site. However, city officials were working hard to find another site that did not have as much controversy. Concurrent to the fight, private Negro housing was being built in Cherry Hill for Negro war workers at Fairfield (the world's largest shipyard during World War II). Finally the city coerced the feds to move the site to Cherry Hill, thus ending the battle over Negro housing in Northeast Baltimore.

Two other housing projects dotted the landscape of Northeast Baltimore. In 1951 the Freedom Apartments and Shopping Center were built directly west of Armistead Gardens.[37] The complex held 308 duplex apartments and a strip shopping center, both designed by Alexander Smith Cochran. In 1951 the Baltimore Chapter of the American Institutes of Architects awarded Cochran a certificate of merit. Today, these structures are no man's land, devoid of any sense of community. It is a complex that has worn out its use and will be demolished. Another project, Hollander Ridge, was built in 1970 and demolished in 2000. This project was forty-seven acres, and 1,000 units of subsidized housing divided into one twenty-story high-rise and more than a dozen low-rise buildings. It was a miserable failure from its inception.

By World War II much of Northeast Baltimore was developed. However, several large tracts were still ripe for development. In the 1950s, much development occurred as ranch, duplex, and rowhousing. By the sixties and seventies, only rowhouse and garden apartments were being developed. Post-World War II development in the outlying regions of Northeast Baltimore had an indirect impact upon the health and well being of Northeast Baltimore. These new suburban neighborhoods—new in form, type, and relationship to city and country—adapted to the changing times. This time, though, the physical transformation was quite different and not as great as farmland transforming into suburbs. This time, the change was generational change.

With the help of conservation groups such as the Herring Run Watershed Association, wildlife such as these new-born screech owls are making a comeback in Northeast Baltimore. (Author's photo)

WALKING THROUGH TODAY 1945-2005

Post-1950 Northeast Baltimore had over forty years of suburban development under its belt. Generational change created a population mix of all ages. Houses were well worn, and neighborhood mainstreets were mature. Northeast Baltimore was one generation too old to be new and the residents too new to remember how neighborhoods were made.

Nevertheless, the region didn't stop changing. New neighborhoods were built, especially east of Gardenville, and in the northern sections off Old Harford Road and Walther Avenue. Infill added to older neighborhoods. Change continually remodeled and updated the older houses. Changes in the neighborhoods paralleled the change along the streets. The arterial and the lateral roads refurbished its buildings and signage created whole new streetscapes. Concurrently traffic engineers straightened curves, widened roads, changed traffic patterns, and added lights and signs. Lastly Northeast Baltimore had to redefine itself politically. Dynamic neighborhood organizations emerged to tackle the physical, environmental, and social issues of Northeast Baltimore. These organizations mark a new era of local organization and sophistication.

Northeast, though, didn't change in a vacuum. No longer was it the shining new city/suburb—the achievement of municipal efficiency. Not longer was it on the edge of urban and rural. By 1962 it became an inner beltway neighborhood. Fiscal and economic energy lay beyond the beltway.[1] As cornfields had enticed development dollars and government subsidies, the older neighborhoods relied on strong homeownership and rising property taxes to sustain itself. Thus, 1962—the year of the beltway—marked a turning point in Northeast's history. No longer was Northeast's twenty or so neighborhoods influenced by the push of Baltimore, but by the pull of the new suburban frontier. Its urbanization (though masked in a suburban mask) was complete.

Again, the automobile changed the landscape. When the streetcars screeched to a halt and Harford and Belair Roads were widened, Maryland was building a whole new

Panaromic view of present-day Baltimore as seen from atop Clifton Tower. (Author's photo)

road system based upon the limited access highways. These limited access highways became funnels for thousands of automobiles. First, they connected economic regions in Maryland. However, with the 1956 and 1958 National Highway Acts, the federal government bore 90% of the construction costs. America changed.

The creation of the limited interstate highway system was the largest earthwork campaign in history. Between 1958 and 1974, 43,000 miles of multi-lane highways were built at a cost of seventy-four billion dollars.[2] However, much of the U.S. interstate system was built on prior local efforts. In 1953, the State Assembly adopted Governer McKeldin's Master Highway Plan. The plan recommended rebuilding 3,100 miles of existing highway and building 300 miles of new asphalt.[3] In 1952 the bay bridge was opened. In 1954, the Baltimore Washington Expressway was completed.[4] Three years later I-70 connected Baltimore to Frederick and the Harbor Tunnel was completed. In 1962, the Baltimore Beltway and the Jones Falls Expressway opened. Finally in 1971, I-95 connected Baltimore to Washington, D.C. With their four-leaf clovers, and capacity for traffic unbeknownst just thirty years earlier, this new road system created offshoot development and changed Northeast Baltimore in two ways.

First, strings of asphalt touched the eastern edge of the area. Attached to the highways were the on and off ramps for Moravia Road, Erdman Avenue and Pulaski Highway. Industrial zones clustered like barnacles around the quick access to the highways. The newest industrial zone was Moravia Industrial Park. By 1963 the industrial "park" had nine tenants, and eight sites available for development.[5] Its selling point was the proximity to I-895, and the proposed East-West Expressway. In addition, the older industrial sites that strategically situated themselves near rail was boosted by the accessibility of truck transport. Interestingly, Northeast's first economic reason for

being, the Principio Iron Company, had been located in the exact same area.

Secondly, I-895 and I-95 exits into Northeast Baltimore bore their own commercial strip on Moravia Road. The hotel perched on top of the hill directly north of Moravia Road serves no Northeast neighborhood, just motorists. At Moravia Park Road and Moravia Road, three gas stations and a fast food restaurant (currently McDonalds) act as gateways into and out of the neighborhood. More out of place with Northeast's character is the split-level office building that faces the highway and is mostly vacant. Also, the gambrel roof-shaped salt storage tanks directly west of I-95 and north of Moravia Road conveniently symbolize the importance of the highways.

In addition, I-95 and I-895 had a big impact on Pulaski Highway heading into the city. Here, many of the automobile-oriented businesses lost their customers. The strip tried to renew itself, but never regained its earlier economic fervor. Today, many early remnants of the auto era exist, but house diverse elements such as adult video shops, strip clubs, and carpet warehouses. In addition, the city of Baltimore has built its incinerator and its impound lot. Once this strip was the Old Post Road that connected Baltimore to Boston. Now it is a strip lined with many commercial and industrial uses that we don't want in our neighborhoods.

By the 1950s, the shopper was dependent on the car. Shopping with the car became the norm and retailers reacted accordingly. They withdrew from the main streets and congregated in strip malls, larger strip malls, and finally indoor shopping malls. Of course, with the car a consumer could "consume" more goods. Thus, the strip mall created seas of parking along with bigger stores. At least twelve different strip malls were built in Northeast Baltimore; today, most are more than seventy-five percent vacant.[6] Inadvertently, due to the early efforts of zoning, not one strip mall is

Typical shopping center design of the late 1950s was designed for the automobile and stands in stark contrast to the traditional neighborhood mainstreet. (Author's photo)

located on the Harford Road. Only when one passes over the city line does one see strip malls. Most strip malls are located along the Belair Road corridor and east on the medium-stripped roads such as Edison Highway, Erdman Highway, Moravia Road, and Sinclair Lane. All these roads were designed or upgraded by the traffic engineer. In 1951 Freedom Shopping Center was opened on Erdman Avenue. Alexander Smith Cochran designed this strip center.[7] In 1956 the Northwood Shopping Center was built, with the Hecht Company as the anchor. In 1959, Moravia Mall was built on a twenty-five-acre site and anchored by a three-story department store.

In order to compete with the new strip malls, which were successful in the beginning, old retailers reinvented their storefronts with a menagerie of different materials. Many residences on the Harford and Belair Roads were transformed into commercial and retail spaces and multi-unit dwellings. Once a certain number of cars traveled daily upon the street, the value of residential properties greatly diminished. In addition, signs became billboard size, lights became brighter, and store fronts were refurbished. Early in the 1950s commercial additions were streamlined with utilitarian remnants into the Art Moderne movement. The next wave of additions built new façades and claimed success under the "International" style. In reality, it had nothing to do with style and everything to do with money. Later, in the early seventies, T-1-11 and perverse mansard shingle-style façades were placed upon the structures. Today, most changes resemble the historic details found on the street.

Belair Road also became a magnet for car dealerships and affiliated industry. Today there are three large and successful dealerships on the Belair Road.

Signs too popped up. These signs became larger as traffic became faster. Today there are dozens of billboards along the corridors. In turn, signs on older ma and pa businesses began to grow in order to capture the attention of commuters whizzing by. As the years were marked with outward growth, and more sophisticated shopping experiences, the old commercial corridors began losing much of its staple businesses.

Nevertheless, the old mainstreets of America are coming back and being reclaimed as integral to healthy communities. The New Urbanism (which is really a way of saying urbanism) movement sees mixed-use developments as essential to the health and vitality of its vision of building new old towns. In 1980 the National Trust For Historic Preservation created its Mainstreet Program, which to date is the most successful commercial revitalization program in the country. These ideas are seen on the corridor. In 2000 Baltimore created its own MainStreet Program modeled after the National Trust for Historic Preservation MainStreet Program.

The neighborhoods physically changed in several ways. First infill construction occurred on many of the sporadically located lots within the pre-World War II neighborhoods. Here, they were houses that reflected the prefabricated construction materials and house design of the fifties through the eighties. Many were built in the same square footage as some small rowhouses in Baltimore. However, they had their yard, carport or garage, and full basement. Their modern characteristics are noticeable, though their position on the street is in character with the streetscapes.

In addition to the style, the post-World War II house transmogrified by reacting to the technological advances occurring almost daily. In the 1949 Housing Act the feder-

This business, located on the Belair Road, changed its design to attract drive-by customers. The storefront window is tilted so that merchandise is visible to passing drivers. (Author's photo)

al government created a firm foundation for post-World War II housing. This act legislatively supported large-scale housing developments. Most directly affecting Northeast Baltimore was the federal government's involvement in building technology. The act stated that the government will "encourage and assist in the use of new designs, materials, techniques, and methods of assembly of home-building materials and equipment, and the increase of efficiency in residential construction and maintenance." This no-frills thinking created no-frills houses.

The houses of the late 1940s and early 1950s were approximately ten percent smaller than the houses of the 1930s.[8] Most of these early post-World War II houses measured between 650 and 1,000 square feet.[9] To help cut costs and create an open interior, walls were eliminated, windows were enlarged, and sliding glass back doors became the norm. Through the glass door, the backyard became a private outdoor room, adding space to the house. The kitchen became the center of the house, in which the housewife had visual contact with every other room as well as the backyard.

Outdoor space transformed also. The house of the 1920s and 1930s had the garage in the backyard and the porch in the front yard. In the late fifties, they switched places. The garage became a side appendage as the front yard gave way to the driveway. Many times the garage was used as another room and the car sat out on the driveway. This led to deeper setbacks for houses in order to avoid having the automobile hang over onto the sidewalk. Sheds, barbecues, patios, and pools became permanent ornaments in the backyard. However, one of the most important features of the yard was the space in which the house could expand. Not only did additions find themselves tacked onto these little houses, the new houses became bigger.

By the 1960s and 1970s the house grew not only in size but also in complexity. New uses needed new rooms. Family rooms and formal parlors, dining rooms and kitchen nooks were mandatory. Television rooms and club basements, workshops, and even sauna rooms were built. The rise of bigger and more complex houses paralleled other factors. The outdoors "backyard" could not compete with the television, video, and air conditioner. The sidewalks could not compete with the treadmill and CD player. As commutes became longer and more people spent time in cars, they spent less time outdoors. The television room with instant access to anywhere only competes with other television rooms of other family members. The house has stopped becoming a retreat from the stresses of the world, but the portal, the gateway into the electronic world. As we separate ourselves more from social institutions, we tend to pump electronic societies into our homes. The bedroom, once the ultimate retreat from the world, has become a television room. Times have changed, the house has changed, and the "style" or fashion of the house reflects both.

Wide streets characterize post-World War II duplex developments such as this one at the intersection of Woodring Avenue and Harford Road. (Author's photo)

Whole neighborhoods were built on land leftover from the truck farm era. Here, Cape Cods, ranch houses, split-level, and modern single family homes were built. New "townhouses" were constructed and marketed for a lower middle class than the previous generation of townhome buyers. Townhomes in fact are rowhouses and differ in name only. Developers, building in suburbia, did what they could to separate themselves from the urban connotation. And a rowhouse neighborhood meant a Baltimore neighborhood. This paralleled the earlier efforts of suburbanizing the urban neighborhoods with such names as boulevards and exotic names like "The Alameda" and "Beverly Hills."

The first post-World War II detached houses were very small, simple Cape Cods. They were one- to one-and-a-half-story houses, three bays wide and topped with a gable roof. In many ways they mimic the simple shape and massing of Colonial Revival houses. Little or no ornaments were used. Interesting, like the term bungalow, the definition of Cape Cod has evolved or devolved to mean a small house. Most Cape Cods were infill. The next phase of Cape Cods was quite bigger, and had a distinctive entranceway, front porch, and vestibule. In addition, second-story dormers were placed in the finished attic space.

The ranch house became the second house to appear in post-World War II Northeast Baltimore. The ranch house in form sprawled out and was significantly wider than the Cape Cod. However, it was one story high only. In style precedent, the ranch house came from California, hence the name. These houses hung low to the ground capturing the horizontal lines, which were explored through the bungalow. The main feature was the garage with its doors. The front porch had turned into a concrete slab with utilitarian pillars. The cornice had been replaced with gutter troughs and windows were all single pane, with a "picture window" connecting the living room with the out-

Garden Apartments, as a residential building form, innundated Northeast Baltimore after World War II.
(Author's photo)

side. Materials of surfaces ranged from brick, siding, flagstone, and now vinyl and aluminum siding. These houses evolved quickly into the ubiquitous split-level house.

The split-level clung to its desire for low-hanging horizontal lines. It still capped itself with the low-pitched roof and overhanging eaves. It this sense, it wanted to be a ranch house. But on the inside it wanted to be a full three floors much like the earlier foursquare houses. In the split-level, the first floor was dedicated to the garage and workshop, play, television, or recreation room. Up one flight of steps the second floor entailed the living room, dining room, and kitchen. Access to the backyard was usually on this level. Over the garage and on the third level lay the bedrooms and bathrooms. Here were the sanctuaries from the noisy house. From the split-level, the houses became bigger, more complicated, and artistically designed.

The 1970s saw a flourishing of shed-like houses, where the roof was a combination of several shed roofs differently angled to one another. Here, the roofs made the house look more geometric, where the outside captured the shape and rooms on the inside. Each room could be read from the outside. On the inside, the floorplan was complicated with several stairlandings, at least three levels of living space. The spaces were opened and differentiated with visual components, such as stepping up or down into the living room from the dining room. These houses were quite a bit larger than the split-level houses which were that much larger from the simple Cape Cods.

In all, these houses read like post-World War II houses and carry with them the common thread of little or no ornamentation. In addition, such things as ceiling height and window size are all similar, thanks to the standardization of building practices worked out with the help of the federal government. They fit into the Northeast area, making this area an incredible menagerie of housing styles from the turn of the century to the 1970s. They have become wellworn and welcome components to the neighborhoods.

In addition, a new building type on the landscape was constructed—the garden apartment. These first started appearing on the edge of the city's landscape in the mid-1920s and took off in the 1930s with the help of federal subsidies and the Works Progress Administration efforts to jump-start the economy. The garden apartment was suburbia's apartment. It could not be built in the city. It needed a large contiguous tract of land. It needed nature to be part of its design. It was placed on the outskirts of cities usually near streetcars. Baltimore received many garden apartments prior to World War II. But not one of them landed in Northeast Baltimore. Most pre-World War II garden apartments were built in Walbrook and the Charles Street Corridor. Northwood and Loch Raven Apartments were built in 1938, and the Samester Apartments in Northwest Baltimore were built in the 1930s. Baltimore also had a vernacular form of the garden apartment that mimicked the massing and design on the rowhouse. They differed from rowhouses by the ubiquitous balconies on the second and third levels.

Finally, in the late 1960s through the 1970s, most of the residential development in Northeast Baltimore was constructed as garden apartments and townouses. Most were located off Moravia Road, and several complexes were near Perring and Northern parkways. This time though, they were not built near mass transit nor were they part of a larger landscape. Just as the automobile usurped the streetcar, parking diminished the green spaces. Now the garden apartment became parking lot apartments. The suburban amenity of luscious greenery was now gone. They were built as temporary living spaces for young couples and affordable housing for the working class. In addition, many were built after the 1972 Housing Act, which allowed landlords to get a government paycheck for Section 8 housing. This created a rush of garden apartments built for quick profits and quick life.

These apartment buildings, usually three stories high, each with their own balcony, sit not in a garden, but a parking lot. By the time this late 1930s building type came to Northeast Baltimore, it evolved into a developer's complex created to suck up short-term profits from low- to middle-income folks as well as government subsidies. Today, the only wholesale demolition in Northeast Baltimore is occurring in two places—Hollander Ridge, which has garden apartments, and the garden apartment complex off Frankford Avenue.

The rowhouse, as it crossed over the year 1950, kept its scale and massing. However, the style mimicked much of the detached houses. In the 1950s and early 1960s

Francis Werneth and his 1959 DeSoto return to their native home each year for the Lauraville Country Fair. (Author's photo)

many of the rowhouses were built in the same style and siting as their earlier Colonial Revival cousins. The Welsh Construction Company was the biggest developer of these houses.[10] These developments were extensions of Belair-Edison. By the 1970s most ubiquitous was the mansard shingled-style roof, which plopped itself on the building like an awkward ten-gallon hat. Porches were no more, and in many cases the front door was couched into a vestibule. These traits, along with the sheathing materials such as the shingled roof, T-1-11, and aluminum and vinyl siding make these townhouses stand out from their earlier predecessors.

More importantly, these new townhomes had a different relationship to the street. From a distance many look like garden apartments. In fact, their street siting and layout is closer to the garden apartment than the older rowhouses. First the alley was completely eliminated. Some open up onto green commons that are bound by backyards. Second, the street was widened for front-end parking. Thus, the front yard and sidewalk are dwarfed. Many are sited on cul de sacs and turn abouts. They were built as developments with well over six rows developed at a time. And lastly, they were built mostly near garden apartment complexes and serviced not by mainstreet retail but by strip malls. With these changes, there were also changes occurring on the older houses.

After World War II the lumber and hardware industry continued an incredible marketing campaign to sell home repairs as a hobby. Tool makers created a line of electric tools marketed to the homeowner. Pamphlets and brochures pictured happy husbands and fathers painting, sanding, cutting, and hammering towards a better house. Do-it-yourself books flooded the market and new and older homes were being redone at a phenomenal rate. In addition, by the 1960s and 1970s many of the homes were in need of rehabilitation. Cedar shake shingles were cracked and warped. Windows lost their balance weights and were drafty in the winter. Porch columns and screen doors needed replacing. And they were replaced with modern materials. The house's skin was renewed first with asbestos shingles, aluminum, and vinyl siding. Porches were rebuilt with concrete, brick, or filigreed aluminum iron columns. Even some houses were clad in T-1-11. Some porches turned into extra indoor living space. Wood windows were replaced with aluminum insulated windows. Storm windows were added. The ubiquitous air conditioner unit stuck out of bedroom windows, producing a sea of late-night white noise. And many backyards became homes of the new sun deck.

The changes that occur to the houses are markers of health and vitality. They are value manifest and, en masse, they indicate for realtors, prospective buyers, and tax assessors the health of the neighborhoods. Nonetheless, if some new building materials are juxtaposed with old materials, then the neighborhood reads as sliding downhill. Thus, T-1-11 stuck within porch posts, laminate plane solid doors, pressure treated porch steps, and front porch flooring all signal decline. It is written in the culture.

By 2003, historic preservation interests have settled into the lower neighborhoods of Northeast Baltimore. Lauraville was listed on the National Register of Historic Places on December 28, 2001. Mayfield will be listed in 2003 and Arcadia and Beverly Hills are actively pursuing historic designation. The neighborhoods around Hamilton have started a home and garden tour. The popularity of historic preservation highlights quality craftsmanship and values the older building materials and styles. As a whole, streetscapes fifty, seventy, or ninety years old delight neighbors and make the homes a place for community organization.

As the neighborhoods embraced their physical history, demographic and social change took place between 1990 and 2000.[11] Some neighborhoods changed from predominately white residents to predominantly African-American residents. Others blossomed into diverse enclaves. Still others showed very little change.

Belair-Edison showed the greatest change in race, generational change, and increase in population. From 1990 to 2000 whites decreased from a population of 10,571 to 3,162. The African-American population increased from 4,255 to 12,869. Total population increased from 15,015 to 16,523. Generational change also had a turnover effect. Belair-Edison lost 1,400 residents over the age of sixty-five. Lauraville, too, increased its population from 4,294 to 4,375 and demonstrated a decrease in the whites with a proportionate increase in African-Americans.

Newcomers to Northeast Baltimore take advantage of recreational facilities. Soccer games in Clifton Park have become a popular attraction for Baltimore's Latin American and Carribbean communities.
(Photo by Robert Wallace)

Waltherson too, gained in total population (5,623 to 5,907) but decreased in white population (4,923 to 3,246). There was a loss of 404 seniors, but a gain of 366 people between the ages of forty-five and sixty-four. In almost all neighborhoods the largest loss in age category was twenty-five to thirty-four. 44,630 people between the ages of twenty-five and thirty-four left the city. They undoubtedly took their children to "better" schools. The largest increase citywide was the age between forty-five and sixty-four years old.

Other neighborhoods like Arcadia, Beverly Hills, Woodring, and Mayfield saw slight gains in the racial mix, which equaled approximately two-thirds white to one-third African-American. Other neighborhoods changed very little. Armistead Gardens went from zero African-American families to six, whereas Morgan Park went from six white families to fifteen. Though demographic change has been significant in 2003, Northeast Baltimore is more diverse than ever, and has seen a significant increase in building activity and real estate value. The dynamics of change are always based upon conscious and unconscious past actions. Thoughtful communities respond. Northeast

Baltimore saw the creation of diverse community organizations: Harbel, Harford Road Partnership (HaRP), The Herring Run Watershed Association, NOGLI, Belair-Edison Housing Services, and Northeast Goodneighbors. These organizations responded to specific events that manifested general issues. They all complement each other either by working in different areas, or by tackling different issues.

Northeast Goodneighbors, the newest ad hoc organization, responded to a specific event, which revealed an underlying angst. For over two centuries, the threads of racism intertwined themselves into the development and culture of Northeast Baltimore. Race issues are poignantly revealed in the ACLU's 1996 housing discrimination lawsuit against Housing Authority Baltimore City (HABC) and the U.S. Department of Housing and Urban Development. The lawsuit proved that city-wide housing policies enmeshed with other governmental policies created pockets of segregated and extreme poverty.[12] A consent decree ordered HABC to create forty new or renovated public housing units in areas of Baltimore that had minority populations of less than twenty-six percent and poverty rates below ten percent. Ten of these units were slated for Northeast Baltimore. Northeast communities became enraged.

In October of 2000 Northeast communities heard about the plan at a public meeting at Hamilton Middle School. Hundreds showed to protest the HABC's buying and managing ten units in Northeast Baltimore. Reasons for the protest were numerous, although the emotional state was the same. Mayor O'Malley calmed the crowd by saying, "I'm confident there's some way we can abide by the consent decree, however outmoded it is to the current demographic realities of our neighborhoods."[13]

After the ground swell of emotion, reasons against the effort coalesced into concise statements. Many pointed out that Northeast Baltimore demographics have changed greatly in ten years, making the consent decree criteria null and void. Others pointed out that the consent decree itself was based on unconscious racist principles. The Mayor bluntly attacked the decree: "I don't buy the argument that to live in a neighborhood more than 26% African American is a bad neighborhood. That's bull--."[14] However, the most vocal statement against the decree was that people just don't trust the Housing Authority of Baltimore City, or HUD, to maintain these new properties. With 2,800 vacant, abandoned, and uncared for HABC housing units scattered throughout the city, this fear was real. In August 16, 2002, the solution was announced in the *Sun* papers. St. Ambrose Housing, a respectable non-profit housing corporation, will own and manage the sites. This plan has not caused a firestorm.

However negative this episode, positive and thoughtful responses appeared. The emotion exhibited over the consent decree concerned many citizens in different ways. For some, the fear and emotion revealed Baltimore's racist specter. It brought to mind many events in Baltimore's segregated past. Blockbusting tactics of the 1960s and 1970s were on the minds of many folks.

After commiserating in dining rooms, a coherent response with positive action began to appear. Diversity of race, class, ethnicity, sexual orientation, and household type has to be the foundation of sustaining Northeast Baltimore. Moreover, diversity is Northeast's strongest asset. The ad hoc coalition of community activitsts became Northeast Goodneighbors. This group took their dining room discussion and moved it into an auditorium at Morgan State University. On June 19, 2003, they had a forum open to everyone. At this forum the history of Baltimore, racism, and community organization were discussed. The findings of the forum were clear: diversity is Northeast Baltimore, and it must be embraced.

Diversity, according to Northeast Goodneighbors, is not just a community of dissimilar people, but the diffusion of power. The decision-making process expands to all groups and ultimately all citizens. Only then does the decision-making process effloresce into truly democratic decisions. Diversity increases the range of possibilities and solutions. It increases the number of ways Northeast Baltimore relates to the city and region. The more threads, the stronger the rope. Diversity of residences then become caretakers to the diversity of buildings. The variety of housing style, type, size, and age can be marketed to the largest possible group: anybody. Northeast Goodneighbors are not alone in their endeavors, but have become part of a nation-wide network of communities celebrating their diversity.

Thirty-two years earlier, in 1969, Harbel was formed. On October 1, 1970, Harbel became a non-profit organization.[15] The Harford Road and Belair Road (hence the name) ministeriums joined forces "to unite organizations in order to define and solve those problems common to the community." The organization assists neighborhoods with commercial development, zoning issues, sanitation, crime through citizens on patrol, and organizing and strengthening neighborhood organizations. They also reach out to individuals through counseling services and social work as well as counsel residents in home ownership issues. And last, they help low-income homeowners by linking them with government services. It is a membership organization, which asks all non-profit organizations to become members. This umbrella organization has grown from an organization of thirteen united churches to an organization directing eight programs, with a thirty-one member staff and an annual budget of $810,000.

Another dynamic organization that directly influenced Northeast Baltimore was the Harford Road Partnership (HaRP).[16] In 1993 a group of concerned citizens came together to work towards improving their commercial corridor: Harford Road. At the time an old, nondescript MTA bus barn sat vacant and deteriorating. The citizens pulled off the near impossible and coaxed a Safeway grocery store onto the site. In addition, the citizens knew very well that a master plan, comprehensive in nature and backed by a local ordinance, was needed in order to redevelop the strip for pedestrians and not only automobiles. Thus, after raising funds they hired the nationally known New Urbanist town planning firm, Duany Plater-Zyberk & Company. In March 1997 they held a several-day charette that brought together stake holders, residents, and governmental departments and created the bones of the comprehensive plan. This plan, once complete, was intricately reviewed by a panel of representatives of neighborhood organizations and other non-profit stakeholders. In June of 1999 a plan was passed through City Council as an urban renewal plan. Today, the law of Baltimore City backs the plan. In 2001, The Harford Road Partnership closed its non-profit doors and merged with NOGLI. Now, the Neighborhoods of Greater Lauraville (NOGLI) offers residential and commercial development assistance to the area.

NOGLI, a composite of six neighborhoods, collectively market and promote the area and administer low interest loans for home buying and renovation as well as market and promote commercial revitalization along Harford Road. Officially an organization on September 7, 2001, their mission statement is as follows:

> The Neighborhoods of Greater Lauraville, Inc. (NOGLI) is a joint project of the communities of Arcadia, Beverly Hills, Lauraville, Moravia-Walther, Morgan Park & Waltherson located in northeast Baltimore City that endeavors to improve the quality of life for residents of the Greater Lauraville area by promoting & marketing the area to prospective buyers and businesses, providing comprehensive homeownership counseling, augmenting community efforts at more effective commercial & housing code enforcement, & working to improve landlord/tenant relations.[17]

The creation of NOGLI establishes a new era of sophistication for neighborhoods wedded with local activism.

Much older than NOGLI and HaRP is Belair Road's version of a community development, marketing, and revitalization organization. More than twenty years ago, the Belair-Edison Community Association spawned the Belair-Edison Housing Services.[18] Today it is known as Belair-Edison Neighborhoods, Inc. The organization has paid staff to counsel homebuyers, build community through organized activities, and create a forum for community information distribution. They—again like NOGLI—have low interest loans for home purchasing and renovation.

In addition, Belair-Edison has become one of Baltimore City's "Main Streets," a citywide program to help revitalize neighborhood mainstreets. Based upon the extremely successful National Trust Mainstreet Program, the city MainStreet Program provides a full-time MainStreet manager (who acts much like a mall manager), façade improvement programs, and funding for promotional activities. More than 100 small businesses line the commercial corridor. Again, the efforts of many of Northeast's neighborhoods have embraced a wholistic approach that commerce and residential areas complement each other and create whole neighborhoods.

To confront environmental issues, the Herring Run Watershed Association was created. Lynn Kramer, one of the first organizers of the Association, began the effort in 1992 with a stream survey. With help and technical assistance from the national organization Save Our Streams, Kramer helped to gather over one hundred volunteers to conduct a visual assessment of the stream. Here, the surveyors were identifying areas of erosion, large accumulation of trash, fish migration barriers, and the smell of open sewers. With the survey finished, it turned into a report for the City Council, who then requested that the Department of Public Works fix many of the storm and sanitary sewer problems.

In January 1993 the report spawned an organization committee. From this committee spawned an all-volunteer organization until 1997, when they raised enough funds for staff. To date, they have planted thousands of trees, kept vigilance for traces of broken sewer lines, conduct a yearly park clean up, and put on an annual festival in the park.

Today it is a membership organization that also receives grants. With their efforts hundreds of folks enjoy the park everyday. However, in early 2003 Herring Run Watershed had a devastating crisis. For six days in February, 35,000,000 gallons of raw sewage flowed into the Herring Run. Several days later they discovered another blockage in the sewer, which ultimately dumped millions more fecal material into the Herring Run. During the summer of 2003 the park was more quiet than usual.

However, under threat of a federal lawsuit, the City of Baltimore will spend approximately $900,000,000 to overhaul its aging sewer system. Baltimore's sewer system carries approximately 250,000,000 gallons of waste per year and is composed of 3,100 miles of pipes.[19] New sewage pipes will be replaced along the valley bed of the Herring Run all the way to the Back River treatment plant. In the summer of 2003 the Herring Run Watershed Association hired long-time community and environmental activist Mary Roby as the Executive Director.

The Twenty-First Century and the Promise of Possibilities

Thus, Northeast Baltimore is not only part of Baltimore's 252 neighborhoods, but part of a five-county region that relates to a global composite of regions. Moreover, it is a conglomeration of neighborhoods whose relationships encompass far more than the mind can know.

For one hundred and seventy years (1780 to 1950), Northeast Baltimore grew on the rules of expansion. But as Baltimore headed into the 1950s and 1960s, forces of unpronounced proportions drastically changed Northeast interaction with the Baltimore metropolitan region. Ironically, the forces that built Northeast Baltimore are now threatening it. Neighborhoods cannot move to the outlying regions, but people can. Twenty-first-century Northeast Baltimore *won't grow* on the rules of expansion, but will survive on *new rules* of sustainability.

NOGLI, Belair-Edison Neighborhoods Inc., Harbel, the Herring Run Watershed Association, Northeast Goodneighbors, as well as the active neighborhood associations, with their hard work, dynamic creativity, and pools of intelligence, point the way to a prosperous future. Their creativity and energy are finding new ways to market our communities by promoting diversity which means diverse stakeholders and house types, small and large business of all kinds, and a healthy mixture of race, ethnicity, and class. Activist-based organizations will help create equilibrium with nature and act as watchdogs for our environment. Neighborhood associations with modern communication technology will create a virtual presence, through the internet and e-mail network systems, that will help maintain healthy and vibrant neighborhoods. Glimpses of history are glimpses of the future—our future.

NOTES

Abbreviations

BCA—Baltimore City Archives, Baltimore, Maryland.
BCSC—Baltimore City Superior Court, Clarence Mitchell, Jr. Courthouse, Baltimore, Maryland.
CHAP—Commission for Historical and Architectural Preservation, Baltimore, Maryland.
EPFL—Enoch Pratt Free Library, Baltimore, Maryland.
HSBC—Historical Society of Baltimore County, Cockeysville, Maryland.
MHS—Maryland Historical Society, Baltimore, Maryland.
MSA—Maryland State Archives, Annapolis, Maryland.

Introduction

1. T. S. Eliot, *The Complete Poems and Plays, 1909-1950* (New York: Harcourt, Brace and Company, 1961), 147.
2. Ibid., 144.
3. William Cronon, *Nature's Metropolis: Chicago and the Great West* (New York: W.W. Norton & Company, 1991), 48.
4. William Wordsworth, *Wordsworth Poetical Works Preface to Lyrical Ballads, with Pastoral and Other Poems* (Oxford: Oxford University Press, 1936 reprint, 1978), 735.
5. Donald McQuade, ed., *The Harper American Literature* (New York: Harper & Row, 1987), 975.
6. Ralph Waldo Emerson, "Nature," *The Selected Writings of Ralph Waldo Emerson* (New York: The Modern Library, 1940 reprint, 1950), 12.
7. Ibid., 10.
8. Daniel Boorstin, *The Americans: The National Experience* (London: Lowe and Brydone Ltd., 1965), 93.
9. John Pendleton Kennedy, *Baltimore Sun* (July 13, 1839), Cemeteries—Greenmount Cemetery, Vertical Files, EPFL Maryland Room.
10. M. C. Robbins, "American Parks: Druid Hill Park, Baltimore," *Garden and Forest* (June 13, 1894), 233.
11. Mark Miller, *Mount Washington: Baltimore Suburb* (Baltimore: GBS Publishers, 1980), 14-17.

Chapter One—Before There Was a City, 1659–1781

1. Charles G. Steffen, *From Gentlemen to Townsmen: The Gentry of Baltimore County Maryland, 1660-1776* (Lexington, Kentucky: University of Kentucky Press, 1993), 8.

2. Ibid., 12.

3. Block quotes from Steffen, *From Gentlemen to Townsmen*, 10.

4. Ibid.

5. Ralph Semmes, "Aboriginal Maryland, 1608-1689, part one," *Maryland Historical Magazine* 24 (September 1929): 195.

6. Steffen, *From Gentlemen to Townsmen*, 11.

7. William B. Marye "The Baltimore County Garrison and the Old Garrison Roads," *Maryland Historical Magazine* 16 (June 1921): 126.

8. J. Thomas Scharf, *History of Baltimore City and County* (Philadelphia: Louis H. Everts, 1881; Baltimore Regional Publishing Company, 1971), 35.

9. Ibid.

10. Marye, "The Baltimore County Garrisson": 126 fn32. Native American inhabitants of Baltimore County were the result of English settlement. With land purchases from the Native Americans, European diseases devastating the Native population, and political involvement of the Maryland province, the Native Americans were forced off their lands and settled in a hopscotch pattern. The Native inhabitants of Baltimore County were the result of the 1652 peace treaty with Marylanders as well as the 1675 defeat of the Susquehannocks by the Iroquois Nation.

11. Marye, "The Baltimore County Garrisson," 126 fn32.

12. Ibid., 110-11, fn 4.

13. Robert Barnes, *Baltimore County Maryland Deed Abstracts* (Westminster, Maryland: Family Line Publications, 1996). The deed information concerning the Baltimore County Rangers was taken from this document.

14. Henry C. Whitely, "A Historical Sketch of the First Iron Works in Maryland," *Pennsylvania Magazine of History and Biography* 11 (1887): 10. See, also, Maryland Commission of Confiscated British Property, "Inventory of Kingsbury Furnace," 1781, MdHR 6636-58-76/4 184, S1004, Confiscated British Property Papers, MSA.

15. Whitely, "A Historical Sketch," 5.

16. Barnes, *Deed Abstracts*, 118.

17. Ibid., 188.

18. John McGrain, *From Pig Iron to Cotton Duct: A History of Manufacturing Villages in Baltimore County* (Towson, Maryland: Baltimore County Public Library, 1985), 20.

19. Whitely, "Historical Sketch," 8.

20. Maryland Commission, "Inventory of Kingsbury Furnace," MSA.

21. Ronald Lewis, "Slavery in the Chesapeake Iron Industry, 1716-1865" (PhD diss., University of Akron, 1974), 38.

22. Paul Travers, *The Patapsco, Baltimore's River of History* (Centreville, Maryland: Tidewater Publishers, 1990), 8.

23. "The State of Robert Long Case Before His Excellency the Governor and Council," 1770, MdHR 66636-62-60, S1024 1/84, Chancery Papers, MSA.

24. McGrain, *From Pig Iron to Cotton Duct*, 20.

Chapter Two—Creation of Borderland Communities, 1781–1852

1. Robert J. Brugger, *Maryland: A Middle Temperament 1634-198* (Baltimore: Johns Hopkins University Press, 1988), 773.

2. Sherry H. Olson, *Baltimore: The Building of an American City* (Baltimore: Johns Hopkins University Press, 1980; 1997), 26.

3. Ibid., 19.

4. Ibid., 21-22.

5. Ibid., 22.

6. Clayton Colman Hall, ed., *Baltimore: Its History and Its People*, vols. I-III (New York: Lewis Historical Publishing Company, 1912), 86.

7. Ibid., 51.

8. Ibid.

9. Robert L. Raley, "The Baltimore Country House 1785-1815" (master's thesis, University of Delaware, 1959), 41.

10. Frank A Cassell, *Merchant Congressman in the New Republic: Samuel Smith of Maryland 1752-1839* (Madison: University of Wisconsin Press, 1971), 43.

11. Ibid., 143.

12. Lawrence Hall Fowler, "Montebello," *Architectural Review* no. 11 (November 1909): 147.

13. Ibid., 146.

14. Ibid., 147.

15. Copy of hand-typed biography of Henry Thompson, date unknown, Clifton folder, A to Z files, CHAP.

16. Architects Michael Trostle and Peter Pearre, in the 1990s, conducted a thorough architectural evaluation of the mansion and drew floor plans depicting the mansion during 1800, 1812, and 1852. Michael Trostle, *Floor Plans Clifton Mansion*, date unknown, Trostel and Pearre Architects, Baltimore.

17. Francis Beirne, *The Amiable Baltimoreans* (New York: E.P. Dutton and Company, 1951), 98.

18. Heinz Park is a triangular strip of park land between Walther Avenue and Harford Road. The Columbus Monument was moved to the current location in 1964. In 1997, the Commission for Historical and Architectural Preservation, under the direction of Kathleen Kotarba and the Arcadia Improvement Association, restored the monument.

19. Newspaper advertisement, 1805, Belmont, Passano Historic Structures Index, MHS.

20. Raley, *Baltimore Country House*, 107.

21. Karen Lewand, *North Baltimore: From Estate to Development, Baltimore Neighborhoods: A Community Fact Book* (Baltimore: Baltimore City Department of Planning and the University of Baltimore, 1989), 53.

22. Research notes, Mount Deposit, date unknown, Passano Historic Structures Index, MHS.

23. Colwill Stiles Tuttle, *Francis Guy 1760-1820* (Baltimore: Maryland Historical Society, 1981), 58-59 and 81.

24. Henry Chandler Forman, *Tidewater Maryland: Architecture and Gardens* (New York: Bonanza Books, 1956), 156-57.

25. Lee McCardell "When Going to Jerusalem Was A Baltimore Custom," *Evening Sun* (January 15, 1941), Baltimore—Suburbs, Vertical files, EPFL.

26. Forman, *Tidewater Maryland*, 160.

27. Ibid.

28. Henry Chandler Forman, *Early Manor and Plantation Houses of Maryland* (Easton, Maryland: 1934; Baltimore: Bodine, 1982), 292.

29. Hamilton Owens, *Baltimore on the Chesapeake* (Garden City, New York: Doubleday, Doran & Company, Inc., 1941), 227-30.

30. Ibid., 229.

31. Charles B. Duff, "Getting Away From It All," Walters Art Gallery, 1997.

32. Block quotes from Richard Parkinson, *Tour in America, 1798, 1799, 1800: Exhibiting Sketches of*

Society and Manners (London: J. Murray, 1805), 161-65, 175, 212-13, 192, 194, 73, and 40.

33. Newspaper advertisement, 1821, Orange Hill, Passano Historic Structures Index, MHS.

34. *Genealogy and Biography of Leading Families of the City of Baltimore and Baltimore County, Maryland* (New York: Chapman Publishing Company, 1897). These numbers are based upon averages taken from families living in Northeast Baltimore that were recorded in this book.

35. Virginia Gatch Markham, *Descendants of Godfrey Gatch of Baltimore County, Maryland* (Baldwin, Kansas: Privately printed, 1972), 8, 15, 19, and 35.

36. *Genealogy and Biography*, 28.

37. Ibid., 315; James Bertram, "Man In the Street: Erdman," *Baltimore Sun* (October 21, 1951).

38. Scharf, *History of Baltimore City and County*, 930. See also *Genealogy and Biography*, 546.

39. John McGrain, *An Agricultural History of Baltimore County Maryland* (Perry Hall, Maryland: Accent Printers, 1990), 40.

40. Ibid., 34.

41. Hall, *Baltimore*, 34.

42. Barbara Mallonee, Jane Karkalitus, and Nicholas Fessenden, *Minute by Minute: A History of the Baltimore Monthly Meetings of Friends, Homewood and Stony Run* (Baltimore: Baltimore Monthly Meeting of Friends, 1992), 3.

43. Ibid., 51.

44. "History of Friends Burial Ground: 2506 Harford Road, Baltimore, MD," Friends Burial Ground folder, A to Z files, CHAP.

45. Mallonee, et al., *Minute by Minute*, 6.

46. Ibid., 4.

47. "History of Friends," CHAP.

48. Scharf, *History of Baltimore City and County*, 931.

49. Markham, *Descendents of Godfrey Gatch*, 31.

50. *American Methodist Bicentennial 1766-1966* (Baltimore: Baltimore Conference Methodist Historical Society, 1966), 46.

51. "Guilded Gleams," hand-written document, 1967, Herring Run Park folder, A to Z files, CHAP.

52. Scharf, *History of Baltimore City and County*, 930.

53. Robert Taylor, *1857 Map of the City and County of Baltimore, Maryland* (Baltimore: Robert Taylore, 1857), Flat files, EPFL Maryland Room.

54. Scharf, *History of Baltimore City and County*, 929.

55. William Hollifield, *Difficulties Made Easy: The History of the Turnpike of Baltimore City and County* (Cockeysville, Maryland: Baltimore County Historical Society, 1978), 2.

56. Scharf, *History of Baltimore City and County*, 848.

57. "Summer Retreat, or Herring Run House," *The Whig* (June 17, 1808).

58. McGrain, *An Agricultural History*, 13.

59. Brugger, *Maryland*, 208.

60. McGrain, *An Agricultural History*, 40.

Chapter Three—A Thriving Borderland Region, 1852–1898

1. Scharf, *History of Baltimore City and County*, 929.

2. Names and occupations were identified in the *The Maryland Directory* (Baltimore: J. F. Lewis & Co., 1878, 1879, 1880, and 1882) and the G. M. Hopkins, *1877 Atlas of Baltimore County, Maryland* (Philadelphia: G.M. Hopkins, C.E., 1877). A database was created that included names, occupations, year,

and location of entries Northeast Baltimore residents found in the 1878, 1879, 1880, and 1882 Maryland directories. Names from this database were cross-referenced with names found on the 1877 G. M. Hopkins map of Baltimore County. What emerged was an 1877 land-use map showing pockets of commercial and retail activity.

3. Biographical information, Dielman-Hayward File, John Henry Keene file, MHS.

4. Richard Henry Spencer, ed., *Genealogy and Memorial Encyclopedia of the State of Maryland* (New York: American Historical Society, 1919), 708-11.

5. Michael R. Farrell, *The History of Baltimore's Streetcars* (Sykesville, Maryland: Greenberg Publishing Company, 1992), 69.

6. Scharf, *History of Baltimore City and County*, 930.

7. Newspaper advertisement, 1864, Hall's Springs, Passano Historic Structures Index, MHS.

8. Block quotes from newspaper advertisements, 1861 and 1871, Hall's Springs, Passano Historic Structures Index, MHS.

9. *Industries of Maryland* (New York: Historical Publishing Company, 1882), 360.

10. William Kelly, *Brewing in Maryland from Colonial Times to the Present* (Baltimore: Kelly Publishing, 1965), 289.

11. G.M. Hopkins, *Baltimore County Atlas of 1877* (Philadelphia: G.M. Hopkins, 1877), Flat files, EPFL Maryland Room. Names identified were cross-referenced with the 1878, 1880, and 1882 Maryland directories.

12. *Industries of Maryland*, 189.

13. Hopkins, *Baltimore County Atlas*.

14. Kelly, *Brewing in Maryland*, 214-19.

15. Scharf, *History of Baltimore City and County*, 930.

16. Eric Holcomb and Walter Leon, *Belair-Edison: Historic Survey 1994* (Baltimore: Commission for Historical and Architectural Preservation, 1994), 78.

17. William Stump, "John Henry Raspe," *Baltimore Sun* (June 22, 1952); Baltimore-neighborhoods-Raspeburg, Vertical files, EPFL Maryland Room.

18. *Genealogy and Biography*, 142-43.

19. Biographical information from *Genealogy and Biography*, 315, 64-65, 508, 316, 260, 600, 972, 142, and 376.

20. Ibid., 376-77.

21. Block quotes from Lizette Woodsworth Reese, *A Victorian Village: Reminiscences of Other Days* (New York: Farrar and Rinehart, 1929), 135, 140, and 133.

Chapter Four—The Tentacles of the City

1. Joseph Arnold, "Suburban Growth and Municipal Annexation in Baltimore, 1745-1918," *Maryland Historical Magazine* 73, no. 2 (June 1978): 113.

2. Ibid., 116.

3. Jane Bromely Wilson, *The Very Quiet Baltimoreans* (Shippensburg Pennsylvania: White Mane Publishing Company, 1991), 89-90.

4. Ibid., 56.

5. Ibid., 71 and 75.

6. Ibid., 68 and 48.

7. Eric Holcomb and Walter Leon, *Belair-Edison*, 34-35.

8. *Matchett's Baltimore Directory for 1853-54* (Baltimore: Matchett, Baltimore Director Office, 1854), 18.

9. Scharf, *History of Baltimore City and County*, 586.

10. John P. Foote, "Colorful, Bustling San Domingo," *Baltimore Sun* (April 30, 1961), Baltimore—Neighborhoods—San Domingo, Vertical files, EPFL Maryland Room.

11. Lee McCardell, "North Avenue," *Evening Sun* (September 18, 1940), Roads—Baltimore—North Avenue, Vertical files, EPFL Maryland Room.

12. Stephens Berge, *Edward Berge, The Sculptor: A Short Biography*, date unknown, Edward Berge, Vertical Files, EPFL.

13. Kelly, *Brewing in Maryland*, 371-85.

14. "Trotting Season," *Baltimore County Union* (May 25, 1872).

15. Kelly, *Brewing in Maryland*, 410-15.

16. "A Fight At Darley Park," *Baltimore County Union* (April 20, 1872).

17. "Riot At Darley Park," *Baltimore County Union* (May 17, 1873).

18. Newspaper clipping, 1906, Parks—Baltimore—Darley Park, Vertical Files, EPFL.

19. Farrell, *Baltimore's Streetcars*, 40.

20. Hall, *Baltimore*, 413-23.

21. Helen Hopkins Thom, *Johns Hopkins: A Silhouette* (Baltimore: Johns Hopkins University Press, 1929), 1.

22. Ibid., 45.

23. Ibid., 72.

24. Ibid., 77.

25. "Improvements at Clifton Park, Country Residence of Johns Hopkins, Esq.," *Baltimore Sun* (February 5, 1852), Clifton folder, A to Z files, CHAP.

26. "Evening Rides About the City," *The Maryland Farmer* (November 1872), 29.

27. Andrew Jackson Downing, *The Architecture of Country Houses* (1850; New York: Dover Publications Inc., 1969), 285.

28. Research notes, Montebello, Passano Historic Structures Index, MHS.

29. Hall, *Baltimore*, 455-60.

30. Research Notes, Historic Architects—Edmund Lind folder, A to Z files, CHAP.

31. "Evening Rides About the City," *The Maryland Farmer* (November 1872): 29.

32. Reese, *A Victorian Village*, 105.

Chapter Five—Democratizing the Suburban Dream, 1898–1941

1. United States Department of Commerce, *16 Census of the Unites States 1940: Housing First Series Data for Small Areas, Maryland* (Washington, D.C.: United States Government Printing Office, 1942), 18, 21-22, 64, 69-73. The number of dwelling units were derived from housing block statistics of census tracks in Northeast Baltimore.

2. George W. Bromley and Walter S. Bromley, *1898 Atlas of Baltimore County, Maryland* (Philadelphia: Bromley, 1898), Library, HSBC; idem, *1914 Atlas of Baltimore County, Maryland* (Philadelphia: Bromley, 1914), flat files, CHAP. The total number of subdivisions in Northeast Baltimore was derived from counting the subdivisions within Northeast Baltimore that were listed on the *1898* and *1914 Atlas of Baltimore County, Maryland*.

3. Arnold, "Suburban Growth," 119-20.

4. Sam Bass Warner, *Streetcar Suburbs* (Cambridge, Massachusetts: Harvard University Press, 1978), 2.

5. Farrell, *Baltimore Streetcars*, 75.

6. Ibid.

7. Robert Moses, "Baltimore Arterial Report" (October 9, 1944): 14-15.

8. Ibid.

9. Chester Liebs, *Main Street To Miracle Mile: American Roadside Architecture* (Baltimore: Johns Hopkins University Press, 1978), 17.

10. Figures taken from Olson, *Baltimore*, 288-89.

11. "Annual Report, 1911," 89, Maryland State Roads Commission, Annapolis.

12. Hollifield, *Difficulties Made Easy*, 77 and 80.

13. "Improved Streets, The City Has Placed in the Annexed Section," *Baltimore Municipal Journal* (February 1916): 16.

14. Ibid.

15. "The Alameda," *Baltimore Municipal Journal* (May 15, 1914): 10.

16. "Border Route," *Baltimore Municipal Journal* (March 20, 1914): 2.

17. "Arterial Highways Entering Baltimore," *Baltimore Municipal Journal* (November 15, 1929): 14.

18. Roderick Ryon, *West Baltimore Neighborhoods: Sketches of Their History* (Baltimore: University of Baltimore, 1993), 15.

19. Olmsted Brothers Landscape Architects, *Report and Recommendations on Park Extension for Baltimore* (1926; Baltimore: Friends of Maryland's Olmsted Parks and Landscapes, 2001), 14.

20. Holcomb and Leon, *Belair-Edison*, 7.

21. Clark Hobbes, "The Lock Raven Boulevard, So-Called," *Evening Sun* (October 7, 1938): Streets—Loch Raven, Vertical files, EPFL Maryland Room.

22. Carroll E. Williams, "Signs Lacking, Autoists Miss Good Highway," *Baltimore Sun* (November 18, 1946); Streets—Erdman, Vertical files, EPFL Maryland Room.

23. "More Candle Power for City Streets," *Baltimore Municipal Journal* (September 20, 1929): 19.

24. Ibid.

25. Ibid.

26. Stanley K. Schultz, *Constructing Urban Culture: American Cities and City Planning, 1800-1920* (Philadelphia: Temple University Press, 1989), 196.

27. Ibid., 197.

28. Ibid., 198. See also Benard Crozier, "Department of Public Works," *The Government of a Great American City*, 182-83.

29. *Arcadia: 15 Years of Progress 1923-1938* (Baltimore: Arcadia Improvement Association, 1938), 6; Arcadia folder, A to Z files, CHAP.

30. Joseph W. Shirley, "City Planning," in *The Government of a Great American City*, ed. Frederick Philip Stieff (Baltimore: H.G. Roebuck and Son, 1935), 261-69.

31. Jefferson C. Grinnalds, "Zoning," in *The Government of a Great American City*, ed. Frederick Philip Stieff (Baltimore: H.G. Roebuck and Son, 1935), 270. See also "Zoning Ordinance Adopted," *Baltimore Municipal Journal* (May 25, 1923): 5.

32. James Vincent Kelly, "The Municipality's Park Problems," in *The Government of a Great American City*, ed. Frederick Philip Stieff (Baltimore: H.G. Roebuck and Son, 1935), 286.

33. For more information, see Olmsted Brothers Landscape Architects, *The Development of Public Grounds for Greater Baltimore* (1904; Baltimore: The Friends of Maryland's Olmsted Parks and Landscapes, 1987).

34. "Picturesque Herring Run," *Baltimore Sun* (May 8, 1913), Parks—Baltimore—Herring Run, Vertical files, Maryland Room, EPFL.

35. "Plan to Make Clifton Park Golf Course Country's Model," *Baltimore Municipal Journal* (May 9, 1930): 9.

36. Kelly, "Park Problems," 287.

37. Idem, 295.

38. See, also, Michael Grimes, "The Development of Baltimore's Northwest Corridor, 1919-1930," working paper for *The Society for American and Regional Planning History*, 1990; located at CHAP.

39. Olson, *Baltimore*, 220.

40. For a comprehensive list of Building and Loan Associations, see *Building and Loan Associations* (Baltimore: Central Insurance Company of Baltimore, 1934).

41. Jackson, *Crabgrass Frontier*, 193.

42. Lewis Mumford, *Sticks and Stones: A Study of American Architecture and Civilization* (New York: Dover Publications, Inc.), 163.

43. Gwendolyn Wright, *Building the Dream: A Social History of Housing in America* (Cambridge, Massachusetts: MIT Press, 1981), 196-97.

44. Pamela H. Simpson, *Cheap, Quick, and Easy: Imitative Architectural Materials, 1870-1930* (Knoxville: University of Tennessee Press, 1999), 21.

45. Carolyn M. Goldstein, *Do It Yourself: Home Improvement in 20th Century America* (New York: Princeton Architectural Press, 1998), 49.

46. Clay Lancaster, *The American Bungalow 1880-93* (New York: Abeville Press, 195), 19.

47. Ibid., 39.

48. "New Type of Bungalow Popular Baltimore Home," *Baltimore News* (February 26, 1910), Suburban development folder, A to Z files, CHAP.

49. "Bungalow Covers a Variety of Styles," *Baltimore News* (April 25, 1914), Suburban development folder, A to Z files, CHAP.

50. Ibid.

51. Virginia Scott Jenkins, *The Lawn: A History of an American Obsession* (Washington, D.C.: Smithsonian Institution Press, 1994), 183.

52. Ibid., 187.

53. Ibid., 35 and 45.

54. Ibid., 54.

Chapter Six—Mainstreets

1. The number indicates a comparison of buildings marked on the *1898 Bromley Atlas of Baltimore County* and the *1914 Atlas of Baltimore County*.

2. The number of businesses came from a comparison between *Maryland, Delaware, and District of Columbia State Gazetteer and Business Directory 1894* (Baltimore: R.L. Polk & Company of Baltimore, 1894) and *Polk's Baltimore City Directory 1928* (Baltimore: R. L. Polk & Co., 1928).

3. *Polk's Baltimore City Directory 1917* (Baltimore: R. L. Polk & Co. of Baltimore, 1917).

4. "Harford Road Now Section of Beautiful Suburban Homes," *The Union News* (May 30, 1930), Harford Road folder, A to Z files, CHAP.

5. Ibid., 2.

6. Ibid., 3.

7. Ibid.

8. Research notes, Parker, Thomas and Rice folder, A to Z files, CHAP.

9. Robert Headley, *Exit: A History of Movies* (College Park, Maryland: Robert Headley, 1974), 47, 45, and 54. This book is an invaluable source for the history of movies and movie theaters in Baltimore. All information on movie theaters comes from this book.

10. "Northeast Improvement Association," *Baltimore Sun* (August 16, 1906).

11. "Harford Road," CHAP.

12. "St. John's of Hamilton United Methodist Church: 75th Anniversary" (Baltimore: The Anniversary Committee of the St. John's of Hamilton United Methodist Church, 1978), 1-4.

13. "Harford Road," CHAP.

14. *God at Work in Calvary 1915-1965 Jubilee Celebration* (Baltimore: Calvary Lutheran Church of Hamilton, Baltimore, Maryland, 1965), 7.

15. "Harford Road," CHAP.

16. Leah M. Reese, *A History of Messiah 1872-1972* (Baltimore: Church of the Messiah, 1972), 25.

17. See n2, this chapter.

18. See n1, this chapter.

19. John A. Jackle and Keith Sculle, *Fast Food: Restaurants in the Automobile Age* (Baltimore: Johns Hopkins University Press, 1999), 38-39.

20. Headley, *Exit*, 104.

21. Ibid., 66.

22. Ibid., 123 and 106.

23. "St. Anthony of Padua Jubilee Celebration souvenir pamphlet," 1934, St. Anthony of Padua folder, A to Z files, CHAP.

24. Research notes, architects (historic) folder, A to Z files, CHAP.

Chapter Seven—Diversity in City Suburbia: Subdivisions Mature into Neighborhoods

1. "Realty Boom Now on Harford Road," *Baltimore News* (March 29, 1913), Suburban development folder, A to Z files, CHAP.

2. For more information, see Mary Ellen Hayward and Charles Belfoure, *The Baltimore Rowhouse* (New York: The Princeton Architectural Press, 1999).

3. Holcomb and Leon, *Belair-Edison*, 15-24.

4. Ibid., 5-15.

5. George W. Bromley and Walter S. Bromley, *1896 Atlas of Baltimore City, Maryland* (Philadelphia: Bromley, 1896), flat files, CHAP.

6. Baltimore City Land Records, Liber SCL 2930, folio 105 and 202, BCSC.

7. *1914 Bromley Atlas of Baltimore County*, CHAP.

8. "New Development in Northeast," *Baltimore News* (March 28, 1913), Suburban development folder, A to Z files, CHAP.

9. Department of Commerce, *16 Census*, 21 and 68-69.

10. Block quotes from "Evergreen Lawn," *Baltimore News* (April 2, 1910), Suburban development folder, A to Z files, CHAP.

11. Ibid.

12. "The Fast Growing Town Of Hamilton And Some Of Its History," *The New Era* (January 17, 1914): Suburban development folder, A to Z files, CHAP.

13. "Build New Suburb On Harford Road," *Baltimore News* (May 7, 1910), Suburban development folder, A to Z files, CHAP.

14. Ibid.

15. Newspaper clipping, *News American*, circa 1911, Overlea folder, A to Z files, CHAP.

16. "Belair Road Has Rapid Growth," *Baltimore News* (March 29, 1913), Suburban development

folder, A to Z files, CHAP.

17. *Arcadia: 15 Years of Progress 1923-1938* (Arcadia Improvement Association).

18. James Bertram, "Man In the Street: Heckel ," *Baltimore Sun* (October 28, 1951).

19. "New Development in Northeast," *Baltimore News* (March 28, 1914).

20. *Arcadia: 15 Years of Progress 1923-1938*.

21. "Beverly Hills: Baltimore's Best Kept Secret," *Baltimore Sun* (March 3, 1996).

22. "Waltherson Observes First Anniversary," *Baltimore American* (July 10, 1938), Baltimore—neighborhoods—Waltherson, Vertical files, EPFL Maryland Room.

23. Lewand, *North Baltimore*, 44.

24. "Whites Still Oppose Site For Morgan," *Afro-American* (May 5, 1917).

25. "Whites Still Fighting Morgan College," *Baltimore Afro-American* (March 15, 1918).

26. Permit Block files, RS 48, Series 59, block 5370, BCA.

27. Baltimore City Land Records, Liber SCL 4179, folio 255, BCSC.

28. *Increasing the Light: Epiphany Lutheran Church 1908-1958* (Baltimore: Epiphany Lutheran Church, 1958), 11.

29. Ibid., 37-38.

30. "Belmar: The Scene of Great Activity," *Baltimore News* (March 27, 1913), Suburban development folder, A to Z files, CHAP.

31. R.L. Polk, *Polk's Baltimore City Directory, 1903* (Baltimore: R.L. Polk And Company, 1903).

32. Eric Holcomb, "From Herring Run to Cherry Hill: Politics of Racism and the Location of War Housing for African Americans," 1996, unpublished article, Compliance files, Cherry Hill folder, CHAP, 1 and 3.

33. Flier advertising rally, June 10, 1939, Armistead Gardens folder, Compliance files, CHAP.

34. "Housing Plan Brings Howls of Derision," *Baltimore Sun* (June 11, 1939).

35. "Armistead Annex Open to More Workers," *Baltimore Sun* (November 30, 1941).

36. Holcomb, "From Herring Run to Cherry Hill," 1 and 3.

37. Christopher Weeks, *Alexander Cochran: Modernist Architect in Traditional Baltimore* (Baltimore: Maryland Historical Society Press, 1995), 85.

Chapter Eight—Walking through Today, 1945–2005

1. Olson, *Baltimore*, 360.

2. Leland M. Roth, *America Builds: Source Documents in American Architecture and Planning* (New York: Harper and Row, 1983), 517.

3. Brugger, *Maryland*, 577-78.

4. Ibid., 812-14.

5. Brochure, "Moravia Park Industrial Park," 1963, Moravia Park, Vertical Files, EPFL.

6. Author's windshield survey of strip malls in Northeast Baltimore, 1999. In 2004, many of these strip malls are home to storefront churches. At least four strip malls have been fully converted to church use.

7. This project won a Baltimore Chapter AIA Certificate of Merit in 1951 for the apartments connected to Freedom shopping center located on Erdman Avenue. The shopping center won an honorable mention award in 1951. For more information, read Christopher Weeks, *Modernist Architect in Traditional Baltimore* (Baltimore: Maryland Historical Society Press, 1995).

8. Larry R. Ford, *Cities and Buildings, Skyscrapers, Skid Rows and Suburbs* (Baltimore: Johns Hopkins University Press, 1994), 163.

9. Ibid.
10. Holcomb and Leon, *Belair-Edison*, 11.
11. Census 2000 Summary File 1, U.S. Census Bureau, July 3, 2001. This is a pdf file located at www.baltimorecity.gov/government/planning/census/index.html (2002).
12. Eric Siegal, "Census Changes Outpace Court," *Baltimore Sun* (August 8, 2002).
13. Idem, "City's Plan For Housing Is Revised: New Approach Aims To Help Poor Buy Middle-class Homes," *Baltimore Sun* (January 7, 2001).
14. Ibid.
15. "Harbel Community Organization," Harbel Community Organization, www.harbel.org (August 2003).
16. Printed brochure Harford Road Partnership, Harp folder, A to Z files, CHAP.
17. Harford Road Partnership and Neighborhoods of Greater Lauraville, "Neighborhoods of Greater Lauraville, Baltimore, Maryland, U.S.A," www.greaterlauraville.com (August 2003).
18. "Belair-Edison," www.belair-edison.org, Belair-Edison Neighborhoods (September 2003).
19. Laurie Willis, "Herring Run Overflow Could Result In Fines," *Baltimore Sun* (February 28, 2003).

INDEX

25th Street, 130, 135
33rd Street, 129, 133, 135

African-Americans: farm workers, 42-43; housing for, 226-27; in Northeast Baltimore, 64-65, 80; population change, 239-42; slavery, 12-13; suburban development, 215-18
agricultural societies, 55-56
Ailsa Heights (housing subdivision), 200
Ailsa Terraces (housing subdivision), 200
Alameda, The, 127, 128-30, 133, 191
Alsop, George, 5
Altoona Park (housing subdivision), 204
American Farmer, 55, 56
American Turf Register, 56
Andrew, (Bishop) J.O., 49
Andrew's Memorial Methodist Church (also St. Andrew's Chapel), 49, 72, 182
Annex Improvement Commission, 127-28
annexation: of 1888, 86-87; of 1918, 121-23, 167
Anthonyville neighborhood, 220-22
Arcadia Improvement Association, 140-41, 211
Arcadia neighborhood, 209-12, 239, 240
architecture (house types and styles): alley houses, 74; bungalow, 155-64, 196, 198; Cape Cod, 235; cottage, 155-56, 161; duplex, 155, 198; foursquare, 155, 163-64; house plans, 234; I-house, 155-56; ranch house, 235-36; rowhouse (also townhouse), 74, 155, 185-95, 226, 235; shed-like house, 236; split-level, 236; Victorian, 156-7, 198
Argonne Drive, 135
Armistead Gardens (housing project), 223-27, 240
Armstrong, Thomas, 70
arrabers, *xii*, 81
automobiles: influence in Northeast Baltimore, 123; influence on shopping, 231-32; use in Baltimore, 125-26

Back River Neck, 7-9
Baird, James, 70
Baltimore City government: Annexation Improvement Commission, 127-28; Commission on City Plan (see city planning); Department of Public Works, 130-32; Mainstreet Program, 233, 243-4; park plan of 1904, 128; role in development of Northeast Baltimore, 120-21; Sewage Commission, 140; Topographical Survey Commission, 141
Baltimore County: development, 3-9; Electric and Water Company, 175; government, 52; iron industry, 10-13; Rangers, 6-9; Turnpike Company (see, also, turnpike companies), 51-52
Baltimore Orioles, 99
Baltimore Town (and City): development of, 9, 10, 17-18, 83; as seen from Northeast Baltimore, 38-39; influence upon Northeast Baltimore, 85-87
Baltimore Water Company, 103-104
Barnum, David, 30
Bass, George, 70
Bauernschmidt, John, 197
beer gardens, 63
Belair-Edison Housing Services (also Belair-Edison Neighborhoods Inc.), 241, 243, 245
Belair-Edison Improvement Association, 89
Belair-Edison neighborhood, 137, 191-95, 239
Belair Parkside neighborhood, 137
Belair Road (see, also, farm villages and mainstreets): development of, 51-52, 60, 63, 73-75, 89, 127-28, 135, 179-80, 232; real estate development on, 125, 182; stagecoach, 87
Belgravia (housing subdivision), 220
Belmar (housing subdivision), 220
Belmont estate, 19, 20, 27-30
Beverly Hills: neighborhood, 212, 239, 240; Neighborhood Association, 212

Biddison family, 45, 87
billboards, 232
Bishop, Jr., William, 68
Black and Decker, 153
Blake, Eubie, 218
Bowly, Ann Lux, 25
Bowly, Daniel, 25, 33, 43, 52
Bowly, James, 80
Bowley's Lane, 51, 60, 63
Bowley's Quarters, 34
Brehm, George, 74-75
Brendan Avenue, 63
breweries: on Belair Road, 63; Brehm's Brewery, 63, 75; Burton Brewing Company, 75; Darley Park brewery (see, also, Darley Park Beer Garden), 63; on Harford Road, 63; Huebner brewery (also Hertlein's brewery), 63, 73; Maryland Brewing Company, 75; Neisendorf's brewery, 74-75; Vonderhorst brewery (also Eagle Brewing Company), 63, 73, 99; Weber's brewery, 63, 66, 69-70
Bridges, Josiah, 9
Broadway, 130
Broom, Mary, 80
Brown, William, 80
building and loan associations, 149-51
building technology (development of), 151-54, 233-34
Burgan family, 45
Berge family, 98

California Grove neighborhood, 205
Calloway, Cab, 218
Calvary Lutheran Church, 179
Campbell, Archibald, 28
Carswell, Stanley, 210
Cedonia neighborhood, 137
cemeteries: Baltimore Hebrew Congregation Cemetery, 88; Biddison family cemetery, 87; B'nai Israel Congregation Cemetery, 88; Gontrum family cemetery, 87; Holy Cross Cemetery, 101, 130; Immanuel Lutheran Cemetery, 88; Jerusalem Evangelical Lutheran Cemetery, 87; Laurel Hill Cemetery, 88-89; Most Holy Redeemer Cemetery, 73, 88; Oak Hill Cemetery, 88
Cherry Hill (housing project), 226-27
Chetwynd, William, 10-11
Chew, Samuel, 11
Christopher, F., 70
Church of the Messiah Episcopal Church, 179
Ciconia (housing subdivision), 204
city planning (Baltimore): City Plan Committee (1918-1932), 131-32, 135, 141-42; comprehensive, 132, 142; Major Street Plan, 131-32; Commission on City Plan (1910-18; 1932 on), 131, 141-42
Clairmont estate, 19
Clifton estate, 19, 25-27, 36, 85, 91, 105-13
Clifton Park, 81, 92, 130, 145-47
Clifton Park Golf Course, 145-47
Cobb, Daniel, 27
Cochran, Alexander Smith, 227, 232
Coldspring Road, 135
Coldstream estate, 19, 30-31
Coldstream-Homestead-Montebello neighborhood (see, also, Homestead), 190-91
Coleman family, 80
Colonial Mortgage Company, 75
Columbus monument, 27-28
commercial signs, 232
Concrete Block Manufacturers' Association, 153
Corse farm, 80
Corse, George, 79
Corse, William, Sr., 34-35, 46
country estates: architecture, 18-20; development of, 15
crossroad villages (see farm villages)

D'Anmour, Chevalier, 27-29
Darley Hall estate, 7, 48, 92
Darley Path, 7-9, 51
Darley Park beer garden, 100-102, 130
Dayton, Elizabeth, 80
deed covenants, 197
Distance family, 80
Dobler, (Judge) John J., 197, 199
Downing, Andrew Jackson (A. J.), *xix-xx*, 94-95, 112-13, 116
DuBois, W. E. B., 218
Durkee family (also Durkee Enterprises), 174-75

Echodale Road, 135, 200
Echodale Terrace (housing subdivision), 200, 204
Edison Highway, 134, 232
Edwards, Moses, 9
Epiphany Lutheran Church, 183, 218-20
Erdman Avenue, 46, 60, 74, 136, 182, 199, 230, 232
Erdman family, 45-46, 77
Erdman, George, 74
Enock, Richard, 6
Ensor, John, 48
Eutaw estate, 67
Eutaw Heights neighborhood, 137, 210
Eutaw Methodist Church, 49-50, 63, 66
Evergreen Lawn (housing subdivision), 202-4
E. Eyring and Sons, 175

Fair Oaks estate, 70
Fairlea (housing subdivision), 222
farm villages (see, also, mainstreets): development of, 15-16, 47, 60-76; on Belair Road, 50; on Harford Road, 50-51
Farmers' and Gardeners' Beneficial Society, 50, 72
Federal Highway Act of 1956, 139
Federal Home Loan Bank Act, 1934 (also Federal Housing Act), 151
federal savings banks, 151
Fells Point, 130
Finlay, John and Hugh, 31
First Presbyterian Church, 179
five-mile house, 70
Foote, John, 97
Forrestor family, 45, 87
Fort McHenry, 38
Frankford neighborhood, 137
Franklin Avenue (also Frankford Avenue), 60
Freedom Apartments, 227
Freedom Shopping Center, 227, 232
Freeman, Francis, 6
Friz and Friz (architects), 183, 219
Fullerton neighborhood, 208
Furley Hall estate, 19, 33-35, 46, 52
Furley Square, 222

G. W. & Son Blacksmiths and Wheelwrights, 72
Gallagher, E. J., 134, 149, 190-91, 193
garage (building type), 212
garden apartment, 155, 237-38
Garden Club of America, 165
Gardenville, 45, 60, 63-65, 66, 72, 75, 137, 180-83, 222
Garrett family geneology, 114-15
Garrett, John Work, 105, 113-17
Garrett, Mary, 114, 117, 197
Garrison Road, 7
Gatch, Conduce, 49
Gatch family, 45
Gatch Memorial Methodist Church, 49, 75, 182
Gatch, Nicholas, 75
Gatch, Philip, 49
Gay Street, 63, 130
Gebb, Henry and Mary, 80
Georgetown, 60, 74-75, 137, 180-83
Gittings, James, 52
Glenham Belford, 137, 204
Glenmore estate, 70
Golden Ring Road, 60
Gontrum, (Judge) John, 79, 87
Gontrum's tavern, 72
Gorsuch, Robert, 6

Gorsuch, Jr., Robert, 91
Gorsuch, Thomas, 48
Grace Lutheran Church, 177
Green, Amon, 68
Green, James, 68
Green, Samuel, 68
Grimes, James, 80
Grindon Building Association, 203
Grindon Lane, 60
Guy, Francis, 31-32
Gwynns Falls Parkway, 133

Hall's Springs Hotel and Tavern, 66-68
Hall, William Carvel, 66-68
Hamilton Addition (housing subdivision), 204
Hamilton Amusement Company, 174-75
Hamilton Avenue, 60, 70, 179, 202
Hamilton Building Association, 204-5
Hamilton, Caughy, 70
Hamilton Hall, 177, 179
Hamilton Improvement Association, 176, 224-25
Hamilton: mainstreet, 172-75, 204; neighborhood, 137, 176, 202-205
Hamilton Park (housing subdivision), 137, 204
Hamilton Presbyterian Church, 174, 177
Hamilton Women's Club, 177
Harbel Community Organization, 240-41, 242, 245
Harford-Echodale- Perring Parkway neighborhood, 204
Harford Road (see, also, farm villages; mainstreets; and turnpike companies: Baltimore and Harford Turnpike): development of, 7, 38, 43, 50-52, 60, 70, 87, 92, 127-28, 135, 137, 179; real estate development on, 125, 232
Harford Road Partnership (HaRP), 240-43
Harker, (Major) Howard, 69
Harris, David, 31-33
Harris, J. Morrison, 78-79
Hazlewood Heights (housing subdivision), 222
Heckel family, 209
Heinz Park, 28
Herman family, 74
Herring Run, 5, 10, 12, 51, 63, 68-69, 104, 135, 180
Herring Run House, 54
Herring Run Park, 5, 143-44
Herring Run Watershed Association, 241, 244-45
Hertlein, Gottfried, 73-74
historic preservation, 239
Hoddinott: brothers, carriage manufacturers, 71; family, 70-72
Hollander Ridge (housing project), 227, 237
Hollingsworth, Jesse, 12

Homestead estate, 19
Homestead: mainstreet, 169; neighborhood, 91-96, 102
Hooker, Thomas, 6
Hopkins, Johns, 27, 105-13, 130
Housing Authority Baltimore City (also Baltimore Housing Authority), 223-27, 241
horsecars (see, also, streetcars): Hall's Springs Railway (also Baltimore and Hall's Springs Railway), 87, 95, 102, 123-24; on Harford Road, 124-25; Stockton, Falls & Company stagecoach, 54
horse racing, 54
hucksters (as an occupation), 80-81
Huebner, John, 73

Idlewild (housing subdivision), 204
International Order of the Odd Fellows (I.O.O.F.), No. 114, 72
Interstate: creation of, 230; I-70, 230; I-95, 230-31; I-895, 230-31
iron industry, Baltimore County, 10-13

Jackson, Edward B., 91
Jerusalem Evangelical Lutheran Church, 50, 72, 182, 222
John Carroll's Fish House, 54
Johns Hopkins University, 107-8
Johnson, William, 79

Keene, John Henry, 65-66
Keene, Jr., John Henry, 65-66
Keene, Laura, 65
Keene, Robert Goldsborough, 65
Kennard and Company (realtors), 208, 220
Kenwood Avenue, 60
King, Henry, 9
King, William, 10
King, Susanna, 10
Kingsbury Iron Furnace, 10-13, 54
Knox, Julius, 78
Kolb, Henry, 208, 220, 222
Kramer, Lynn, 244

Lachenmeyer family, 97-98
Lake Clifton, 85, 104
Lake Montebello, 85, 104
Lamley, George, 74
Lancashire iron furnace, 11
land tracts: Come by Chance, 9; Darley Hall, 9; Edward's Enlargement, 9; Gardeson, 9; Gorsuch Point, 10; Grindon, 11; Kingsbury, 9-12; Long Point, 11; Maiden's Hill, 10; Mason's Oats, 11; Mount Hayes, 9; Pemblicoe, 8; The Plains, 11; Roger's road, 11; Sheredine's Bottom, 11-12; Sheredine's Discovery, 11; Sidmore's last, 45; Whetstone Point, 10; Wilmot's Neglect, 11
Lanham Act of 1940, 223
Lauraville: mainstreet, 169, 172-75; neighborhood, 63-65, 70, 200-2, 204, 239
Lauraville Park (housing subdivision), 200
lawns: development of, 164-66; zoning requirements, 166
Lawrence, Sally Dorsey, 65
Lind, Edmund (architect), 115
Lloyd, Edward, 55
Loch Raven apartments, 237
Loch Raven Boulevard, 134-35
Loch Raven water supply, 104
Long, Robert, 12
Lord Baltimore, 9

Macht, Ephraim, 193, 195, 201
Magruder, Hugh (builder-architect), 177
mainstreets (see, also, farm villages): development on Harford Road, 169-74; on Belair Road, 169-70; on Harford Road, 169-79; Program, 233
Mansell, Norman T. (architect), 219
Maryland Agriculture Society, 55-56
Maryland Farmer, 109-111, 116-17
Maryland state legislation: on Baltimore City annexation, 86; on establishment of Baltimore water company, 103-4; Governor McKeldin's Master Highway Plan, 230; on private turnpike companies, 52;
Maryland Jockey Club, 100
Maryland State Roads Commission, 127, 128
Matthews, Samuel, 80
Mayfield neighborhood, 104, 196-200, 239, 240
McCallister, William, 176
McCormick, Jr., Alexander, 73
McCormick, Margaret, 79
McDonald family, 70
Mckewin, C.W. (architect), 190
Merchants and Manufacturers Association, 121, 140
Miller, George, 100
mills: Coxon's mill, 63, Eutaw grist mill, 63; Green's cotton mill, 49, 63, 68; Ivy mill, 63, 69, 215; J. Russell's mill, 69; mill towns, 63; owned by William Carvel Hall (also Columbia mill), 68
Montebello estate, 19, 20, 23-25, 85, 113-17
Montebello Park (housing subdivision), 200-2
Moore, Robert, 70
Moore's Run, 141
Mount Deposit estate, 19, 31-33

Moravia Road, 50, 135, 230-32
Moravia Mall, 232
Morgan Park neighborhood, 215-18, 240
Morgan State University (college), 63, 69, 215-16
movie theaters: the Arcade, 174; the Belmar, 182; the Cameo, 174-75; the Community (later the Avon), 174; Earle, 182; Northway, 175; Overlea movie house, 180; Paramount, 182; Vilma, 182
Muller, L.P., 68
Municipal Arts Society, 140
Murphy family, 218
Mutto and White (architects), 179

National Bureau of Standards, 151
National Highway Acts of 1956 and 1958, 230
National Home Builders' Association, 150
National Register of Historic Places, 239
National Trust Main Street Program, 233, 243
Native Americans: Algonquins, 5; conflict with, 6-7; settlement patterns 3, 5-6; Nanticoke Tribe, 7; Susquehannocks, 5-6
Neidhart, Frederick, 78
Neighborhoods of Greater Lauraville (NOGLI), 241, 243, 245
Norman Avenue, 133
North Avenue, 87, 130
North Harford Road neighborhood, 137
Northeast Baltimore: and the Civil War, 76-77; annexation (see annexation); development of, 17-18, 44, 59-60, 229; population, 41, 76, 239; as picturesque landscape, 35-39; race issues, 241-42; residents of, 76-83; road development, 127-39; sewer development, 140-41; suburbanization of, 119-21, 208-9; topography, 4-5; water development, 141
Northeast Goodneighbors, 241-42
Northeast Improvement Association, 175
Northern Parkway, 135, 170
Northwood Apartments, 237
Northwood Shopping Center, 232
Novak, Frank, 194

Old Har Sinai cemetery, 74
Old Harford Road, 60, 70-71
Old Main Road, 52
Old Philadelphia Road (also Old Post Road), 40, 51-52, 135
Oldton, (Captain) John , 7-9
Olmsted (brothers, landscape architects): Frederick, 128-29, 133, 143; firm, 143; plan, 143
Orange Hill farm, 40-44
Otto, John, 78
Overlea: housing subdivision, 208; neighborhood, 124, 170, 180-83, 206-8

Park Course Resort, 100
Parkinson, Richard, 40-44, 52, 59
parks (development of), 143-47
Patapsco Meeting of the Religious Society of Friends, 48
Patapsco Valley, 5
Patterson, William, 30-31
Perlman Street, 189
Perry Hall Road, 52
Potter, Martin, 54
Powellnaron neighborhood, 218-20
Powell, Mr. and Mrs. Frederick, 219-20
Principio Iron Company, 10-12, 52
Pulaski Highway, 5, 10, 230-31
public housing, 223-27

Raspe, Henry, 66, 75-76
Raspeburg, 75, 180-83, 208
Raspeburg, John, 60
real estate development (innovations in), 148-50
Regester, Samuel, 80
religious denominations: Baptists, 18; Episcopalians, 18; German Calvinists, 18; Lutherans, 18, 47, 50; Mennonites, 18; Methodists, 47, 49-50; Presbyterians, 18; Quakers, 18, 47-49
Reese, Lizette Woodsworth (poet), 80, 117
Richard Estates (housing subdivision), 200
Richardson, (Captain) Thomas, 6
Ridgely, John, 54
road development (see, also, Northeast Baltimore): prior to the 1918 annexation, 127-30; with the rise of the automobile, 130-39
Robards, Thomas, 9
Robertson Realty, Inc. (advertisement), 213, 215
Roby, Mary, 244
Rockdale (housing subdivision), 222
Rosekemp (housing subdivision), 200
Rosemout Avenue neighborhood, 137
Royston (housing subdivision), 204

Safeway, 243
San Domingo neighborhood, 91, 96-99
Sargeant, (Reverend) Thomas, 49
Save Our Streams, 244
Schaffler, Franklin, 80
Schrotke, Otto, 219
Seidel, John, 74
Seigman's Beer Garden, 101
Sheredine, Thomas, 11
Sheredine's Bottom, 11-12
Sholler, Christian, 80
Sinclair Lane, 232
Sinclair Nursery, 55
six-mile house, 70

Sligh, Thomas, 45
Smith, (Captain) John, 3-4, 5, 10
Smith, Nathan L., 132
Smith, Robert, 44, 55
Smith, (General) Samuel, 12, 20-25, 67, 105, 113
Smith, William, 67
South Clifton Park neighborhood, 189
Southern Avenue, 60
Spear (Smith), Margaret, 22, 113
St. Anthony of Padua Roman Catholic Church (also St. Anthony's), 72, 182, 221
St. Dominic's Roman Catholic Church, 177-79
St. John's United Methodist Church, 177-78
St. Michael's Church, 183
State Roads Commission, 128
street lighting, 138-39
Sterret, (General) Joseph, 33
Stewart, Ann, 33
Stirling, Archibald, 105, 115
Stockton, Falls & Company stagecoach, 54
stone cutters, 98-99
streetcars: Baltimore City Passenger Railway, 124; Baltimore Consolidated Railroad Company, 124; Baltimore Gardenville and Belair Electric Railway, 123; Baltimore and Lorely Electric Railway, 123-24; Baltimore and Northern Electric Railway, 124; Central Railway, 124; City Passenger Railway, 102, 123; development of, 123-25; Hall's Springs Railway (also Baltimore and Hall's Spring Railway), 87, 95, 102, 123-24
strip malls, 231-32
Surrey estate, 33
Sydenham hospital, 216

Tames, John, 70, 78
Tames Lane, 60, 70-72
Taylor family, 45
Taylor, John, 6
Taylor, Richard, 48
taxpayer buildings, 170, 172
Tenant, (Colonel) Thomas, 28
Thomas, Philip, 11
Thompson, Henry, 25-27, 36, 38, 105
Tiffany family, 92, 105, 113-14
Tormey, Francis (architect), 183
Towson Avenue (also Taylor Avenue), 60
truck farms, 40-45
turnpike companies: Baltimore and Harford Turnpike Company (also Harford Road Turnpike) 26, 52; Baltimore and Havre de Grace Turnpike, 52; Baltimore and Jerusalem turnpike company, 52, 123; Fredericktown Turnpike Company, 52; lack of development, 96; Reisterstown Turnpike Company, 52; Yorktown Turnpike Company, 52

Underwood, Noah, 44
U.S. Department of Agriculture (USDA), 165-66
U. S. Housing Acts: of 1937, 223; of 1949, 233
U.S. Golf Association, 165

Valley View Park (housing subdivision), 222
Vonderhorst, John, 99

Walther Avenue, 133-34, 137, 200, 213
Waltherson neighborhood, 137, 204, 213-15, 240
Waverly, 117
Webb and White (realtors), 200
Weber, Frederic, 69-70
Wegefarth, Dr., 202-3
Welsh Construction Company, 195, 238
Welsh, Daniell, 9
Westphal Lawn (housing subdivision), 204
Watkins, Francis, 6-7
White, Lucius (architect), 182
White Tower restaurant, 182
Whitney, Joseph, 44
Whitridge, Horation, 49
Whittiwicks, John, 11
Wilson Heights neighborhood, 222
Wirt, William, 27, 36-39
Woerner, Otto, 74
Woodholme neighborhood (also Woodhome Heights), 137, 205-6
Woodlea (housing subdivision), 222
Woodring neighborhood, 137, 206, 240
Woodrow (housing subdivision), 221-22
yellow fever, 43

Zink, John, 175
zoning: system, 142; ordinance, 190

ABOUT THE AUTHOR

ERIC L. HOLCOMB (b. 1966) moved to Baltimore in 1990. He received his B.A. in English Literature at St. Mary's College in Maryland and his M.A. in historic preservation at Boston University. He spent many years working in the building trades, including a year with Gibbons of Baltimore Church Restoration Company and a year with Tidewater Restoration Services. From 1994 to 2004, he worked as a city planner in historic preservation for the Baltimore City Commission for Historical and Architectural Preservation (CHAP). In 2004, CHAP staff merged with the Baltimore City Department of Planning where he continues to contribute to the revitalization of historic Baltimore. He and his wife are currently raising two boys, Eliot and Emerson.

THE Center for American Places is a tax-exempt 501(c)(3) nonprofit organization, founded in 1990, whose educational mission is to enhance the public's understanding of, appreciation for, and affection for the natural and built environment. Underpinning this mission is the belief that books provide an indispensable foundation for comprehending and caring for the places where we live, work, and explore. Books live. Books endure. Books make a difference. Books are gifts to civilization.

With offices in Santa Fe, New Mexico, and Staunton, Virginia, Center editors bring to publication as many as thirty books per year under the Center's own imprint or in association with publishing partners. The Center is also engaged in numerous other programs that emphasize the interpretation of place through art, literature, scholarship, exhibitions, and field research. The Center's Cotton Mather Library in Arthur, Nebraska, its Martha A. Strawn Photographic Library in Davidson, North Carolina, and a ten-acre reserve along the Santa Fe River in Florida are available as retreats upon request. The Center is also affiliated with the Rocky Mountain Land Library in Colorado.

The Center strives every day to make a difference through books, research, and education. For more information, please send inquiries to P.O. Box 23225, Santa Fe, NM 87502, U.S.A., or visit the Center's Website (www.americanplaces.org).

About the Book:

The text for *The City as Suburb: A History of Northeast Baltimore since 1660* was set in Sabon. The paper is acid-free Thai A, 140gsm weight. The book was printed and bound in China.

For the Center for American Places:

George F. Thompson, President and Publisher
Randall B. Jones, Independent Editor
Amber K. Lautigar, Publishing Liaison and Assistant Editor
Ernest L. Toney, Jr., Chelsea Miller Goin Intern
Kristine Harmon, Manuscript Editor
Gwen M. Stamm, Book Designer and Art Director
Dave Keck, of Global Ink, Inc., Production Coordinator